Southern Africa: land of beauty and splendour

Reader's Digest

Southern Africa: land of beauty and splendour

by T. V. Bulpin

Published by The Reader's Digest Association South Africa (Pty.) Limited
130 Strand Street, Cape Town 8001

SOUTHERN AFRICA: LAND OF BEAUTY AND SPLENDOUR
was edited and designed by
The Reader's Digest Association Limited, London
and written by T. V. Bulpin

Seventh Edition Copyright © 1981
The Reader's Digest Association South Africa (Pty.) Limited

ISBN 0 620 04990 1

FRONT ENDPAPER Close-up of lichens on a rock face at
Robberg Point, on the Garden Route in the Western Cape.

REAR ENDPAPER Close-up of bark of eucalyptus tree, on
the Garden Route near Knysna.

The splendour of the land: the majesty of the sea

ON the summit of the promontory of the Cape of Good Hope stands a beacon, weathered by the winds which in these parts seldom die, by the salty spray, by rain, and by the ever-alternating warmth and cold of the days and nights.

The beacon is simply a pile of rocks, towering above the tumultuous face of the sea. For 5000 km southwards there is no other land; no trade routes; no jet aircraft tearing through the sky. There is only a seething wilderness of water, whipped by the howling storms of the Roaring Forties. The cold increases with every kilometre travelled towards the shores of Antarctica – forbidding, repellent, but also alluring with their dangers, secrets and untamed beauty.

To the north lies the whole continent of Africa – vast and sprawling, boisterous and rugged. It has the world's richest and most varied wild-animal population. Looted and stained with blood, it is regarded by many scientists as the cradle of man.

The moods of the sea are equalled by those of the land. The wild flowers and precious stones of the land are matched in beauty by the corals and anemones of the sea. And beneath the sea there rages a struggle for existence just as ruthless as the conflict on land.

The sea is divided by currents and temperature into distinctive zones. The land has its geological, climatic and botanical divisions. Like the fragments of a patchwork quilt, all are connected, but each has its distinctive individuality.

Man, by his various activities, has changed the land and had some effect even on the sea. But in this southern portion of the African continent there are great areas still untouched, or little changed, where the face of the earth may be seen much as it was before the coming of man.

Nature reserves and national parks help nature to maintain its delicate balance. Such preservation provides man not only with recreational space and a revitalising escape from his congested environment, but also with a measure of the worth of his own creations against those of nature.

The purpose of this book is to depict the unspoilt beauty and splendour of the land and the sea, to show how it all came to be there, and to reveal the never-ending creativity of nature.

Where the splendours are

FROM the parched deserts of the west coast to the tropical lushness of the eastern seaboard, Southern Africa is full of scenic contrasts. The richness and variety of the landscape are reflected in the way that this book is divided into 18 major sections. Most of these sections portray the scenic character of a particular region, but others deal with features such as waterfalls, caves and mineral treasures, that are common to many regions. Throughout the book there are detailed maps for both the regions and the general features. In the map on the left, each scenic region is enclosed within a rectangle, and the number in a corner indicates the page on which the detailed map for that region appears. The Drakensberg map, for instance, is on p. 136. Detailed maps for general features appear in the appropriate chapters.

SYMBOLS USED ON THE MAPS

Town...●

National boundary........................ – – – – –

State boundary...............................

River.. _Falls_

Intermittent river............................ – – – –

Lake..

Intermittent lake................................

Ocean current (warm)............................. ⟶

Ocean current (cold)............................. ⟶

Sand dunes...

Mountain peak (height in metres)...............1615▲

Site of interest...................................★

Acknowledgments

The author and editors wish to express their gratitude for
the invaluable contributions, information and advice given in
compiling this book by the following authorities. Their papers and
writings are the detailed standard sources on the relevant subject.

A. Batten and H. Bokelmann, authors and illustrators of *Wild Flowers of the Eastern Cape*.

F. von Breitenbach, of the Department of Forestry, author of *Southern Cape Forests and Trees*.

The Reverend A. T. Bryant, author of *Olden Times in Zululand and Natal*.

R. A. Dyer, L. E. Codd and Professor H. B. Rycroft, editors of the *Flora of Southern Africa*.

D. F. Ellenberger, author of *History of the Basuto*.

D. H. Kennelly, author of *Marine Shells of Southern Africa*.

D. P. Liebenberg, author of *The Drakensberg of Natal*.

K. T. Lilliecrona, author of *Salt-water Fish and Fishing in Southern Africa*.

C. T. A. Maberly, author of *Game Animals of Southern Africa*.

Professor Edgar Mountain, of Rhodes University, author of *Geology of Southern Africa*.

Professor H. P. Riley, of the University of Kentucky, author of *Families of Flowering Plants of Southern Africa*.

Professor E. S. W. Simpson, of Stellenbosch University, particularly for his advice on geology.

Professor J. L. B. Smith, author of *The Sea Fishes of Southern Africa* and *High Tide*.

R. Summers, author of *Ancient Ruins and Vanished Civilizations of Southern Africa*.

Dr A. J. Tankard, Geologist, S.A. Museum.

Dr F. C. Truter, Director of the Geological Survey of South Africa, and his staff, particularly J. de Villiers, Chief Geologist, and P. H. Vermeulen, Editor of Publications.

Dr B. Tyrrell, author and artist of *Tribal Peoples of Southern Africa*.

Dr H. Wild, Senior Botanist, Branch of Botany and Plant Pathology, Zimbabwe.

Contents

Where two oceans create two different worlds

The continent of Africa is the great wedge which divides the Atlantic from the Indian Ocean; but oceans are simply man-made divisions of the sea. The sea itself does not recognise them. It knows only the currents, which flow through it like powerful rivers.

THE DUTCHMAN'S HAUNT The Cape of Good Hope, looking southwards. The legendary Flying Dutchman is said to be spending eternity trying to round these shores in his spectral ship. It is here that the Benguela and Moçambique currents meet.

From the unrelenting deserts of the west to the tropical lushness of Natal, the sea rules the land

IT MAY SEEM strange but it is perfectly true that any account of Southern Africa, whether of its scenery, vegetation and animal life, or of its uproarious history, must start with the sea. Through the temperature of its currents sweeping along the coast, the sea controls the weather on land, and so plays a vital part in creating and modelling the landscape. All forms of life, their distribution and well-being, are also controlled by the same potent influences of temperature and rainfall.

Southern Africa, lying south of the Zambezi and Kunene rivers, is peculiarly exposed to the conflicting powers of two major sea currents, one warm the other cold. They give this southern end of the African continent a range of climate and habitats so extreme that on the same line of latitude there is a full gamut, east to west, from fever-ridden swamplands, through forest, savanna, grassland and semi-arid wilderness to desert, complete and relentless.

These habitats, and their permutations, provide homes for a fantastic variety of 20 000 species of plants. The number of different species of insects and reptiles is still to be counted. Bird life is prolific, with 829 recorded species. Southern Africa excels, too, in the number and diversity of its mammals. It is the cul-de-sac of game migrations from the rest of Africa, as well as the nursery of its own species; and it has over 200 species of mammals, from swamp-living hippopotamuses to creatures of the desert, who go through life without ever getting wet.

The continent of Africa is the great wedge which divides the Atlantic from the Indian Ocean; but oceans are simply man-made divisions of the sea. The sea itself does not recognise them. It knows only the currents which flow through it like powerful rivers; the foodstuffs they carry to support marine life; and the all-important differences in temperature which control the character of life in the sea and, by aiding or resisting the process of evaporation, the climate of both sea and land.

In the Indian Ocean, the warm, west-flowing Equatorial Current collides with the land mass of Madagascar. The current divides. One flow passes the northern point of the great island and reaches the coast of Africa at the cape called by the Portuguese

Cabo Delgado, where the current is once again forced to divide. One stream turns further northwards and becomes known as the East African Coast Current. A second division swings south and, as a 100 km wide river in the sea, it flows down the coast of Moçambique.

From October to February this Moçambique Current is at its most powerful, flowing at a speed of over 6 km per hour and with a temperature of around 28°C. From May to August the current is at its weakest – about 4 km per hour and cooling to about 24°C.

The Moçambique Current is reinforced by the second main division of the original Equatorial Current which found its way around the southern end of Madagascar. The united waters continue their way down the coast of Africa, slowly cooling but, in their northern extent, essentially forming a tropical current washing a tropical coast. The lushness of this coast is

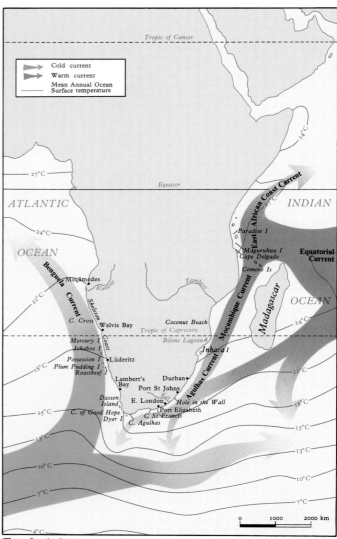

THE SEA'S INFLUENCE Contrasting sea currents produce on land habitats ranging from parched desert to steaming swampland.

a direct result of the heavy evaporation of water from the warm sea. On both sides of the shoreline, life flourishes in conditions of plentiful food and languorous climate. Hot and sometimes uncomfortably humid for man, especially in the northern parts, it is an ideal habitat for a considerable variety of plants, insects, birds and game animals.

Where life abounds

It is in the shallow waters of the continental shelf, however, that life flourishes to an extent which makes anything on land insignificant by comparison. All over the world, such shallow waters around the verges of continents are the most prolific homes of life. It is estimated that four-fifths of all the earth's plants and animals live in these littoral areas. Mineral foods wash off the continents and feed the minute drifting plants and animals, known as plankton, carried along by such currents as the Moçambique. The density of

plankton is more than astronomical. The pure plankton, including the prodigiously abundant copepods, which spend their whole lives drifting and grow to a size as large as a small grain of rice, live in vast communities of up to 105 000 individuals per cubic metre. Mixed with these shrimp-like creatures are the larvae of sponges, clams, snails, starfish, crabs, barnacles, shellfish, fish, anemones, jellyfish and corals, which start their lives as plankton and then either grow into free-swimming forms of life, or attach themselves to some selected base and become permanent fixtures.

Corals dislike water temperatures below 20°C. The northern part of the Moçambique coast therefore provides them with an excellent home, for the temperature is consistently warm and the powerful current serves them with rich stores of plankton food and oxygen. All along this coast the coral larvae settle, forming reefs and submarine platforms which

HAZY HAVEN Bilene Lagoon, on the shores of Moçambique, where warm waters lap a dazzling white beach. Casuarina trees, crowding the shore, murmur in the hot breeze. Fishing boats and piroques languidly ride the waves.

support numerous coral islets. These coral communities are the second most prolific homes of life on earth. They are, in fact, worlds unto themselves. Countless millions of tiny creatures, living in a strange but beautiful harmony, create massive additions to the shores of the earth which are as significant in their own way as mountain ranges.

Corals are members of the division of the animal world known as *Coelenterata*, which includes such creatures as jellyfish, anemones and hydroids. They are simple creatures with prodigious appetites. After their brief free-swimming larval stage, they settle down in water not deeper than 50 m, where sunlight can penetrate, free of mud, sediment or pollution, and in constant movement, with the current bringing masses of food to their waiting tentacles.

A fantasy of coral

Always growing upwards towards the light, and outwards towards the oxygen of the open sea, the coral colonies develop the most remarkable forms and colours. It is difficult to remember that the polyps are

animals and not plants. There are coral trees, shrubs, spires, boulders, fans, brains, toadstools and innumerable other shapes.

Living as tenants in these coral fantasies are a host of other creatures. Even within their armour the coral polyps accommodate microscopic plants called *dinoflagellates*. These boarders are very welcome. They pay their way and flourish by consuming the waste carbon dioxide given off by the polyp. Through the action of sunlight, the carbon dioxide is converted into food for the plants, and oxygen. These little plants act as built-in garbage and sewage-disposal units and it is for them, especially, that the polyps need the rays of the sun. The polyps themselves are dormant during the daylight hours. It is at night that the corals really come to life. In the darkness the polyps stretch out their tentacles and feed.

The warm waters of the Moçambique Current are producers of features other than coral reefs. From November to April tropical storms – cyclones or hurricanes – are born through the mixture of wind and heat.

Tropical seas are always notable for winds, for the parent of winds is heat and they follow the sun as a dog does its master. Currents of air flow like the currents in the sea. The south-east wind blows for ten months of the year along the Moçambique coast. Only in September and October does it die and the north-easter takes over. The south-easter starts off as a cool wind flowing to fill the vacuum caused by the rising of hot air in the tropical areas. As it flows northwards the wind gathers moisture and warmth. When it reaches the area where the sea has a minimum temperature of 27°C, it starts to rarefy and rise. This is a period of frightening instability. The wind mass tends to spiral clockwise in the Southern Hemisphere. If the wind is the dog of the sun, it is at this stage that it sees a cat, slips its leash, and runs wild.

Whirling around trying to catch its own tail, the cyclonic system wanders down the Moçambique channel accompanied by pouring rain and filthy black skies. In the development of the coral coast, such storms play a leading role. They break sections of the reef, and fragments, large and small, are tumbled off, piling up in deep water to provide a base for new reefs, or breaking down into sand which piles up and forms glistening white beaches. Hard coral rock is also formed. Birds roost on the top and their guano, added to chance pieces of drift matter, brings fertility to what now becomes a coral islet. Seeds of grass, shrubs and trees are blown on to it. Coconuts are

---

HOW REEFS ARE CREATED

Coral reefs are sculpted by some miracle of nature from the skeletons of countless millions of tiny, soft-bodied, carnivorous animals called polyps. Each mature polyp has a mouth fringed with tentacles, which catch food and pass it into the mouth. The mouth also voids excretion, sperm and eggs. The chalky skeleton forms a base for some polyps, but with others it is simply a mosaic of hard particles inside the body. Every reef, no matter how vast, begins as a single polyp. Side-shoots sprout from the 'parent', then they in turn produce more side-shoots. All are interconnected by a sheet of tissue that completely covers their skeletons. As the original polyps that began the colony die, their hard skeletons support new layers of living polyps — and so great undersea cathedrals are built up, often fantastically shaped by the currents that sway them.

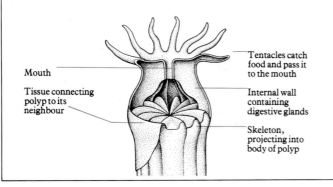

Mouth

Tissue connecting polyp to its neighbour

Tentacles catch food and pass it to the mouth

Internal wall containing digestive glands

Skeleton, projecting into body of polyp

SILVER SANDS Coconut Beach, Moçambique, sheltered by high, glistening dunes, and washed by the Indian Ocean. But there is menace, too, in this scene of serenity. For the multitude of fish attract vicious predators such as barracuda and giant sharks.

carried in by the current. Other colonists arrive.

Seedlings of mangroves sail gaily down the current in a great gamble which can end with their drifting out to sea or being cast up on an evolving shore. They are the pioneer plants in the birth of many new islands. Cast upon these infant islands their roots find the mud, and the growing trees attract to their shelter a numerous community of creatures. Soil is collected and held. Other plants have a chance of taking root. Pandanus and casuarinas grow. Crabs by the million, turtles and countless birds all settle in a garden growing where once the waves and the winds moved unchecked. The shattered coral reef is itself soon repaired. More polyps grow and the only long-lasting result of many a storm is generally what could least be expected – an encroachment of dry land into the domain of the sea.

Fish of the reef

A multiplicity of fish live in the Moçambique Current. Most of them are shallow-water species, and their diversity of shape and colour is the consequence of widely varying rock and coral formations and different bottom deposits, which create a vast number of habitats for plant and animal life. Bright and variegated colours are the rule. Four main varieties live in the reefs: butterflies, damsels, surgeons and wrasse. Most big fish tend to avoid the reefs as it is difficult for them to find food there. Groupers, amberjacks and barracudas, however, manage to prey on the clouds of smaller fish. Giant groupers, particularly, are like stomachs with fins. They simply gulp at anything edible and, with the barracuda, require close watching by any diver.

Some of the smaller fish are so weird in form and colour as to be preposterous. The lionfish, for example, dressed in an amazing collection of spires and spears, drifts lazily and insolently around, confident that any creature eating it, even a giant grouper, would need a stomach made of corrugated iron, for it is almost as poisonous as the dreaded stonefish.

Such creatures, however, are passive and unaggressive, and their armour is purely defensive. The stonefish, of such dreadful reputation among humans who explore coral reefs, is, in fact, totally retiring. Only about 18 cm long, and drab in appearance, it spends its life concealed in crevices waiting for the

CORAL KALEIDOSCOPE The delicate colours of a coral reef in the Paradise Island group shimmer in the sunlight. Such reefs consist of countless living creatures. By day they rest; by night they feed, trapping food with their searching tentacles.

A LIVING TRAP The gruesome stonefish lies perpetually in wait for food. Its spines are deadly to an unwary attacker.

DRIFTING FOOD Plankton, seen through a microscope. They are cannibalistic – and at the bottom of the food chain in the sea.

current to serve it by carrying to its jaws some unfortunate plankton. On its back are 13 viciously sharp dorsal spines, which are capable of penetrating the sole of a normal shoe. The poison they eject rises in the veins like molten lead, producing a numbing agony, and eventually death. One way to counteract its effect is to place the limb in almost scalding water, or near a fire, risking severe burns. For the venom is a protein, extremely sensitive to heat, and a tempera-

ture of 50°C renders it harmless. However, even this simple but painful antidote is rarely possible: the agony of being stung is so great that the victim usually collapses in the water, and dies by drowning.

Beyond the reefs, rock cods, snappers, kingfish, sea-eels or morays and puffers are other major families of fish in the Moçambique Current. To the scientists, pride of place in the whole fish fauna of this current is, however, given to the coelacanth, so

MONSTER FROM THE PAST The coelacanth, which dates back 400 million years. These creatures were thought to have become extinct 70 million years ago . . . until a live specimen was found in 1938. Since then, several more have been caught.

PLACE OF THE SOUND This cliff-bordered island, the Hole-in-the-Wall, is known as *esiKhaleni* (the place of the sound). Rollers thunder through the hole with a roar that can be heard kilometres away. The Hole-in-the-Wall is on the Wild Coast of Transkei.

far not found anywhere else in the world.

The fame of the coelacanth comes from its ancient origin as well as from its rarity. Scientists had long deduced from fossil remains that all land-living creatures had originated from fish-like creatures called *Choanichthyes*. These antique parents existed 400 million years ago and their fossil remains showed little change over a vast period of time. Three major divisions of life, called orders, developed from them. The *Rhipidistra* abandoned water for land and from them came amphibians, reptiles, birds and mammals. The original ancestors are extinct. Another order, the *Dipnoi,* or lungfish, having developed an organ like a lung, were content to remain exactly as they were right up into modern times. Using their lungs they could survive foul waters, geological upheavals and dramatic climatic changes. Working their way high up the rivers of Southern Africa, they were indifferent to droughts. If the river stopped flowing they simply encased themselves in a capsule of mud which was baked rock-hard by the sun, leaving the fish secure inside, snoozing and gently breathing until the coming of the next rains.

The third order, the *Coelacanthini*, contained only one known species. They remained in the water, and all indications were that 70 million years ago they were extinct. Then, in December 1938, a live speci-men was found off East London. Fourteen years later a second specimen was found at the Comoro Islands, and quite a few of these weird-looking primitives obviously still survive in the waters of the Moçambique Current. Their discovery gave scientists the exciting opportunity of testing deductions made from fragmentary fossil evidence. It showed their reconstructions to be substantially correct, and allowed them the opportunity of studying the structure of a creature from a most ancient rung in the ladder of evolution.

Another remarkable inhabitant of the Moçambique Current is the dugong, so often exhibited in sideshows as the original mermaid. In warm waters, and especially wherever suitable edible marine plants such as *Cymodocae* and *Zostera* grow, these strange, strictly vegetarian mammals find a home. Very little is known about them. Totally inoffensive, they live in family units and are especially to be found in the area between the Paradise Island group and the mainland, where the bed of the sea is thickly grown with their favourite foodstuffs. They seem to thrive in water of the same temperature as that desired by the corals. The density of both dugongs and corals dwindles as the current sweeps down the coast, the last extensive coral reef and the last resident dugong population being found at 26° south latitude around Inhaca

MERMAID'S RETREAT Dense vegetation cloaks the beach of Magurukwe Island, off the Moçambique coast. The dugong – a sea-mammal said to be the original mermaid – is common here. Fishing nets are drying in the foreground.

Island, at the southern end of the bay of Lourenço Marques.

In the same underwater grazing grounds as the dugong there also live numerous turtles: loggerhead, green, hawksbill, ridley and leatherback. Their range extends somewhat further south into the cooler waters of the northern Natal coast, but their numbers dwindle as the temperature falls.

When it passes the Natal border south of Inhaca Island, the Moçambique Current undergoes a change of name. It sweeps on down the South African coast under the name of the Agulhas Current, although the old name also survives. By the time the current reaches Durban it has cooled to an average of 27°C in summer and 21°C in winter. The population of marine life has slowly changed with the temperature. The beautiful coral reefs have vanished. Salmon, grunter, kingfish and stumpnose have become the dominant fish species. Sometimes, the ocean can be darkened by the presence of vast shoals of sardines. The seasonal perambulations of these little fish are quite as astonishing as the world of the coral reefs.

The sardines live for most of the year in the waters of the Southern and Western Cape. Towards autumn each year the sardines that will spawn gather in prodigious shoals and begin a leisurely 1500 km journey up the waters of the Agulhas Current. Apparently, their spawning process requires water of a warmer temperature than that of their usual home. It is difficult to convey some idea of the size of these shoals. The Milky Way itself cannot equal them in sheer numbers. Their usual pattern is a succession of shoals which, as far north as Port St John's, keep a few kilometres out to sea. Then, depending on the current, they move inshore and hug the coast as far as Durban. First come small vanguard shoals, then vast shoals of countless millions of little fish, then straggling shoals.

Ordeal of the sardines

The spectacle is staggering. A hungry canopy of seabirds poises over the shoals, diving, gorging, and floating heavily on the surface. Around the fringes prey a vicious crowd of predators – kob, leervis, bonito, tunny, barracuda, snoek, kingfish, queenfish, prodigal son, sharks, skates and rays.

The shoals at the end of the run are accompanied by enormous concentrations of gannets. These birds gorge themselves to such an extent that at times they lose the ability to fly and cover the sea in huge floating masses, squawking, groaning as though with 'crop-aches', and complaining of inability to consume more. The predatory fish have the same experience. They lurk on the fringes, stuffing themselves to bursting point, never daring to tear into the centre of the shoal for fear of suffocation from the little fish clogging their gills. Human anglers crowd the coastline, fishing for the game fish in what is one of the world's principal fishing events.

Somewhere about the latitude of Durban, the sardines complete their great swim. The water has perhaps reached its optimum temperature for them, and the time of spawning is over. They swing southwards again, disperse and move swiftly down with the current. What percentage of fish survive the double journey is unknown. But each female lays about 100 000 eggs. If only two of these ever reach the happy stage of themselves breeding in these annual nuptials, then the quantity of sardines will remain constant. The other 99 998 sardines can be eaten.

By the time the Moçambique Current passes the mouth of the Kei River it has changed its nature from tropical to temperate. All along its journey it deposits on the beaches a great variety of shells. The Wild Coast of Transkei is a particularly productive

Cape gannet *(Sula bassana capensis)*

Gannets: byword for greed

A gannet colony is one of the noisiest, most aggressive places on earth. Thousands of bills open and close in raucous, yelping, screeching discord. Thousands of huge, clumsy, webbed feet seem to be a constant threat to the eggs. The birds are ready to gulp down anything that looks edible – their very name has become a byword for greed – and chicks have a survival rate of only about 5 per cent in their first year.

Each nesting site is only a bill's length from the next, and an elaborate social system has had to evolve or the species would have fallen victim to its own ferocity long ago. It can be seen in operation in any of the large gannetries on the rocky offshore islands between Algoa Bay and Walvis Bay. A bird arriving back at its colony immediately points its bill skywards, revealing the black line that runs down its breast. This appeasement gesture convinces the other birds that it is not going to attack them, so they allow it to waddle to its own nest. Any bird not announcing its peaceful intentions in this way would have to run a gauntlet of razor-sharp beaks.

Gannets in their greatest quantities feed on the teeming fish stocks of the cold Benguela Current, which sweeps along the western coast, and take their prey with spectacular dives. The waters around the islands are alive with splashes as the gannets plunge from heights of up to 30 m, their wings half closed to form living arrowheads. They do not appear to go far beneath the surface, nor do they remain submerged for long. Like pelicans and boobies, gannets have inflatable air sacs under the skin, which bring them swiftly bobbing to the surface.

Gannet chicks, fed by both parents, leave the nests and make their own way to the sea about 90 days after hatching. They are black, with white spots. The all-white plumage, with black-tipped wings, comes only with maturity.

BRUCE'S BEAUTIES A giant wave thunders towards the shore at Cape St Francis, where the rollers are believed by many to be the world's best surfing waves. Known as Bruce's Beauties, they can surge for more than a kilometre without breaking.

COLLECTORS' DREAM A mother-of-pearl-coated perlemoen lies beside a piece of sea bamboo. The Wild Coast is rich in shell treasures. Although scavenged by commercial shell gatherers, the beaches are littered daily with new specimens.

area for collectors. Jeffreys Bay, south of Port Elizabeth, is another area renowned for its varieties of shellfish, and although commercial shell gatherers constantly scavenge the beach to supply conchologists and curio manufacturers, the tide each day deposits many more specimens.

Jeffreys Bay lies on the east side of Cape St Francis. Here, in the winter months (May to September) when a north-westerly wind blows, coupled with a ground swell at low tide, there builds up what is considered by many devotees to be the world's perfect surfing wave. These rollers surge in from the outer ocean with immense and relentless power. Riding these wild waves is an experience which attracts surfers from all over the world. Every skill of their sport is needed. Huge tubes, breaking symmetrically, carry a surfer at such speed that most actions have to be on the reflex. The full power of the sea seems to be symbolised in these majestic waves. They were discovered by an American film producer, Bruce

Brown, who used them in his surfing film *Endless Summer*. Known as Bruce's Beauties, the rollers do not break quickly, but keep their tube shapes for nearly a kilometre.

Slightly smaller waves, known simply as Bruce's, thunder towards shore at Super Tube Point on Jeffreys Bay. In Seal Bay, west of Cape St Francis, some of the loveliest of all waves may be seen, too broken for surfers but each one sweeping in like a line of armoured knights, with plumes, pennants and banners trailing behind them, charging upon a trembling shore.

Onward flows the Moçambique Current down a rocky and steeply sloping coast. Then the great continent of Africa suddenly subsides gently into the sea like a huge man sighing as he relaxes in a pool of water. Without any drama of cliffs, the continent simply vanishes below the waves at Cape Agulhas, and spreads out in a vast submarine plain.

This undersea projection of Africa lies about

NO-MAN'S-LAND The Skeleton Coast, where hot desert meets cold sea along an inhospitable shoreline. Here there is no drinking water or food. On the beach lies a wreck – a reminder of the many disasters that have befallen seafarers on this coast.

60 fathoms beneath the surface and extends nearly 250 km to the south. Over this so-called Agulhas Bank the Moçambique Current eddies and swirls, with a prodigious fish life feeding on the rich food stores washed off the African continent and nourishing the plankton. This abundance of life makes the Agulhas Bank one of the world's principal commercial trawling areas. For the great ocean current, this is almost the end of its long journey. Ahead of it lies the Cape of Good Hope, and there the Moçambique or Agulhas Current, now old, relatively cool and weak, collides broadside on with the powerful young Benguela Current.

Quite overwhelmed by that vigorous new river in the sea, the Moçambique Current bends southwards, hesitates, and then loses itself in the icy waters of the southern sea. In the shallow waters of the Agulhas Bank, along the coastline from Cape Agulhas to the Cape of Good Hope (especially in False Bay, the great line-fishing area), it leaves its rich variety of marine life. But it leaves the creatures of the sea with a parting gift, for they are sustained by inexhaustible stores of plankton and primitive life killed by the collision of the warm and cold currents. False Bay, as the terminal point of the Mocambique-Agulhas Current, teems throughout the year with a confused and unnatural mixture of warm and cold water marine

life. Such varieties seldom encounter one another, so that there is a great feasting on what are to them exotic dishes.

Birth of a current

The Benguela Current is totally different but equally decisive in its influence on marine life and the whole nature of the south-west coast of Africa. While the Moçambique Current has its start in the warm waters of the Equator, the Benguela Current starts in the Antarctic. Gigantic segments of pack-ice break away from the land mass and flow off to the east on a restless journey, drifting slowly around the globe. A huge reservoir is formed of water not only cooled by the ice, but also enriched with a prodigious store of chemicals carried by the ice off the mainland of Antarctica, or deposited by previous icebergs and swirled up from the depths of the sea.

The end of Africa, projecting into this moving mass, with the weight of the Moçambique Current flowing down its east coast, deflects a portion of this Antarctic Drift into a northerly flow. This, the Benguela Current, reaches the Cape of Good Hope with a temperature of about 10°C. The Moçambique Current, its waters still above 20°C in temperature, hits it broadside and the collision sends the Benguela Current up the west coast of Southern Africa on a long journey towards the Equator.

This cold river acts as an effective wall dividing the Indian and Atlantic oceans. Few forms of marine life can survive changes of more than 5°C in the temperature of water. A river of cold water such as the Benguela Current, forcing its way through a warm sea, is therefore a barrier almost as solid as a stone wall to marine life. Warm-water fish simply double in their wake and head for home and familiar temperatures as soon as they find their noses pushing into the fringes of the cold stream.

In its own right, however, the Benguela Current has a population of sea creatures whose numbers make even the Moçambique Current seem sparsely inhabited by comparison. As it flows up from the Antarctic this current carries with it 20 times the amount of nitrogen found in parallel latitudes in the Mocambique Current. All told, it has so rich a store of chemicals that it has been well described as a meadow of the sea; and on its pastures there feeds such an

BREAKFAST TIME Early morning on Marcus Island, at Saldanha Bay... and jackass penguins huddle together in groups or waddle about in pairs, as if to discuss the first meal of the day. In the background, cormorants gather for their flights out to sea in search of fish.

Captain Benjamin Morrell. Seal-hunter who missed a greater prize.

The Great Guano Rush

In the year 1828 an American sealer, Captain Benjamin Morrell, reaped a rich and bloody harvest of pelts from the islands that lie off the Atlantic coast of Southern Africa. The voyage paid him handsomely, but the captain could have become one of the world's richest men if he had realised the value of the prize that lay literally beneath his nose.

On Monday, October 6, 1828, Captain Morrell made the following entry in the log of his ship, the *Antarctic*:

'October 6th Monday. Arrived at Ichaboe Island; about one mile in circumference and one-and-a-half miles from the shore. The island is formed of volcanic materials and its shores are resorted to by a multitude of fur-seals. We took about one thousand of their skins in a few days. The surface of this island is covered with birds' manure to a depth of twenty-five feet.'

It was the last, almost casual, remark that contained the clue to Ichaboe's real treasure.

On his retirement, Captain Morrell wrote a book of his travels, *A Narrative of Four Voyages*. It was published in 1832. Not much notice was taken of it then. But in 1835 the first shipment of guano was made to Europe from Peru. The Incas had discovered the richness of guano as a fertilizer, and the Spaniards had found the islands off the Peruvian coast so thickly covered that they jocularly named them the *Sierra Nevada* (snowy mountains).

The Peruvian guano was received by European farmers with tremendous enthusiasm. It was without doubt the richest of all fertilizers. The trouble was that the deposits were controlled by monopolies. A worldwide search commenced for alternative supplies. It was then that Morrell's book was dusted off somebody's shelf and in 1842 the description in it of Ichaboe was pointed out to a Liverpool merchant. A small company was hastily formed and three vessels set out to look for the island.

One vessel met with an accident. The second found nothing. The third reached Table Bay on February 15, 1843. Her master, Captain Parr, met the crew of an American whaler and they gave him the location of Ichaboe. He sailed there immediately and reached the place without difficulty. To his glee he found that Captain Morrell had made a curious mistake for a Yankee: he had underestimated. Ichaboe (it is said that the name came from a Hottentot word sounding like Itshabo) was covered in 60 ft (20 m), not 25 ft, of guano, a truly incredible mound of pungent ammonia-scented fertilizer. It was estimated to weigh 800 000 tons.

Queueing for a fortune

Parr loaded his ship, the *Ann* of Bristol, and sailed for home with the news. Confronted by such a chance of fortune, the company promoters immediately set to arguing about a division of the profits. They rushed to litigation and the publicity drew the attention of a flood of fortune-seekers. In the whole history of commerce, the guano rush that followed has never had its parallel. Ship after ship arrived. The few good loading places on the north side of the island were soon snapped up. Departing ships sold their places to the highest bidders, and there were queues of waiting ships. The scene was grotesquely picturesque. A British naval frigate had to be despatched to impose order.

'Imagine,' wrote her captain, Sir John Marshall, *'a fleet of about 225 sail, some of them old and rigged out for the occasion, many with masters of irregular habits and insubordinate crews, seamen and labourers amounting to about 3 500 men of the lowest and most drunken class, crowded together in certainly the most boisterous anchorage in the world.'*

On the island a tent town had been pitched, and according to a visitor, Charles Andersson, 'the scenes of drunkenness and debauchery they sheltered would have disgraced the lowest house of vice'. He went on:

'Spirits in much greater quantity than were allowed by the

regulations were issued to the men, with the connivance of the mates, though not with that of the masters, and bacchanalian orgies were held in the encampment abominable beyond belief, which would call up a blush even on the face of the most abandoned.'

A committee of control was appointed by Sir John Marshall. The tent town was pulled down, and from then on naval patrols cleared the island each night of skulkers. All seamen were driven back to their ships, taking with them a good many women who had contrived in some mysterious way to reach this little island.

By January 1845 there were 450 ships at anchor around Ichaboe. Over 100 000 tons of guano had already been removed, while another 200 000 tons were carried away by the end of the year. Guano then sold for £8 a ton.

Charles Andersson has left another piquant description of the scene in his book, *The Okavango River* (1861):

'On a fine, calm day it was pleasant to stand on the summit of the rocky islet, and look down on the busy hive below. One might then see one party in a pit, amidst clouds of dust, digging guano, while another was shovelling it into bags and further on, perhaps, a band employed in wheeling or carrying sacks to the shore, where a long row of men would be seen running along with others on their shoulders, tossing them into the boats at the stage ends, and returning rapidly for more. Then again, the deeply laden boats pulling off to the vessel, and the crew on board heaving up the cargo to their well known chant, just reaching the ear of the listener on land, and contrasting well by its lulling sound and effect with the stirring life which it softened and harmonised, added greatly to the picturesqueness of the scene. On some of the fine days referred to, which occurred generally after bad weather, not less than 2000 tons have been shipped in the course of twelve hours.'

It was certainly a surprising sequence of events — icebergs carrying chemicals into the sea; the plankton proliferating on the chemical foods; the Benguela Current carrying the plankton up the west coast of Southern Africa; the pelagic shoals of fish flourishing on the plankton; the seabirds feeding on the fish; man carefully collecting their guano and shipping it for thousands of kilometres to Europe and America; farmers eagerly buying it as one of the richest of all fertilizers; crops such as grapes thriving on it; fine wines being drunk at glittering banquets with not much thought to their background.

Ichaboe and other guano islands such as Malagas were reduced to well-swept tidiness. With a squawk of relief the birds returned. An estimated 230 000 gannets nest on Ichaboe, as well as 8000 penguins and about 2600 cormorants. About 2000 tons of guano are collected each year and this is sold at the current price of R64 per ton. The original estimated 800 000 tons which covered the island at the time of the first rush would have yielded at least R51 million. No pirate ever left a treasure on any island comparable with this.

immense concentration of plankton that the water carrying them, compared to the clear blue of the Moçambique Current, is often a leaden, opaque, grey-green in colour. In this ocean meadow, extending for 3000 km up the west coast, a swarming mass of shoal fish such as pilchards, sardines, anchovies, mullet and mackerel wander about like vast flocks of sheep, feeding to capacity. These are pelagic fish — that is, fish which live on the surface of deep waters as distinct from littoral fish, which inhabit the marginal shallow water or littoral.

The variety of fish species found in such cold waters is limited, but their quantity is overwhelming, and it is from these shoals that the fishing industry draws its bulk supplies for canning factories along the coast, for factory ships and refrigerated bulk carriers, and for hundreds of highly sophisticated fishing craft sent into these waters from Japan, Korea, Spain, Soviet Russia and other fishing countries as well as South Africa.

Feeding on these shoals are a host of other creatures. Rock lobsters scavenge the sea bottom, keeping it clear of dead fish. Cape fur seals in huge numbers have their rookeries on rocky islets and at such shore sites as Cape Cross. Seabirds, notably penguins and gannets, make their nests on such islands as Dassen, Ichaboe, Malagas, Marcus, Jutten, Plumpudding, Roastbeef, Mercury and Dyers, and yield each year a highly valuable deposit of guano which is used as a fertilizer, expecially for the vineyards of the Cape.

Dassen Island was described by Cherry Kearton in his book, *The Island of Penguins*, as the naturalist's eighth wonder of the world. Lying in the full stream of the Benguela Current, 78 km north of Cape Town, it is just the top of a submerged hill, 3,25 km by 2 km in extent and only 30 m above sea level. This sandy pancake of a place is nevertheless considered a paradise island by the jackass penguins, and this is their principal breeding ground. Sadly depleted by the oil pollution of passing tankers, and a variety of other factors such as massive competitive fishing by humans, the number of nesting penguins is down to about 100 000. During the breeding seasons, in February and September, there are few spectacles in natural history more captivating and droll than the antics and social behaviour of this quaint community of birds. The booming sound of their massed donkey-like braying call merges strangely with the roar of the surf.

Gannets, possibly the most beautiful of all seabirds, and certainly among the greediest, nest in their

BAY OF PLENTY Cormorants crowd the cliffs of Bird Island, in Lambert's Bay. Cormorants are unusual among seabirds, because they have no oil glands to waterproof their feathers. They spread their wings out to dry: otherwise they would become waterlogged.

own communities on such islets as Ichaboe, Malagas, Mercury and Possession. Another notable bird of these waters is the Cape cormorant which nests principally on Penguin Island (Lamberts Bay), Jutten Island and Ichaboe. These black-plumaged, duck-like seabirds are the most numerous of the flying predators of the southern coast of Africa. Flying in disciplined groups, V-formations or line ahead, they cover vast distances in search of suitable feeding shoals, gather above the fish in thousands, feed, and then return to their roosts at dusk, flying steadily and purposefully in their tight formations low over the sea, their powerful wing beats just skimming the surface of waters glowing with the colours of a sunset sky.

Islands of treasure

The rocky little islands scattered along the west coast of Southern Africa can be ranked among the genuine treasure islands of the world. The first profit ever made from the settlement at Cape Town came from sealing, for the pelts of the Cape fur seal have been highly valued from early times. Before Van Riebeeck settled at the Cape, French and Danish sealers paid regular visits to the islands each winter season. This activity continued into modern times with about 70 000 seals, mostly pups, slaughtered annually to supply the market for pelts. The carcasses are frozen and exported to Greenland as food for Eskimoes.

Guano (the Spanish word for manure), collected from the islands is an even more valuable harvest from this productive 'meadow' of the sea. It was discovered almost by accident, by an American sealer, Captain Benjamin Morrell, who in 1828 was cruising up the coast hunting for pelts. Each seal nursery yielded him a bloody increase to his cargo. On one island, Possession, he found a mystery. It was completely deserted and covered with the bodies of an estimated 500 000 seals whose deaths he attributed to a plague, or else what he called a 'spurt' of sand from the adjoining desert coast. The likeliest-sounding modern explanation of the mystery is that the seals were poisoned by some massive gas bubble, rising from the seabed.

On the same voyage, Captain Morrell entered a casual note in his log to the effect that the island of Ichaboe was covered by vast deposits of bird manure. The discovery meant little either to him or to the world at the time, but it was to lead to one of the most colourful episodes in South Africa's history: the Great Guano Rush. (See box, pp. 26–27.)

Ichaboe and the other 15 principal guano-producing islands off the coast of Southern Africa have an estimated combined population of 375 000 gannets and 205 000 penguins. Over 1 million cormorants live around the coast, many of them nesting on wooden platforms obligingly built by man at such places as Cape Cross Lagoon and Walvis Bay. In return, the birds reward the platform builders with valuable deposits of guano. The collection and marketing of this guano each year is a highly profitable operation.

The Benguela Current moves up the coast at a speed of about 3 km an hour. Its width is never more than 150 km, and its dense marine and bird life is therefore confined to a long ribbon of cold water contained by a howling desert on the coast to the east and the warmer waters of the South Atlantic on the west. The cold stream of water not only resists evaporation but also actually condenses any moisture from sea breezes trying to reach the land from the warm South Atlantic.

As a barrier, the Benguela Current remains relentless. In its depths it is subject to occasional disturbances as a consequence of its own teeming population. Countless dead plankton, diatoms, microscopic sea plants, fish, carcasses of seals, birds and rock lobsters rain down in a ceaseless drizzle, forming a greenish-coloured mud in which feed vast colonies of bacteria. These bacteria produce sulphuretted hydrogen which accumulates in the mud. Occasionally a sneak intrusion of warmer water from the western ocean disturbs this established state. The gas bursts out of the pockets in the mud and bubbles up through the water. Fish and marine plants are killed. They litter the beaches with their carcasses, while uncanny islets of sulphurous green mud appear suddenly above the surface of the sea and then disappear after a few days with equal abruptness.

The temperature of the Benguela Current remains cold all the way up what is called the Skeleton Coast. Then, at 15° south latitude, near Lobito in Angola, it reaches the end of its flow. It encounters the warm waters of the Equatorial zone and subsides beneath them, merging with the vast pool of cold water which lies in the dark depths of all great oceans, even in regions of the greatest surface temperatures. Its legacy to the land mass of Southern Africa would be hard to exaggerate. Just as the Moçambique Current brings humidity to the lush and tropical eastern coast so, on the west, all is parched, withered, stony and dry. The Benguela Current creates a harsh unrelenting world in which life, if it is to survive at all, must take on strange forms.

The Cape, a romantic land of legend, set between two mighty seas

According to a poetic legend, the Cape of Good Hope is the home of the savage and barbaric giant Adamastor, who rebelled against the gods and, as a punishment, was cast down to the end of the African continent. There, his sullen spirit lurks around the great sandstone cliffs.

FAIREST CAPE Pounded by huge rollers, and with Table Mountain, free of clouds, brooding over all in the distance (top centre), the Peninsula recalls Sir Francis Drake's words: 'The fairest cape we saw in the whole circumference of the earth.'

31

*A workshop for storms, where
a banished giant rages in
fury against the shore*

STORM-LASHED, mountain-shadowed, majestic even at its most peaceful, the Cape of Good Hope thrusts down from Africa like the continent's last challenge to the eternal ocean.

According to Luis Vaz de Camões, the poet genius of Portugal, it is the home of the savage and barbaric giant Adamastor, who rebelled against the gods of Ancient Greece, and as a punishment was cast down to the very end of the continent. There, his body 'turned to rocks all rough and strange' and formed the peninsula of the Cape, with the mass of Table Mountain as his tomb. His sullen spirit still lurks around the great sandstone cliffs, and the Peninsula is his workshop for storms. He roams over the face of the southern seas, dressed in howling gales and dark storm clouds.

The Cape has always been rich in legends. The Arabs of the days of Sindbad spoke of Table Mountain as a magnet which drew their dhows to inescapable doom. The pioneer Portuguese navigators encountered such fearsome storms that, from the disappearance of Bartholomew Dias, European discoverer of the Cape of Good Hope, was born the legend which Wagner set to music in the form of *The Flying Dutchman*. It told of the sea captain who defied fate by swearing to double the Cape in the face of contrary winds, and was condemned for ever to be blown back.

These ancient tales blend perfectly with the appearance of the Cape. It lies at the southern end of a perfect textbook peninsula. Long and narrow, with a backbone of sharply defined mountain peaks, it probes into the southern ocean like a half-curved finger. The sea lashes against it, and great rollers relentlessly pound at its rocky shore. Only a solid foundation of granite gives it the strength to defy innumerable storms.

Rounding the Cape

Winds blow almost incessantly here, while the sea around it has the turbulence of the meeting place of two great ocean currents, the warm Moçambique and the cold Benguela.

To generations of sailormen, the Cape of Good Hope also marked the blending point of the cultures of the East and West. Outward bound, the doubling of the Cape turned the traveller's back on his own homeland; ahead lay new experiences, new people and new challenges. Homeward bound, the rounding of the Cape turned the traveller's face towards familiar places. The sweet sounds and smells of home started to whisper gently in on the breezes. The homesickness of innumerable travellers has been blown away by the winds of the Cape.

Modern geographers mark Cape Agulhas, at the southern end of Africa, as the actual meeting place of the Indian and Atlantic oceans. This is pure convenience; there is no difference in water on either side of the imaginary line drawn due southwards from Agulhas. Obviously, there never could be a straight line of division anywhere in the sea. But it is at the Cape of Good Hope that the nature of the sea changes, and the barrier interposed by the continent of Africa between East and West has its end.

On the summit of the Cape promontory, weathered by salty spray, rain and the alternating warmth and cold of the days and nights, there stands a beacon. Climb up to it, and southwards over the seething face of the ocean for 5000 km there is no other land; no trade routes; no jet aircraft tearing through the sky.

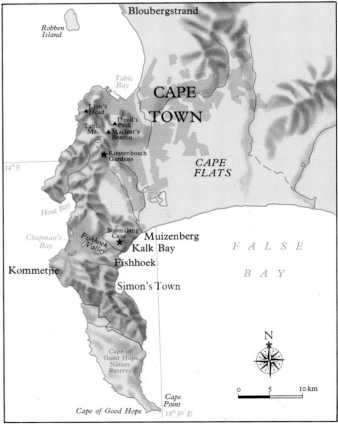

DEFYING THE SEA A solid granite base gives the Peninsula the strength to resist howling winds and pounding seas.

TAVERN OF THE SEAS To seafarers of old, Table Mountain was as welcome a sight as their favourite inn. This view, with Devil's Peak on the left and Lion's Head on the right, is from Bloubergstrand, across a 15 km stretch of Table Bay

Only a wilderness of water; the tumult of the Roaring Forties; the increasing cold with every kilometre travelled; and then, at last, the shores of Antarctica – forbidding, but alluring in their dangers, secrets and untamed beauty.

In that desolation of snow and ice, pollution and despoliation are still the work of only a few whalermen. The winds and the currents pressing in upon the shores of Southern Africa are clear and fresh. Through the keen air you can see into the verges of eternity. The clarity of the water is darkened only by the richness it carries of plankton and fish.

Behind the Cape lies the whole continent of Africa. Vast and sprawling; boisterous; brutal in its history; well looted; well stained with blood; regarded by many scientists as the cradle of man. Certainly it has the richest and most varied of all populations of wild animals.

A ruthless struggle for existence

The contrast between land and sea is startling, but so are the parallels. Both are on a gigantic scale. Both are majestically beautiful. Beneath the sea there rages a struggle for existence just as ruthless as the conflict on land. The moods of land and sea are matched; the wild flowers and precious stones are equalled in beauty by the corals and anemones.

In fairly recent geological times the Cape Peninsula formed a pair of islands, divided by a narrow rift (now the Fish Hoek Valley) through which the sea had forced for itself a short cut from east to west. Even now, with the Peninsula attached to the mainland by the Cape Flats, a low-lying former part of the sea floor, it is tremendously influenced by the sea. In summer there is usually a difference of at least 6°C in sea temperatures on either side of the Peninsula, with the warmer eastern side supporting a marine life very different from that on the western side.

In these summer months, from November to March, the south-east wind is persistent, often reaching 40 km per hour, with periodic tantrums which reach 120 km per hour. Trees grow at an angle, hoping to get away from the relentless and venomous south-easter. Man plans his activities in any natural lee. Nevertheless, it is a dry, healthy wind so far as the Peninsula is concerned. It carries rain far inland but brings to the Peninsula some

FISHERMEN'S HAVEN Hout Bay, with the start of Chapman's Peak on the right and the Sentinel at the other end. *Houtbaai* was named 'wood bay' because the forest there provided timber for the repair of ships in former years. Today it is an important fishing harbour.

Grey plover (*Pluvialis squatarola*)

Fugitives from the Arctic

As summer approaches, flocks of small birds appear on the beaches and inland waters of Southern Africa. They are waders, fleeing from the deadly grip of winter in the Arctic, where they have raised their young in the tundra and along the riverbanks.

On their prodigious journeys, many of these birds exchange their summer plumage for a more workaday travelling costume. In its homeland, in Siberia and northern Russia, the grey plover is handsomely spangled with grey on its wings and back, and almost black on breast and body. The curlew sandpiper, from Siberia, is particularly handsome in the breeding season because of the rich chestnut colour of its breast and body. And the sanderling is resplendently russet at home in the Arctic. But out of the breeding season all three take on a drab, camouflaging grey-brown and white plumage.

With the coming of winter they begin to leave, to take advantage of the bounty of spring in the north. By early May most of them have gone. The shores of Southern Africa will see them no more until the following spring.

remarkable cloud effects. It disperses flying pests, smog and pollution so effectively that it is known as the Cape Doctor, and is well liked by flowering plants, many species of which use it as a medium for distributing their seeds.

The winter wind is the north-wester. This is far less persistent, although its gales can be of great violence and it is the bringer of rain to the moderate annual extent of 35 cm at the tip of the Cape. Throughout the year, there is seldom a day when there is no wind at the Cape of Good Hope.

The tip of the Peninsula is exposed to enormous pressures from wind and sea. Surging in upon Cape Point comes the full weight of the great rollers created in the clash of two great ocean currents and a

A world of colour at the Cape

The full glory of the Cape wild flowers comes from August to November. These are idyllic months in this realm of the flowers. The rains of winter are over; the winds of summer are still to come. A time of colour and sweet scents.

The small-petalled oxalis

The glowing mesembryanthemum

Disa uniflora, the 'Pride of Table Mountain'

The fragrant, white everlasting *Helichrysum vestitum*

The sweetly scented and luxuriant *Lampranthus glaucus*

Disa ferruginea, a Cape orchid

The cancer bush, *Sutherlandia frutescens*

The everlasting *Helipterum*

Dimorphotheca, in the spring

HAVEN FOR PLANTS A tranquil scene in the botanical gardens at Kirstenbosch, with the tree fern *Alsophila dregei* on the left and arum lilies at its foot. The gardens provide a sanctuary for thousands of different species of plants—all of them native to South Africa.

complex pattern of winds. Steep cliffs, detached rocks and oddly shaped pinnacles have been eroded into the granite shoreline. Beneath Cape Point itself, and along the coast, there are sea caves, one of them 61 m deep and with a mouth 12 m in diameter.

On top of this granite basement, the higher levels of the Peninsula consist of sedimentary sandstone and quartzite. The sandstone is a coarse-looking rock composed of large grains of sand stained red and brown by iron. Manganese is also present and provides dark-coloured layers.

Paradise for flowers

The thin layer of soil on top of this rock is acid and contains little organic matter. A human gardener would look at it with distaste and go elsewhere to do his planting. Nature, however, makes of this unpromising-looking soil a paradise for the ancient type of vegetation known as Cape Schlerophyll, and 1800 species of plants flourish in the area of the Cape of Good Hope Nature Reserve at the end of the Peninsula.

Animal life has always been sparse, and confined mainly to small creatures which can shelter from the winds below the level of the shrubs. Baboons have always been present, probably flourishing because they can move at will to sheltered places. Larger animals tended to migrate into the Peninsula in the winter months and then get out with the coming of the south-easter.

Both sides of the Cape Peninsula have handsome bays and beautiful beaches. Especially notable are the long beaches at Chapman's Bay on the western side and Muizenberg on the eastern side. All beaches have fine sand of almost dazzling whiteness. The Muizenberg beach stretches in a magnificent curve for over 30 km to the verges of the Hottentots Holland Mountains.

Rock pools, especially on the western coast, shelter a vast number of seaweeds, anemones and shellfish. On the eastern side, where the water is usually calmer and very clear, there are submarine forests of marine growths, with vividly coloured sea urchins and numerous little fish. The lovely perlemoen shell is

found all around the Peninsula, and in June the delicate paper nautilus shells are washed up on the Muizenberg beach.

The mountain backbone which runs the length of the Peninsula is full of caves. Between Muizenberg and Kalk Bay there are 86, some of them probing deep into the mountains, others, such as Boomslang Cave, finding an involved way from one side of a high ridge to the other.

Tavern of the seas

Table Mountain is one of the most spectacular of all landfalls. It is only 1087 m high but, with its slopes leading directly into the sea, it looms up as a massive pile of rock, an unmistakable beacon on the shipping route around the southern end of Africa. Like a gigantic inn sign, the mountain offered earlier travellers shelter from the storms, recreation on shore for sea-weary legs, foodstuffs from the hunting and farming activities of man and, of major importance, fresh water from numerous streams to replenish supplies which had usually become foul by this stage of a long sailing-ship journey.

The influence of Table Mountain on the history of Southern Africa has been considerable. So far as the city of Cape Town is concerned, there is no doubt that without the mountain it would never have been there. The great natural harbour of Saldanha, 120 km up the west coast, offered far superior shelter but there was no drinking water. Table Bay had the disadvantage of inferior shelter, but the sweet water of the mountain and the ease of identifying the landfall were the deciding factors.

Nature was particularly ingenious in the creation of Table Mountain.

If everything – shape, height, orientation, and the very particular nature of the prevailing summer wind – did not each contribute exactly to the whole effect, then nothing very special would be achieved. But each component is exactly right. Table Mountain not only has its shape but also its tablecloth, and in the laying of this large-scale piece of napery, nature contrived matters with a real touch of humour.

The mountain was created about 150 million years ago as part of what is known to geologists as the Cape System. It started as a thick deposit of silt eroded off the African mainland and deposited beneath the sea.

BROKEN GIANT The skeleton of the steamer *Kakapo* thrusts above the sands of Long Beach. The ship foundered here on her first voyage in May 1900. Behind the wreck towers the majestic Chapman's Peak and to the right soars Noordhoek.

39

The weight of this load of silt eventually became too great. The bed of the sea simply collapsed to form a trough under the silt. As the silt subsided it was caught in a vice-like pressure from the sides of this trough, which tended to close inwards. The upper levels of the silt were forced above the surface of the water and this was the birth of the Cape System.

In the paroxysm of birth, the deposits of silt were warped, buckled and twisted. As they emerged from the sea the silt was in three series. On the top was what is known as the Witteberg Series. Contained in its muds were the remains of numerous plants. Below it was the Bokkeveld Series, full of shallow-water fossils. At the bottom was the Table Mountain Series. No fossils have been found in its silts, but many striated and glacier-scarred pebbles are the sure signs of an ice age at the time of deposition.

The Table Mountain Series consists of thick beds of silt, hardened into white quartzite and sandstone of a colour often made red, orange or purple by the iron oxide and silica which cement the grains of sand. A vast layer of this colourful sediment once covered the area of the adjoining Cape Flats and ran as far as the mountains on the horizon. Erosion steadily removed the upper layer of the Bokkeveld and Witteberg Series, as well as everything covering the Cape Flats.

Table Mountain, its two companions, Devil's Peak and Lion's Head, and the range which makes a backbone for the Cape Peninsula, were left isolated, and assumed their present shapes as the consequence of continuing erosion. The process continues, with further change accelerated by man.

The ice age may have inhibited the presence of life at the time the materials of Table Mountain were laid down. Since it emerged from the sea, however, the mountain has become the home for an extraordinary variety of living things, especially plants. At least 2500 known species of plants are found on its slopes, their distribution controlled by considerable differences in soils and climate at varying altitudes, and by the shelter against or exposure to wind, sun and rain found on different sides of the mountain. The western side of the mountain is considerably drier than the eastern.

Throughout the year, Table Mountain is the scene of a magnificent display of flowering plants. Spring is the peak period, but in every month there is something beautiful to be seen and it would be rash to single out any species as being exceptional. The rocky slopes can produce flower displays to match those in any cultivated garden. Even the faces of the precipices have their disas, 20 different species of what is known as the Pride of Table Mountain, clinging to the rocks wherever the water of cascades keeps them moist. But for sheer fame, somewhere very near the head of all the species must be the celebrated silver trees whose leaves, shimmering in the sunshine, are in perfect harmony with the towering precipices of sandstone.

The silver trees originally grew only on the windswept mountains of the Cape Peninsula, with Table Mountain their particular home. They flourished on the nutrients found in decomposed sandstone. And they needed the winds. The south-easter, so hostile to other plants, blew fungus parasites away and was essential to their seeding. There are male and female trees. The male produces flowers in late spring. The female produces cones in which the seeds ripen. When the seeds are ready and the wind is at the correct velocity, the cones open. The seeds, each with a built-in parachute, are blown forth on a great adventure, with only an infinitesimal chance that they will land on some spot where a chain of favourable circumstances will allow them to take root. An adult silver tree is the almost unreal product of an almost impossible series of coincidences.

Laying the tablecloth

The south-east wind of the summer months is the great servant of Table Mountain. It lays the tablecloth, blows away most pests, and keeps the mountain top reasonably moist until the rainy season proper comes in winter and deposits about 1400 mm of water to keep the streams in spate.

The tablecloth is the real crowning glory of Table Mountain. Properly laid – not too thick or too thin – it is one of the great natural spectacles of the earth. Bushmen, Hottentots, the first Europeans, all viewed this phenomenon and speculated on its origin. European sailors noticed that the first sign of the coming of the tablecloth was generally a wisp of cloud appearing on the saddle of land connecting Devil's Peak to Table Mountain. This wisp steadily expanded until it filled the saddle, reached the table top, and then rolled neatly over the full length from Maclear's Beacon, the highest point in the east, to the point now occupied by the upper cableway station in the west. On this saddle of land there is a prominent rock, providing some shelter and with a few convenient boulders scattered around as natural seats. A stream of fresh water flows near by. This is the site of the legend of Van Hunks, the Devil and the beginning of the tablecloth. (See box, overleaf.)

THE TABLECLOTH Cloud drapes over Table Mountain. The tablecloth is laid. Sometimes the cloud lies placidly; at other times it is in ceaseless turmoil, buffeted by severe south-east winds. In the foreground are two former signal cannon.

The real cause of the phenomenon is the south-east wind. This wind prevails from October to April. It starts as an offshoot of the anti-cyclones which girdle the Southern Hemisphere between 35 degrees and 40 degrees south latitude and whirl around in an anti-clockwise direction with the spin of the earth. Travelling from the south, this powerful but shallow stream of wind reaches the mountain ranges which line the southern end of Africa. Piled up against this barricade, the wind searches for a gap. It sweeps around Cape Hangklip, picks up velocity from the cornering effect, veers south-east in direction, and hurtles over the warm waters of False Bay, picking up a high content of moisture.

In this vigorous, moisture-laden state, the wind collides head-on with the mountains of the Cape Peninsula. The only escape is for the wind to rise steeply, forcing it into a sudden drop in temperature. The moisture content immediately starts to condense into a thick white cloud. This condensation would produce a cloud on the top of any mountain, but it is precisely at this stage in the sequence that nature has been droll. At just the right height for moisture to condense comes the top of Table Mountain, perfectly placed to catch the bulk of the white cloud.

In a thickness determined by the height of the wind (a factor itself determined by the velocity forcing the wind up the mountain mass), the cloud rolls over the summit, drapes itself neatly over the northern edge like a waterfall, and then abruptly disappears in an almost straight line where the increasing temperature of lower altitude causes the moisture to once again dissolve.

From far out across the sea, the sight of the landfall of Table Mountain with its cloud is an experience which has excited countless travellers since it was first seen, probably by some Phoenician or Arab explorer. The first European navigator to see it was Bartholomew Dias of Portugal, when he passed that way in 1488. Thenceforth, the first sighting of Table Mountain became a great event on every voyage between East and West.

Flowering plants and aromatic shrubs cover the entire area. There is no part of the earth with a richer variety of wild flowers. The Cape Peninsula and the adjoining Western Cape form a floral kingdom, with the bulk of Table Mountain towering above like the throne of some mythological king of gardeners. The shade of the mighty Adamastor has settled in a home that befits one who defied the gods.

41

How the mountain got its tablecloth

In Cape Town long ago there lived a retired pirate by the name of Ort van Hunks. Having made enough money from his roguery on which to turn honest, he had settled in Cape Town, the Tavern of the Seas, the place in which he thought he would be socially most acceptable. He bought land just above the great company garden and lived there well enough, with fine, strong slaves to do the work for him while he watched things grow and indulged his weaknesses, like sitting smoking and thinking of his past deeds.

The trouble with Van Hunks was his wife, a great, fat vrou with extra petticoats swelling her out until she could hardly pass through a doorway. He had married her thinking it would be nice to have so much to be close to during cold winter nights. But her tonnage had gone to extremes. She was a hard housewife besides, always nagging at her slave-girls to polish this and rub that, and elbowing Van Hunks out of his own hearth and home for fear his tobacco ash would fall on the fine yellowwood floors. So Van Hunks, in self defence, found a hideaway.

High up on the saddle of land connecting Table Mountain to Devil's Peak there is a clump of trees. Amongst them, in the shade, is a giant rock called Breakfast Rock, shaped like a semi-circular couch with a low, flat rock in the centre. It is the kind of place, indeed, which seems to say: 'Stay and rest a little while.' And Van Hunks, having found it, was content. Here no one would disturb him, for the burghers thought anybody who went toiling up the slopes of Table Mountain to be a madman. At times, sitting on their verandas in the evening, watching the blue shadow of the mountain creeping off across the sand flats, they would say: 'Well, yes. Perhaps another day we'll climb up to the top and have a look around.' Then the vrous would say: 'Ach, yes. It would be nice, but you must wait, yes, until it's cooler.' So they waited, and in Cape Town long ago you could spend a lifetime doing that and never notice it.

So Van Hunks had things to himself and spent his time up there in contented dreaming, with his pipe in his mouth and a heap of strong rum and tobacco on the rock before him. Beneath him lay the romantic Cape in all its calm serenity. Through the glittering silver trees he could see the tiny, whitewashed houses of Cape Town, gathered snugly around the castle, all speckled with green-blue oak-leaf shadows and the golden sunbeams in between. In the bay the sloops and the wealthy Indiamen lay resting on the tide, while their crews plied backwards and forwards to the beach with long strings of water caskets and loads of meat and greens.

Thus it was, on a day when the sea was laughing and as blue as the sky above, that Van Hunks went puffing up the mountain. Reaching the saddle he lay down for a while on his fat belly and drank deeply of the brown, peat-stained mountain streamlet, bubbling up close to the rock on its first joyous bid for life. He drank slowly, in great, greedy mouthfuls, swallowing loudly and then waiting a little while to feel the crisp coldness go twisting all the way down until even the laziest little toe, secure in the biggest boot, would feel like turning over and saying, 'Uh Huh!'

A visitor for Van Hunks

Then he got up with a heavy sigh and after muttering: 'Ach. Thunder. It's a long way,' which he always did at this point, he sat down on the rock, unpacked his tobacco and crook-pipe and set the two working harmoniously with a pleasant, acrid smell. He leant back, closed his eyes and started to daydream of the wealth of the ships in the bay below him. Suddenly he was rudely aroused.

'Morning mynheer!' said an irritatingly chirpy voice. 'And a very good morning it is to be sure.'

Van Hunks cleared the smoke and the dreams from his eyes in consternation. Before him he found a plump little man, stylishly attired in a black cocked hat with an ivory buckle, a red waistcoat, black pantaloons with a green stripe, and hose and shoes to match. Van Hunks grunted his astonishment: 'Who the thunder are you?'

The little man smiled and doffed his hat with an exaggerated gesture. 'Some call me good old Nick, others – well, other things. I at times come up for air and a pipe.'

He nodded behind him at Devil's Peak and readjusted his wig, which had come a bit loose with his bow. 'Van Hunks is your name I believe. I have heard of you. I have your old partner, Captain Roelof Boons, with me, together with his company.' Van Hunks looked at him sceptically and the little man turned round. 'Look!' he said, 'If you have any doubts as to who I am.' He undid a fastener in the back of his pantaloons and out shot a tail, which he proceeded to twist into an elegant pitchfork shape.

'It doesn't take a tail to make a devil,' said Van Hunks, accepting the matter with resignation and picking up his pipe again: 'You should meet my old woman.'

'Of her I have also heard,' said the little man, sitting down with a great sweep of his coat-tails. Van Hunks motioned him towards the tobacco. The devil loaded up a business-like iron pipe. Van Hunks looked at him appraisingly. 'What's on your mind?' he asked. 'Feel like a game?' He produced his dice set and rattled it.

'Wouldn't mind,' said the little man, 'let's see your money.' He dumped a bag of gold on the rock. Van Hunks sorted out from his pocket a collection of ducatoons, reals and a few diamond rings, some still with fingers in them, which he kept as souvenirs of his pirate days. 'I didn't expect this,' he said, 'so I haven't got too much on me, but it shall be seen, yes, it shall be seen, whether I shall lose what is mine now.' He caressed his dice lovingly for they were well loaded. The devil smiled. 'All right,' he said. 'I'll always give you credit on your soul.'

They made themselves comfortable, but just as they were about to start the little man looked up suddenly and said in surprise: 'Why, bless me! If it isn't St Peter.' Van Hunks turned round in astonishment. 'What! Someone else up here?' The little man leant forward and whispered urgently, 'You say "down here" to him – "up here" to me.' 'Yes,' said the newcomer, 'I have come to warn you.'

'Belay there!' said Van Hunks sharply, mistrusting the tone. 'I trudge up this mountain for no lectures. Those I get at home, yes.'

'Hold your anchors, Peter,' chimed in the little man. 'How would you like to come in on a game?' Peter looked upwards cautiously. 'Well, to tell the truth, I wouldn't mind. Things are quiet lately. How's business with you?'

'Middling,' said the little man, 'enough for the pot, but it's warm work. You don't need tobacco to make you smoke there you know.' He winked at Van Hunks cunningly.

The game begins

So they started the game, and Van Hunks produced a reserve of tobacco and dumped it before the table, and an extra pipe as well.

They played and they smoked and smoked and played and smoked, smoked, smoked and smoked. They knocked the pipes out, refilled, cursed their luck and changed notes and wondered where they could get more change and smoked, smoked, smoked and smoked.

The air grew thicker and thicker and the smoke billowed out of the trees, filled the saddle and covered Devil's Peak, and spread to the top of Table Mountain itself.

The dassies choked and ran for their holes and the lizards blinked, and even the fat cobras slid back into their cast-off skins to save their new ones from getting sooty. St Peter started to flap his wings. 'Glory-be! It's getting dark,' he said, coughing a bit. 'I can't see the numbers on the dice.' He put his wings into low pitch and flapped up a breeze to blow the smoke away, and the more they played and smoked the more he flapped and the harder the breeze.

Down below, in Cape Town, the burghers said: 'We should all be comfortably in bed with our vrous in weather such as this, for it surely is the worst south-easter ever.' So they went inside and locked the doors and shutters, and peeped out at the mountain through the peep-holes their vrous had made to see what the neighbour vrous were doing. But all they could see for their pains was an ever-thickening haze.

In the bay the blue waters churned up into greens and greys, like a ruffled field with white sheep grazing. The fishing smacks scampered in like startled birds and the great Indiamen dropped their spare anchors while their captains rowed back post-haste from the taverns on the shore.

The game went on, and the pipes were lit and lit again, and it was wonderful how that great cloud grew. It spread until it covered the mountain top with an undulating cloth as white as snow. It boiled and twisted and waved, and bubbled and coiled and turned in and out of the crevices. It rose and it fell and it went tumbling over the edge as though it was going to engulf the little town down below. But it never reached there, for Peter's breeze came sweeping down the nek and went booming up Platteklip Gorge like great guns firing. It swept the smoke up and moulded it and patted it, shaped it and modelled it into a great helpless lump which went willy-nilly wherever pushed.

Winner takes all

In the end, Van Hunks stood up and stretched himself. 'Well, gentlemen,' said he, 'it appears I have your money and your halo and your tail besides for surety.' He looked at Peter and Nick inquiringly and they nodded glumly. 'It's been a great game and fine knowing you, but home I must go for it is late and the old woman, yes, the old woman, she awaits, yes, with cudgels she awaits.' He gathered up his winnings, his pipes and his tobacco, put the halo and the tail in his knapsack and went striding off down the zigzag mountain path.

Nick and St Peter looked at each other. 'It appears we've been trimmed,' said Nick. 'Appears so,' agreed Peter, thinking a bit, with his tongue in his cheek, 'but it was a grand game. I could do with more.' 'That's so,' agreed Nick. Going to the edge of the saddle, he shouted down. 'Ahoy there Van Hunks!' And when Van Hunks answered with a faint 'Halloa?' he shouted, 'We'd like another game, as between friends some time. How about it?'

'You can go to blazes,' answered Van Hunks, thinking they might discover his tricks. 'I'm going in any case,' said Nick, 'but come on man, be a sport and maybe we'll come to some arrangement about that vrou of yours, and there's always the matter of your soul.' 'Well,' said Van Hunks slowly. 'I'll consider it, on a nice day mind you. I can't come in winter for I get rheumatism.'

The great cloud of smoke lingered for a while. From their homes the people of Cape Town watched it, full of wonder at what they saw. 'Table Mountain has spread its cloth for tea,' they said. And ever since, this spectacle has reappeared each summer day whenever the great game has been resumed.

The glory of the world's biggest garden

In the Western Cape, nature has created the perfect setting for a garden ... a kingdom of wild flowers which has been carefully protected from drastic variations of climate for the last 200 million years.

VALLEY OF THE WITCH Hemmed in by towering sandstone mountains, the Hex River Valley produces the bulk of South Africa's export grapes. The valley is said to be haunted by the ghost of a witch who killed herself in grief over her lover's death.

45

Where the colours of nature are so brilliant that they embarrass the painter

THE WESTERN CAPE PROVINCE is so different from the rest of Southern Africa as to be almost another land. It is not just that its rain falls in winter rather than in summer. It is not just that its temperate, Mediterranean-type climate and the nature of its soils make it resemble the Atlas Mountain area of North Africa and even parts of Iran. What makes the Western Cape unique is that it has the largest, most spectacular concentration of flowering plants found anywhere on earth.

With more than 16,000 different species, there is just nothing to compare with it. The whole of Europe has only one-tenth of its species. South America, so prolific in its bird life, is a pale inferior. The Western Cape is the undisputed domain of wild flowers, and the reasons for this prolific variety provide a fascinating study.

Visually, the Western Cape is like the elaborate frills of a woman's petticoat, peeping out from below the far drabber garment of the high-lying Karoo. A succession of brilliantly coloured mountain ranges,

separated by deep valleys, hugs the edge of the central South African plateau. Their colours – red, orange, magenta, beige – are almost unreal. Painters are embarrassed by them. A landscape is accused of being exaggerated, until the critic sees the original and realises with a shock that the reproduction was meticulously correct.

The origin of what is known to geologists as the Cape System (or Super group) provides an understanding of its whole appearance. As geological systems go, it is not very old. Perhaps that explains its vivid appearance. It is very much the child of the continental land mass.

Its birth came between 250 and 350 million years ago. Into what seems to have been a shallow sea washing the verges of this land mass, a vast amount of silt was eroded. Rivers carried this spoil of sand down from the continental mass and it spread over the bottom of the sea in three successive principal layers.

The oldest and lowest of the three series consists of thick beds of white quartzite and sandstone, with a glacial band halfway up and several small veins of manganese. It was laid down in shallow water by swift currents. A clue to the climate at the time of this activity comes from the presence of hard, water-worn pebbles, some of them with the scratches left by glacial ice. The scratches explain why no

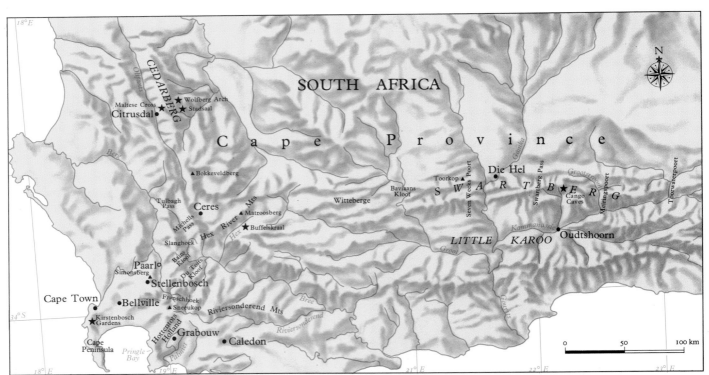

KINGDOM OF FLOWERS Warm, dry summers and ample rain in winter make the Western Cape the world's finest and largest garden. More than 16 000 species of flowers flourish in its rich, fertile soil – ten times as many as in the whole of Europe.

DOMES OF PEARL Nature has sculpted strange granite domes at Paarl (which means pearl). In the rain they glisten spectacularly. Beyond this dome, to the left, is the Franschhoek Valley. Right centre, with its summit shrouded in clouds, is Simonsberg.

fossils have been found in this deposit. There was certainly plenty of life on earth at that time, but it had removed itself to a warmer climate. This part of Southern Africa must then have been locked in ice.

Life returns

Then came a change in climate. The first principal layer, known as the Table Mountain Series, was already about 1500 m thick and pressing down deep into the bed of the sea. On top of it a second series of deposits, known as the Bokkeveld Series, was laid down, also in shallow but obviously far warmer waters. Life had returned to Southern Africa, and the mudstones, shales and sandstones of this deposit, 750 m thick, are rich in fossils of the period known in Europe as the Devonian Age – the period about 345 to 395 million years ago during which the first amphibians began to crawl out of the sea.

Still another change took place. A third series of deposits was laid down, also about 750 m thick and consisting of thin bands of quartzite, sandy shale and the remains of numerous plants. This deposit is

known as the Witteberg Series and it was the end of the sequence.

The mantle of the earth underneath this load of rubble could support no more. Sindbad trying to throw off the Old Man of the Sea would be a good description for the events that followed. The load was insufferable. The mantle of the earth collapsed. The load subsided with a mighty squelch, first into a submarine trough. Then the weight of the silt, pressing against the bottom of the trough, forced the sides to press inwards. Like a banana squeezed in its skin,

Cape sugar bird (*Promerops cafer*)

Bird of the bushes

One of the best known among the birds found nowhere in the world save South Africa, is the Cape Sugar Bird. Without proteas, there would be no Cape sugar birds. And without Cape sugar birds there would be far fewer proteas. This medium-sized light brown bird, with a yellow patch under its long tail, uses proteas as a shelter, as a source of food and for nest-building materials.

More often than not, it perches on the topmost spray of a protea bush. It may be looking for insects on the branches, to feed its young. Or it may be sizing up which flower is likeliest to yield a good supply of nectar. As it probes for nectar, with its long, curving bill, the bird picks up a dusting of pollen on its head and neck feathers. This is transferred as it moves from bush to bush, so that as the bird feeds it ensures the continuation of its own habitat, by fertilizing the plant. The connection between bird and bush goes even further: the Cape sugar bird builds its nest in the depths of a protea, using fluff which it has teased out of the flowers.

Sugar Birds can be identified at most times by the extraordinary gobbling and chattering sounds they make deep in the bushes. During the breeding season, roughly April to June, the height of the flowering season of the proteas, the male birds perform an elegant and entrancing courtship flight with their long tails looping up and down as they swoop and dip above the bushes where the female of their choice watches.

GARDEN OF GRANITE Heavy surf and storms have carved a mass of weird shapes in the rocks at Pringle Bay. Wave-smoothed granite towers above more eroded fragments. Beyond lies the debris of other rock formations, now reduced to grains of sand.

BLANKET FOR A MOUNTAIN A thin blanket of winter snow mutes the riotous colours of the Hottentots Holland mountains. But already the snow is beginning to melt, and in a few days the flowers will peep through, turning the mountains into a vast natural garden.

the sedimentary load was forced upwards.

It emerged above the sea in successive arches and troughs, and started to dry. It was warped, twisted, folded and bent by conflicting pressures and forces. Rain attacked it while it was still soft. Deep valleys were washed into it. Large portions were simply eroded away. Fragments such as Table Mountain were left isolated. Closer to the original mainland, parallel ranges of mountains were left, enclosing deep valleys. Iron oxides in the silt stained the rocks with vivid colours. As a final touch, lichen started to grow in irregular patches of yellow and green on the precipice faces, as though some giant painter had been testing out colours by daubs from his brush.

Nature's masterwork

It was in this strange way that nature created one of the most distinctive and beautiful of all African landscapes. It was not simply an achievement of rugged design. An elegance of shape, a delicacy of arrangement, subtlety of colours and innumerable ingenious little touches combined to give the whole landscape a degree of perfection.

Nature must have been well satisfied with the work. What had been achieved was the perfect setting for a garden. Not just an ordinary garden, but the largest and most varied in the world – a veritable domain of wild flowers, with over 16 000 species flourishing to perfection in a climate of ample winter rain and snow, warm dry summers, balmy springs and autumns. It is also a garden which has been carefully protected for the last 200 million years from any drastic variation of climate. In such a stable setting, plants must proliferate. Species mutate into innumerable forms, their flowers finding endless variations of colour, and all manner of delicate changes of perfume. In Europe, more recent ice ages have wiped out old vegetation, and new plants have not yet had time to produce so many variations.

In the very heart of this great garden lies the range of mountains known as the Hottentots Holland. This short range, 40 km long, is without compare in the whole wide world as a home of flowering plants. From the top of its serrated peaks to the depths of its valleys it is all flowers. To wander along its pathways is a botanist's delight. At any season of the year it is a superb spectacle. There are more than 350 species of heath and, if nothing else grew there, the flowers of these heaths alone would saturate the mountain slopes with varied colour.

Botanically, heaths are members of the *Erica* genus which contains more than 500 species. Most of them

PROMISE OF NEW LIFE It is not just bees that pollinate flowers. These two ladybirds, inside the petals of a *Euryops pectinatus*, will gather pollen on their legs, and pass it on to other plants as they move about searching for the aphids on which they feed.

grow in the Western Cape, with 102 found in the Cape Peninsula alone. For the botanist there is a lifelong study in these plants, while the layman can only marvel at the incredible displays they provide when thousands of one variety all blossom together in some valley or on a mountain slope.

In the Hottentots Holland Mountains, where the *Erica* reach perfection, January sees the pink species, *E. corifolia;* the pink and white *E. longifolia;* the pink *E. savileana;* the scarlet *E. curviflora;* and many others in full flower. In each succeeding month of the year, additional species come into flower. The fading blooms of their predecessors gently seem to dissolve into the fresh new colour of successors, and there is no end to the varieties of shades or the delicacy of nuances.

Reigning over this whole floral kingdom is the king of all flowers, *Protea cynaroides,* the giant protea, the floral emblem of South Africa. In their season, about June, these giant, dark red flowers, notably regal in appearance and reaching 25 cm in diameter, dominate, without any serious rivals, the whole throng of flowering plants growing around them like the nobles and commoners of this domain.

The proteas are the principal and namesake genus

ENDLESS SYMPHONY *(Overleaf)* Nature composes a symphony of colour as the Riviersonderend Mountains, under stormy skies, tower beyond sun-drenched cornland. The 'river without end', which gives the range its name, meanders at its foot.

of the whole family of *Proteaceae*. With more than 130 species the proteas are indigenous to Africa, and most of them are found only in the southern half of the continent. All are handsome, with a presence which makes even the small members of the genus prominent, no matter how dense the surrounding throng of plants.

Proteas were named after the Greek god of the sea, Proteus, who was remarkable for his endless changes of form. There are 32 protea species growing in the Hottentots Holland. The path which leads to the summit of the 1402 m high *Sneeukop* (Snowy Peak), the highest point in the range, is known as Grandiceps Path for, as it zigzags its way to the summit, it passes through a thicket of at least 10,000 bushes of *Protea grandiceps*. In late January the scene is breathtaking. The large, blood-red flowers of *P. grandiceps* are spectacular enough, but blooming in their company are lesser numbers of *P. caespitosa*, patches of bright, brick-red *Erica curvirostris* and groups of the lovely *Kniphofia tabularis* with orange-red spikes on long stalks.

The month of January also sees in bloom a particularly lovely member of the orchid family, *Disa uniflora*, the red orchid known as the 'Pride of Table Mountain'. About 90 different disas grow in Southern Africa. They are particularly fond of cascades and waterfalls where they cling precariously to the face of the rocks, the brilliant colour of *D. uniflora* making them look like the drops of blood left by some fallen mountaineer. The mauve species *D. longicornu* is equally lovely, while *D. cornuta* seems to be made of gold.

February in the Hottentots Holland sees in bloom such flowers as *Mimetes argentea*, an extraordinary-looking plant whose genus is part of the *Proteaceae* family. The 16 members of this genus are confined entirely to the Western Cape. Their flower-tipped leaves have a variety of brilliant colours. In common with the rest of their family they dominate their surroundings with the easy, almost arrogant assurance of an old-time aristocrat.

The rare marsh rose

One of the rarest, if not the rarest of all flowers, is another member of the *Proteaceae* family, the marsh rose, or *Orothamnus zeyheri*. One of the most aloof and elusive of all plants, it is a classic example of adaptability to what seem to be totally impossible conditions. The rarity of the marsh rose, in fact, is perfectly understandable. It simply shouldn't be there at all for it is a most contrary and difficult

plant, its tastes so devised that it likes everything that nearly everything else abhors.

The Hottentots Holland range is exposed to harsh weather. In winter it is saturated with rain, hail and snow. In summer it is exposed to the full violence of the south-east wind. The marsh rose loves all this. It will grow nowhere else but in the teeth of howling gales. By choice it seeks out high saddles in the mountains through which the south-easter howls like Sindbad's genie released from imprisonment in a bottle.

To make the site perfect, it should also be a boggy morass of decomposing sandstone and rotting vegetation. A good, sharp fire should also have swept through the place, burning off all other vegetation, leaving their ashes as a fertilizer, but not burning for quite long enough to have anything other than a beneficial effect on the marsh rose by cracking the tough case of its seeds.

The seeds of the marsh rose, which can lie dormant for years hopefully waiting for such a sequence of events to occur, will then bestir themselves. In the most unlikely looking areas, where they have long been considered extinct, they suddenly reappear, grow into an erect shrub, produce their blood-red flowers and then totally vanish, leaving only a few seeds lying patiently waiting, year after year, for another start to the strange cycle of their lives.

The marsh rose is the only species of its genus. Nature apparently considered that one such difficult plant was enough. All efforts to cultivate them have failed, and it is very unlikely that their lovely flowers will ever find a way into florists' shops.

It is curious that few of the flowers of the Western Cape have a perfume. The aroma of the mountains comes from a variety of shrubs whose odour is a permanent part of their leaves and branches. The *slangbos* (snake bush) is one of these perfumers of the Cape mountains. Particularly beloved by campers and the mountain hermits, this shrub of so pleasant an odour makes a magnificently warm and springy mattress when it is spread thickly on the ground. It is a member of the *Compositae* or sunflower family, which has about 1000 genera and over 20 000 species growing in many parts of the world.

Another characteristic aroma of the mountains originates in the *Rutaceae* family. These shrubs grow

SPRINGTIME WONDERLAND A multitude of daisies wave in the wind. In the centre, a *Protea magnifica* has burst into magnificent bloom. Spring in the Western Cape is a time of vivid colours, when countless flowers are born. More than 16 000 species of wild flowers flourish there.

LAND OF A THOUSAND FACES The Cedarberg range, notable for its bizarre rock formations resembling faces, animals, bridges and archways, stands like a wall over the valley of the Olifants River. In the foreground is a field of ursinias.

in portions of the Western and Southern Cape. They are gregarious and their territory is well defined by their all-pervading odour, pleasantly antiseptic and emanating from the *Agathosma* species of the family.

Agathosma betulina and *A. crenulata* are the round and oval-leafed buchu plants which grow in some of the valleys of the Hottentots Holland, notably in the upper valley of *Riviersonderend* (River without end). Vast quantities of their leaves, particularly those of the oval-leafed buchu, are collected each summer, dried in curing sheds, and then transported by pack animal out of the mountains for export to many countries. They are used as a basis for several medicines (especially those used to treat stomach complaints) and also in a variety of manufacturing processes. The aroma of buchu, slightly but not unpleasantly acrid-sour, is a distinctive perfume of the Cape mountains.

Winter in the mountains is the period of greatest growth for most vegetation. Many species also come into flower. Some of the most spectacular of these are members of the *Leucadendron* genus, another section of the *Proteaceae* family. *L. salignum*, with its cream flowers, and *L. grandiflorum* with its golden flowers, reach perfection in the Hottentots Holland. Further north, in the Cedarberg, *Leucospermum reflexum* has its home. In full bloom, this shrub, with 100 or more of its crimson flowers each lifted

skywards on the end of a vertical branch covered with silver-grey leaves, has something of the appearance of a massed fireworks display.

Above the snow-line

The Cedarberg range is also the home of the rare *Protea cryophila* (snow protea). This protea flourishes above the snow-line of the mountains. Its lovely pure white flowers are similar to large snowballs in size and appearance. It clings to the snow-line of the Cedarberg with such devotion that it has never been successfully cultivated elsewhere. It will not flourish even in the Hottentots Holland, where the forestry department has experimentally tried to grow it, packing it with ice and snow to provide the nostalgic plant with the familiar comforts of home. The plants perk up for a while, then realise they are being fooled and die.

The Cedarberg range is the home of *Widdringtonia cedarbergensis*, the gnarled cedar trees that hug the rocks which have protected them from fires for so many years. It is a massive wall of mountain, so similar in appearance to the Atlas Mountains of North Africa that when a forestry station was established there in 1904 it was named Algeria.

The whole range, 125 km long and 2150 m at its highest point, is a proclaimed wilderness area and a great delight for climbers and walkers. Paths lead to

LONE SENTINEL Looming above an isolated part of the Cedarberg is the Maltese Cross, a 20 m high sandstone formation, carved by unnumbered centuries of wind and rain. It seems to stand guard over other oddly shaped rocks in the area.

all manner of remarkable places and viewing sites. The weathered rock formations of the Cedarberg are extraordinary to the point of being bizarre. The Wolfberg Arch; the Maltese Cross; the complex of caverns and rock shelters known as the *Stadsaal* (town hall); and a vast collection of odd rock shapes, faces, animals, gargoyles, monsters; all are features of this handsome mountain range. The fiery colours of these sandstone formations, the clarity of the air, and the magnificence of the wild flowers contribute to an atmosphere of peculiar enchantment.

Several of the individual peaks of the ranges of the Western Cape have particular character. *Simonsberg*, overlooking the town of Stellenbosch, is one of the most elegant of these mountains. Viewed from Cape Town, across the Cape Flats, it is the mountain which catches the last rays of the setting sun. The renowned Cape Governor, Simon van der Stel, was a great admirer of this lovely sight, and it is his name which was given to it.

Simonsberg looks down on *Franschhoek* (Frenchmen's Glen) where French Huguenot settlers made their homes in the 17th century. On the high peaks on the south side of this valley grow the delicate, delectable flowers known as blushing brides (*Serruria florida*).

These are almost as difficult a crowd of botanical characters as the marsh rose. Taken from their moun-

tain homes, which were windswept, cold and bleak, they were lost. Kind treatment in gardens killed them. For 100 years they were considered extinct. Then they were rediscovered on these mountain summits, and the perseverance of botanists of the National Botanic Garden at Kirstenbosch has contrived to cultivate them. A good whipping by the wind seems to do them good. Coddle them and they wither.

Witch of the mountain

Another peak full of character is the 2500 m high *Matroosberg*, named after a shepherd, Klaas Matroos (Klaas the Sailor), who wandered around its slopes with his flocks in former years. The great dome summit of the Matroosberg is the highest point in the Hex River Mountains. Clinging to this lovely range of red sandstone is the legend of a romantic ghost. On an attic window-sill in the homestead of *Buffelskraal*, the date 1768 and the initials E. M. were carved. The story goes that a girl by the name of Eliza Meiring was courted by so many of the local gallants that she set any would-be suitor the task of obtaining for her a disa from the heights of the mountains. The task was too difficult, and the few who tried soon gave up.

Unknown to her, the one young man she really loved was determined to please her. He fell and was killed. News of the tragedy deranged the girl. She was restrained in the upstairs room. One night she contrived to force open the window, but trying to reach the ground, she too fell and was killed.

It is her spirit, lamenting the death of her lover, which is said to wander along the peaks at night. When the moonlight glitters on the first sprinkling of winter snows, someone living on the valley floor is sure to remark 'the *hex* (witch) is on the mountains tonight'.

The deep valley at the foot of these mountains has an ideal climate for table grapes. There is a long, warm summer and autumn, with little rain. The winter is cold enough to force the vines into a restful sleep. The soil is cool, well-drained and susceptible to irrigation. From the mountains comes pure water with something of the quality of high snows and the peat and iron oxides of the sandstone. Such are the conditions in northern Iran, the traditional home of the vine. From there, man carried the grape to many parts of the world. But there is no area more perfectly contrived by nature as a paradise for vines than this valley.

All man needed to do was discover the suitability of the valley, and find the correct crop. After considerable experimentation, the Barlinka variety of grape was introduced in 1909 from Algeria. It took to its new home with enthusiasm, and the Hex River Valley is today the producer of the great bulk of South Africa's export grape harvest.

To see this valley in June is to witness one of the most exquisite of all botanical spectacles. The first snows of winter generally sprinkle the peaks. The leaves of the Barlinka vines turn an almost unbelievable shade of scarlet. A sea of blood seems to wash against snow-capped mountains.

Through this valley run the principal rail and road routes from Cape Town to the north. To cross the mountains, the railway has to climb 600 m in 10 km, with a gradient of 1-in-40 and so many curves that, if they were put together, a train would do 16 complete circuits before reaching the summit. The Hex River Mountain railway pass provides travellers with a dramatic scenic experience. Railwaymen, however, could be excused for ignoring the scenery. For them, the pass means endless maintenance work.

On the trail of the elands

Passes are of considerable importance in mountain country. Long before man came to the Western Cape, migrating herds of antelope found the easiest ways through the mountains. They blazed pathways which

Royalty and rarity in the colourful realm of flowers.

Erica of Hottentots Holland　　　*Dorotheanthus muirii*

The giant protea, *Protea cynaroides*, king of all the flowers

man followed, and several of them have become the highways of today. The principal route across the Hottentots Holland was originally one of these migratory game paths. The early nomadic Hottentot tribes knew it as *Gantouw* (the pass of the elands). The first European settlers followed their trails, and the scars made by the wheels of wagons are still very clear in the rocks.

The giant protea is often described by botanists as the king of flowers, with the domesticated rose as the queen. Certainly the size and shape of the protea give it a royal look. The flowers, a mass of striking cup-shaped heads, are surrounded by whorls of coloured petals of varying texture. The snow protea is one of the rarest of the protea family, growing above the snowline of the Cedarberg range. The marsh rose is probably the rarest of all South African flowers. Often reported as extinct, it reappears in its favourite haunts then vanishes for years. The exotic-looking crane flower comes from the easterly part of the Cape and is much cultivated in gardens. Pincushions are prolific throughout the Cape.

The pincushion *Leucospermum*

The *Orothamnus zeyheri* marsh rose

Leucospermum reflexum

The crane-like bloom of *Strelitzia parvifolia*

The snowball *Protea cryophila*

Prolific *Gazania krebsiana*

Ursinia cakilefolia

The gradient was murderous, and the summit still seems to be haunted by a sigh of relief lingering on through the years from all the weary animals that laboured to drag vehicles to this high point. For them there was no consolation in a wonderful view of the Cape Peninsula, fading away like a vignette as the rocky sides of the ravine narrowed and closed.

On the summit, a few old cannon still lie where they once mounted guard. Beyond it, a new world opens up for the traveller moving east. 'The New Canaan', Lady Anne Barnard called it when she travelled that way in 1798, and saw ahead of her 'hillock upon hillock, mountain behind mountain, as far as the eye could reach'.

All the early travellers were impressed by this view. Immediately east of the summit of the pass

END OF THE DAY The setting sun flecks the clouds with gold over the valley of the Berg River, and the glory of the evening sky is reflected in the waters of irrigation dams that serve the fruit farms. Fertile land stretches for kilometre after kilometre.

there is a high-lying bowl in the mountains drained by the Palmiet River. The height and situation of the place combine to give it a special quality. It enjoys a freshness to its air, a crispness in winter, a good rainfall, and a dew from the sea breezes. In these conditions the flowers flourish. The wagons of the early settlers travelled axle deep in them for kilometres.

At the far side of the bowl, for some reason, the everlastings have their home. Pink, white and yellow, these strange artificial-looking flowers have been exported for years to Germany for use in the making of wreaths. Beyond this flower-covered rim the landscape falls away abruptly, with another view over a rolling countryside backed by another lovely range of mountains, the Mountains of the River Without End.

Most of the passes through the mountains of the Western Cape find their way through *kloofs* or *poorts*. A *poort* is a natural passage leading directly through a range. A *kloof* is something very special. There is an English dialect word, clough, meaning a deep cleft, and this is the simplest description of what is a most spectacular variety of ravine. Bains Kloof and Du Toits Kloof are two well-known examples of passes leading through such clefts.

Bains Kloof Pass is one of the scenic glories of Southern Africa. It was first explored in 1846 by Andrew Geddes Bain, a classic pioneer road engineer. Before his discovery of this pass, the road to the interior made an involved circuitous journey through what was known as Tulbagh Kloof, and then through Michell's Pass to Ceres and the interior. Working on construction in Michell's Pass, Bain, from his camp at the southern entrance, observed what appeared to be a natural gap in the Elandskloof and Slanghoek ranges which presented so formidable a mountain barrier to road builders.

At the first opportunity, Bain set out to investigate this gap. Starting from the southern side of the mountains he left before dawn one morning, discovered a steep way to the summit and then found himself at the head of a precipitous cleft, worked down the northern slopes by the Witrivier. It was quite a superb piece of scenic dramatics. The pass built by Bain down this kloof is a lasting memorial to a man who could harmonize his designs with those of nature, and leave a twist in a road so as not to disturb some beautiful natural feature.

The *Witte* (white) River which flows down this kloof gets its name from its flurry of cascades, waterfalls and rapids. It has its source high up near the summit of the Slanghoek peak. From there, it leaps downwards in a succession of waterfalls, each with a deep, fern-girt pool at its foot. Gathering tributaries, it then flows into a valley so prolific in wild flowers that it is known as Paradise Valley. The peat-stained, amber-coloured waters of the river form a chain of pools in this flowered setting, with brown trout lurking in their depths and, on the surface, magnificent reflections of the surrounding mountain summits.

At the point where Bain reached the apparent top of the gap, the river swings sharp north and commences a fine series of cascades, losing altitude rapidly. The whole impression of the precipitous kloof is one of wild grandeur. On both sides tributaries rush down to join the main streams, and the connoisseur of waterfalls has quite an experience of discovery and rediscovery in visiting each of these scenes. Carved into the left-hand side of the kloof, the road twists its way precariously downwards. The flowers are a danger to drivers. They constantly tempt the eye away from the road, and no road demands more careful driving than this.

Seven kilometres down the pass, a major tributary reaches the river, flowing down *Wolvenkloof* (Cleft of the hyenas). A pathway up this cleft leads to a magnificent waterfall falling over a precipice which, in February, is ornamented with the bright colours of hundreds of orchids. Baboons bark from the heights, eagles sweep down the valley with the whispering rush of the wind in their wings. Later, in the quiet hours of the night, the beautifully agile mountain leopards, their coats thick and warm against the winter snows, hunt their preserves. Each leopard keeps strictly to its own territory, demarcated by urinating on boundary points and the bones left behind from former feasts. Altogether, a place of solitude and freedom, with the winter winds keen and sharp.

The *Swartberg*, or Black Mountain range, between

WHERE DANGER CAN LURK Streams such as this – a tributary of the Witrivier in Bains Kloof – are where leopards quench their thirst and make their kills at night. The water, cool and inviting, is pure, sweet and abundant with trout.

the Great and Little Karoo, is the most storied, and perhaps the loveliest of these sandstone mountains of the Cape System. Nearly 200 km long and reaching a height of 2325 m, it is a gigantic wall-like barrier with four natural passes allowing roads and railway to penetrate the wall of brilliantly coloured rock.

Land of the ostrich

On the southern side of this range lies the long, narrow 'plain between the mountains' called the *Cango* by the Hottentot tribes, and the Little Karoo by Europeans. There is no landscape like this to be seen anywhere else on earth. It has always been the domain of the ostrich.

Ostriches are common in many parts of Africa, but this plain or basin, 250 km long by 75 km wide, was their particular idea of paradise. They revel in a dry, sunny climate, with water laid on from the mountains through perennial streams. In the wild state they flourished there in thousands. The natural food was to their liking, including pebbles of just the size they needed to aid their digestive processes. Their eating habits are peculiar. Vegetation, seeds, insects, sand, bits of metal, glass, bullets, bones and stones, all provide good food for the bird. The stones, like iron marbles in a rock crusher, are necessary to grind up food in the gizzard of the ostrich.

Hunters soon discovered the ostriches of the Little Karoo. In the late Victorian era, the international demands of high fashion for their feathers became so intense that the idea of domestication came to some of the professional feather merchants. Even today this oddly old-world setting of the Little Karoo, the home of over 60 000 domesticated ostriches, is unique. Attempts at domestication in many other parts of Africa, and in such foreign parts as the Argentine, Australia, America, and even in Europe, had no success. The Little Karoo is their home; they want no other. Their fine feathers still reward farmers with excellent returns for the trouble of keeping the big birds.

Brooding over the Little Karoo, the Swartberg range at one point suddenly divides into a double range. Here lies the lost valley of *Die Hel*, a deep canyon securely held by two great enclosing barriers of rock. The whole setting is wild, and has an almost tangible atmosphere of romance. Leopards

THE HAND OF MAN The natural beauty of the landscape below Simonsberg (on the left) has been enhanced by man. Vineyards and fruit farms, interspersed with clumps of pine, form a delicately interwoven tapestry of mingling colours and shades.

roam the heights, hunting the dassies, baboons and antelope that live in the mountains. Man and leopard fight an endless duel over goats, sheep, donkeys and calves.

Aloes in great variety and number cover the slopes, their red and orange flowers merging with the colours of the sandstone. Tall *Watsonia* species, with flowers in several shades, sway in the winds. Heaths and about 150 species of gladioli turn the wilderness into a garden. Even where mountain fires have raged, some vegetation benefits from the destruction of other plants. Wherever fire has swept a path through the shrubs a trail is left, not of blackened stumps, but a lovely mass of fire lilies which thrive on the ashes of a vanished generation of less fortunate plants. Then, when the fire lilies have had their time, they are succeeded by the painted ladies, which dance all day in the sun and winds in the ruins of the burnt-out plants and the decaying fire lilies.

In former years, travellers found it excessively difficult crossing the Swartberg. A legend tells how a witch, trying to find her way over the range, was baffled near the summit. In her rage she split with her wand a great rock dome impeding her progress. The 2400 m high dome, *Toorkop* (Bewitched Peak), remains today divided into eastern and western pinnacles. They are extremely difficult to climb, and so oddly situated in relation to each other that the peak takes on an entirely different appearance in varying lights and from each point of the compass. The northern aspect is particularly strange. The peak looks like a recumbent face with a bulbous nose, a protruding chin and a cigarette stump between the lips.

Another reputedly enchanted part of the range is *Toorwaterpoort* (Pass of the bewitched water). A hot (45°C) spring reaches the surface here. Subterranean gases also cause periodic surface fires, burning intermittently, like will-o'-the-wisps, and leading to unfounded fears of volcanic explosions.

Toorwaterpoort takes the railway through the Swartberg. The three road passes are among the grandest to be seen, not only in Southern Africa, but anywhere in the world. Meirings Poort, a majestic pass 12 km long, follows the course of the Grootstroom. Crossing this stream 26 times in the course of the journey, the road maintains a nearly

POOL OF GOLD A tangle of *Leucadendron* thrusts gaily upwards in the Bree River Valley. Yellow and orange are the commonest colours of the Cape wild flowers, with white next, then red. Blue is the rarest of all the shades.

64

level altitude right through the range and is hemmed in by vast precipices. The Swartberg Pass, on the other hand, climbs up to the top of the range and is breathtaking in its gradients and views.

The road has to climb over 1400 m to reach the summit from the Little Karoo. The slopes of the mountains are thickly covered with proteas, watsonias and heaths. The views are superb. From the summit the road has to find an involved route down, through a prodigious chasm slashed into the northern side of the range like a wound in the side of a sleeping dragon. The rocks seem to bleed colours of crimson, orange and yellow. At the bottom end of the pass, particularly, the rock strata are warped, twisted and folded.

The classic of all the kloofs of Southern Africa, and one of the most beautiful of road passes, is *Seven Weeks Poort*. There is no doubt of the superlative loveliness of this great cleft through the Swartberg.

Most kloofs are little worlds of their own. This is particularly so if they occur in ranges of mountains looming up from arid plains, provided that the mountains themselves are high enough to touch the clouds. Winter snows and summer rains then saturate the range with water. This is stored in the complex rock formations. Slowly it seeps out in the form of springs. These springs feed streams, and the streams wash the kloofs deep into the mountains. In these kloofs life flourishes. They become choked with vegetation. Birds revel in the warm air and rich food supply of seeds and fruit.

Mammals, insects and reptiles are also attracted. The rock shelters provided snug homes for the early Bushmen and the walls became galleries for their art. Stone Age man was succeeded by the men of the Iron Age. Modern man also discovered the character of kloofs and it is said that Seven Weeks Poort was so named because it took seven weeks for an exploratory party to penetrate its inner recesses.

The first explorers must have found the place only half-believable. Dominating the kloof is the highest peak of the Swartberg, the 2325 m high Seven Weeks Poort Mountain. The great cleft leading through the range at its foot has its precipice faces so warped, twisted and coloured with oxidised iron and manganese, that the whole 25 km length seems to glow as though afire.

MIRRORED MAJESTY Baviaanskloof, one of the most spectacular of the kloofs in the mountains of the Western Cape, is mirrored in a crystal lake. Kloofs are miniature worlds, full of wildlife and vegetation. They are like deep gashes, carved through mountains by the erosive power of water.

Prometheus himself might well have made this place. While searching for a passage through the mountains he at length decided to create one. With a burning wand and a breath of fire he set the rocks ablaze. Then, with a white-hot poker, he cleared a tortuous passage through the glowing coals. Such a passage, made through the coals in a grate, is indeed the nearest thing to Seven Weeks Poort.

In the middle of Seven Weeks Poort there was once an inn. The stone building still stands and serves as a simple, generally abandoned, homestead on a small farm named after the rare *Protea aristata* which grows in the kloof. It is pleasant to think of all the travellers who rested in this little hostelry, exchanging yarns while they sheltered from winter snows. Sitting snug in front of a roaring blaze, drinking the wines and brandies brought through the *poort* by smugglers, they once told tales of the ghost of the toll-keeper who, according to legend, still demands tribute.

Dream time in the gorge

A stream flows directly in front of the old inn. Guests used its cold waters for their ablutions. It carries a flavour of the high mountains where it has its origin. In the air, as well, there is the subtle perfume of many aromatic herbs and flowers, combining with the basic odour of mountains to make the nights singularly balmy.

A tired traveller of yesterday or today would find himself drifting easily to sleep through a darkness not only rich in dreams, but also soporific in its perfumes and stillness; in the echo of half-comprehensible sounds; in the calling of wild creatures and the murmur of the stream, talking endlessly to itself of all the things it has seen on its journey, and all the things it hopes to do.

If roads and inns were only vocal, what a tale they could tell of travellers . . . of dusty-looking tramps . . . of horsemen . . . wagons . . . adventurers . . . runaways and wanderers. The mounds of several graves lie next to this road through Seven Weeks Poort. What sad histories brought these individuals to such lonely unnamed graves is unrecorded. At least they sleep in a setting of such stunning beauty that the absence of a tombstone, or some sad mourner to deposit flowers, is no real loss. The spirit of nature walks softly through this great gorge each night. The winds sigh, the leaves rustle, strange echoes whisper from the rock faces, and for a breathless moment the frogs and crickets and the night birds are hushed into silence, awed by the passing of a power man may sense, but never see.

Flowers splash the wilderness with colour in sun-baked Namaqualand

Hot, stony, wind-cursed, drought-stricken . . . Namaqualand is yet so beloved by flowering plants that, given the least relaxation in the normal rigours of climate, they turn the whole improbable environment into a miraculous garden.

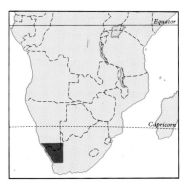

CINDERELLA GARDEN This soil, in the south of Namaqualand, is impoverished. Yet the scanty rains coax forth a wealth of blooms. They grow in frantic haste, grasping as much of life as the climate allows . . . as if aware that nature has set a curfew on their reign.

69

On the doorstep of the desert, a land of tremendous contrasts and contradictions

NORTHWARDS from the great landmark of Table Mountain, the coastal area becomes increasingly arid and rugged with every kilometre travelled. By the time the flat top of the mountain falls below the horizon, the sandy coastal terrace has turned into a wilderness, while just beyond the next horizon the desert begins. The dunes of the Namib probe down a threatening finger of sand as far as the mouth of the Olifants River.

Namaqualand is the name applied to this transitionary region between the desert of the north and the fertility of the south. It has always been a Cinderella part of Southern Africa – an area of tremendous contrasts and contradictions. Harsh and poverty stricken, it yet possesses rich deposits of diamonds, copper and other precious things. Hot, stony, wind-cursed, drought-stricken and sterile-looking, it is yet so beloved by flowering plants that, given the slightest relaxation in the normal rigours of climate, they turn the whole improbable environment into a miraculous garden.

A human gardener simply stands abashed. With all the advantages of cultivation, fertilizers and irrigation, he cannot equal such a display. Uneasily, he realises that his pampered plants would just love to escape from him over the garden wall and in this dismal-looking wilderness find a stony place entirely their own. There they will patiently wait, sometimes for years, for the chance of a perfect climatic sequence. Then, fearful of some sudden deterioration from this perfection, they will grow, flower, seed and die in such haste that their massed stirrings can be softly heard in the silence of the wilderness.

Cavalcade of flowers

The aridity of Namaqualand is dictated by the cold Benguela Current, sweeping up the coast. In a good year perhaps 150 mm of rain will fall in the area. This is exactly what the flowers need. Provided the winds are also tolerant (and they can be searing) then, from mid-July to mid-September, one plant species after the other comes into flower.

Among the earliest to bloom are the white daisies and the oxalis in its various forms and shades. Then come the light purple wild cineraria; the dark purple

everlastings and, especially on sandy soil, the red and orange Namaqualand daisies. Mixed with these are the hazy-blue flax.

The height of the season sees in full bloom the yellow *Carpanthea* species; the many-coloured *Nemesia versicolor;* the dark red *Lapeirousia* species, and the yellow *Sutera tristis.*

Towards the end of the season the yellow *Relhania pumila;* the dark orange *Gorteria personata;* the purple *Lampranthus* species; the dark orange *Gazania* species; the almost fluorescent-coloured *Mesembryanthemum* species; numerous beautifully shaded succulents, and many more flowering species, are all in full bloom.

Why so many plants should struggle to survive in this harsh environment and then, by strange perversity, give the world one of its more glorious botanical spectacles whenever nature shows some compassion, is something of a puzzle. Obviously, they would not continue the struggle unless there were rewards. The absence of grass cover makes it relatively easy for their seeds to find a home. The wind-blown sand provides quick protection by burying the seeds. The stony surface is constantly decomposing and replenishing the thin soil with chemical foods. The drought periods, when there is no vegetation above the surface, destroy insect parasites. The 150 mm of rain, when it does fall at the right time, is a sufficiency. The new growth finds itself at such suit-

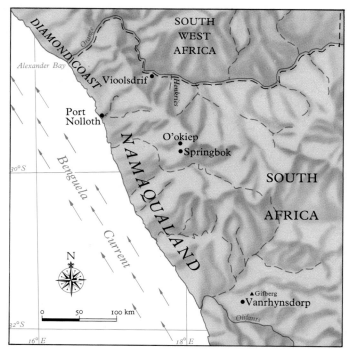

SAVAGE PARADISE Drought-stricken and sterile for most of the year, Namaqualand becomes a flowering paradise after rain.

THE QUIVER TREE The kokerboom is also known as the quiver tree, because from its fibrous core the Bushmen made pincushion-type quivers for their arrows. The trees, which thrive in Namaqualand, store water and can resist drought for years.

POISON MOUNTAIN In the heart of Namaqualand, the sandstone massif of *Gifberg* (poison mountain) looks down on a plain covered with daisies. Chincherinchee flowers flourish on the Gifberg's summit. They are poisonous and can be fatal to livestock.

able seasons to be almost in a virgin landscape.

Provided only that the hot winds of the Namib are suppressed, then innumerable little plants discover this wilderness to be a paradise, and by their joyous growth they carpet the drab, brown surface of Namaqualand with a fantasy of colour.

A considerable variety of oddly shaped succulents also have their home in Namaqualand. The weird *Dioscorea elephantipes* has a body resembling a cluster of rocks, the disposition of an immobile elephant and a seasonal growth of investigatory creepers which explore the surroundings and contribute a mass of diminutive white flowers to the general floral display.

The central area of Namaqualand consists of a rugged mass of granite domes. Baked in the sunshine, these rock masses have held the landscape in subjec-tion for 3000 million years and allowed but little change. It is a hard, hot world of rock and sand, with life difficult for all save the hardiest and most resilient of creatures. Wandering Hottentot pastoralists, the Nama people who gave their name to the area, were the first to explore it, their goats and fat-tailed sheep finding sustenance from the shrubs. These early people observed the green stains in the rocks which betray the presence of malachite ores, and they smelted copper from the surface outcrops, manufac-turing tools, weapons and ornaments.

The Great Copper Rush
Tales of the rich copper mountains of the Nama country lured the first European explorers into these parts. To work the mines, men had to be prepared to

live in almost total isolation from the outside world. Only the richness of the ore bodies, with the O'okiep Mine for long ranked as the richest copper mine in the world, and the demand for the metal at the time of world industrialisation, opened Namaqualand to change and development.

A considerable rush took place to the area in the 1850s. Rumours spread in the outside world that in Namaqualand copper lay thick and pure on the ground, like over-ripe apples in an orchard. The reality ruined many, for although the ore contained up to 31,5 per cent copper, it had to be mined. But

for those prepared to labour hard in heat and drought and follow the malachite lodes beneath the surface, there was fortune. Difficulties of transport, water supply and solitude all had to be surmounted. The more man probed, however, the greater the discoveries of copper and the richer the rewards for toil in the sun.

Northwards of the copper area, Namaqualand consists of a vast, desert plain of granite-like gneiss, with stony ridges of schist and flat-topped heights of limestone capped with Nama rocks. In summer, autumn and winter the whole area seems

PEEPING PETALS *Brunsvigia orientalis* normally allows only its head to peep above the sand. The bulbs remain securely buried, protected from the winds and searing heat. A leaf will be tentatively pushed above the surface when the weather is temperate.

YOUNG AND OLD Bustling spring flowers, *Grielum humifusum*, contrast with the stolid, ancient granite rocks – a characteristic scene in Namaqualand. The growing season is brief. Soon the flowers will wilt and all will be bare rocks and sand.

74

lifeless. A few goats find sustenance, and in the valleys of dried-up watercourses, such as the Henkries, groves of date palms flourish in conditions which they alone consider ideal, their leaves giving shade in the hell of relentless heat, their roots probing down to the heaven of cool underground water.

It is through this hot world that the Orange River forces a way to the sea, its course marking the boundary between Namaqualand and South West Africa while its waters provide irrigation for fields of tropical fruit, dates, citrus, lucerne, corn and vegetables. In the cliffs overlooking the muddy, lukewarm river the decorative Vioolsdrif Stone is found, while the bed and banks are rich in ornamental and semi-precious gemstones.

The coastline of Namaqualand is pure desert. Sand and clammy mist are the two principal features of a landscape which seems totally hostile to any form of life. It is difficult, in fact, for man to comprehend the mood of nature when this part of the world was created. Harsh, grim, ruthless. It was a mood that produced ice-cold seas; oven-baked land; freezing nights; and barrenness, solitude and thirst. Even the few springs that do occur were cynically made salty, as a final torment to life.

Compassion in a tortured landscape

And yet, after it was all made in some burst of spite and anger, nature looked down upon this strangely tortured coastal landscape, and suddenly there was compassion. Too late for tears: no rain, no rivers, no trees, no grass, not even the most hopeful flowers could ever take root in such a place. So nature, in one moment of generosity, sprinkled the place with diamonds as a parting gift and then, with a wry smile, wandered off elsewhere, leaving this desert coast to man.

To the scientist, the precise manner of the coming of these diamonds is a puzzle. In immense numbers, the diamonds occur in the beds of gravel underneath the sands of the coast. In an inexplicable association they are invariably found with the fossilized shells of *Ostrea prismatica*, an extinct warm-water oyster. Such an association can only be coincidental. The oysters could not have lived in the cold waters of the present-day Benguela Current. Even their presence along the coast requires some explaining. Some major change killed them, and at the same time deposited the diamonds.

Another mystery is why man took so long to discover the diamonds. Rumours of the presence of precious stones were common long before the first discovery was made. Prospectors searched and re-searched the course of the Orange River, deluded by tales that the river carried diamonds down from the interior. The same prospectors must have trodden over diamonds lying on the coast, but their eyes were too fixed on distant horizons. It was only in 1926 that Captain Jack Carstens, an Indian Army officer home on leave with his father, a storekeeper in Port Nolloth, found the first diamonds on the beach. And then the whole deposit suddenly became obvious. Another prospector found 487 diamonds under one flat stone. Within a month 2762 diamonds, totalling 4308,9 carats, were found along the shores of Alexander Bay alone.

Scramble for diamonds

A frantic scramble for wealth and a massive interplay of double-crossing took place. With the desert as a stage, man acted out a tragi-comedy of pure venality. The desert might be bleak, but it is nothing compared to human nature confronted by such prodigious wealth. Government was forced to intervene. There was armed rebellion by individual diggers against powerful mining houses who held monopolies over whole stretches of beach. Barbed wire, armed guards, police, watchdogs, machine-gun nests, all were added to the harsh beauty of the desert. The whole area of sandy beach became overnight the most desirable piece of seashore real estate anywhere on earth.

The diamonds found there are gemstones of particularly fine quality. With the fossil oysters they are recovered along the line of an ancient beach, and also by marine dredging. Outside the monopoly areas of the original discoverers' claims, the diamond coast is operated by the Government as a State digging. Barbed wire and guards make it a prohibited area. There are great workings and vast reserves. The output is restricted and carefully controlled so as not to depress the market value of gemstones.

The desert coast of Namaqualand remains little disturbed by this activity. The diamonds are taken out and shipped away; nothing is put back. If man ever removes the last diamond, the winds will soon blow sand over his abandoned workings. Solitude will return. Greed, jealousy, spite and envy will go with man to some other scene of his activity. The desert will remain gazing silently back at the wry smile of nature, although the whole giddy excitement could start again overnight if some other valuable deposits were found. Such riches are perhaps already there, overlooked by men who, on this coast of death, are bedazzled by diamonds.

In the eternal wasteland of the Namib, where no birds sing

The Namib is a world by itself, with the highest dunes of any desert in the world. . . a place of mirages, searing winds, sandstorms and dense fogs.

MOUNTAINS ON THE MOVE The Namib's massive sand dunes, the highest in the world, are constantly on the move. Their architect is the wind, building them up, blowing them down, twisting and moulding them into an ever-changing series of patterns.

*A pitiless desert, on the
edge of a sea that is
teeming with life*

IN THE LANGUAGE of the Hottentot tribes, the word *Namib* means a waterless land: harsh, relentless and a total desert. There is no exaggeration in the use of this word as a place name, for there is no region anywhere on this earth which looks at the sun with a face more scorched, desolate or lonely than the Namib.

A first view of the Namib from the sea is awesome. It is incongruous and baffling to see a desert on the edge of the sea. The prodigious store of water, teeming with life from plankton to fish, birds and seals, is, by a quirk of nature, narrowly separated from utter desolation. A walker along the shore can have one foot in the fertility of an ocean and the other in a region of such aridity that no rain falls from one year to the other.

The sudden contrast between life and death is sombre. It was not always like this. In the age of the Earth, 80 million years is nothing, and it is only within that time that the Namib was formed.

Coast of death

If the temperature of the Benguela Current flowing up this coast of death increased by a few degrees, moisture would evaporate, clouds would form, rain would fall, and the desert would become a garden or even a swamp. On such a precarious edge all life is balanced. A slight nudge by nature to the tilt of the earth and the age of mammals, birds, reptiles or insects has its beginning or comes to an end.

The Namib is a narrow belt of desert 80 km to 160 km in width and more than 2000 km long, from the mouth of the Olifants River in the south to near Mossamedes in Angola. Within this area it is a world by itself with sand dunes heaped up in places to a height of 350 m – the highest dunes of any desert in the world. It is a place of mirages, searing winds, sandstorms and dense fogs.

Most days in the Namib begin with fog. Dawn peers through the mists, pale and colourless. Only towards mid-morning does the mist lift as the ground warms up and causes the bottom layer of the mist to evaporate. The upper layer remains as a cover of low cloud.

With this cover, and the cold sea breezes, the days seldom become too hot. The winter months (May–September) are the warmest, but even then the maximum temperature is usually about 25°C. In the summer months the mists settle thickly, and only an occasional break allows a hot arrow of sunlight to dart through the covering.

With the coming of night, the sun steals away. No birds serenade its passing or plead for a return. The mist settles down as the sands cool. Just as the high mist acts as a sunshade, so this foggy blanket protects the surface from any real cold. The temperature varies little, day and night – one of the few kind

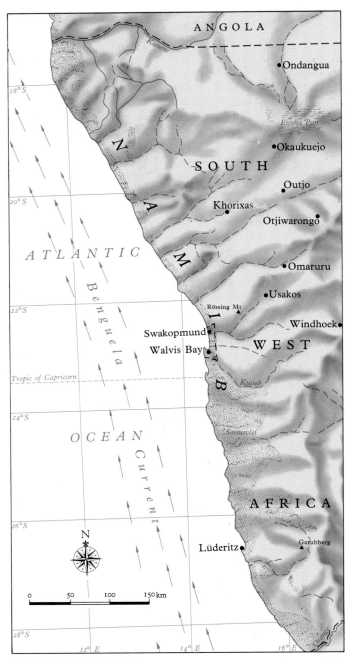

COAST OF DEATH The cold offshore current produces fog but little rain, making the Namib one of earth's most arid deserts.

THE CRUEL SEA A solitary clump of hardy trees thrusts defiantly above this desolate sea of sand on the inland verge of the Namib. In the distance, a seemingly ever retreating formation of rocks.

FACE OF THE NAMIB The rising sun tinges the dunes of the Namib with unreal pinks and purples. And night mist still lurks in the hollows, forming insubstantial lakes, as if to mock anybody rash enough to travel in this forbidding land.

aspects of the otherwise harsh world of the Namib.

The sand grains of the dunes are mainly of quartz, size-graded by wind action interminably rolling them one against the other. They range from 0,5 mm to 0,07 mm in diameter and are subglobular in shape. They originated as fragments carried down by wind and water from crumbling rocks of the uplands.

Creatures of the desert

Millions of tons of this sand accumulated during wet cycles in the history of the Namib. The wind continues its grinding action on the sand, and also constantly carries in more material, including organic matter, alive and dead, animal and vegetable. This organic material is caught in the sand, where it is dehydrated.

On it feed an odd variety of highly specialised little creatures – beetles, fishtails and termites. These manufacture their own water by oxidization from the desiccated diet. In turn, they provide both food and drink for other predators. Spiders, scorpions, crickets, flies, wasps, reptiles and moles, all find sustenance and comfort in the dunes which seem so malignant to the eyes of man.

By burrowing into the sand, the dune creatures can

A LAND OF 'FRIGHTFUL DESOLATION'

'When a heavy sea fog rests on these uncouth and rugged surfaces – and it does so very often – a place fitter to represent the infernal regions could scarcely, in searching the world around, be found. A shudder, amounting almost to fear, came over me when its frightful desolation first suddenly broke upon my view. Death, I exclaimed, would be preferable to banishment in such a country.' CHARLES J. ANDERSSON, *19th-century traveller in The Namib.*

---

find protection and their own ideal temperature. They emerge at will to roam the surface, searching for more food supplies, moving nearer the uplands or the coast as inclination persuades them, but never leaving the dunes, for the sands of the Namib are home to them. Where others find death they find life.

Several inland rivers have to penetrate the Namib on their way to the sea. Their watercourses are dry except in times of heavy upland rain when sudden floods of chocolate-coloured water rush down the

SANDSTORM A few meagre strands of life have survived the rigours of the desert, only to face the menace of the suffocatingly hot wind. What life the wind does not kill it is likely to bury in a tomb of shifting sand.

THE DESERT PAVEMENT Flat, wind-smoothed slabs of rock throughout the Namib are known as the 'desert pavement'. These are remnants of former hills and outcrops attacked by the wind and worn down to the level of the surrounding wilderness.

sandy valleys, reach the sea, stain it brown, and then vanish, leaving behind only a dampness beneath the sands.

On this, some hardy vegetation finds enough refreshment to exist. A number of succulents – mesembryanthemums, anacampseros, huernias, kochias, and salsola species – as well as a few tough grasses, manage to flourish and even produce a few cheerful little flowers as a touch of hope in such a setting.

The sands of the Namib are reddish-brown to yellow in colouring. In between the dunes, in places, there is what is known as a desert pavement of weathered rock fragments, left behind from an ancient land surface now almost completely buried. Eastwards, the great dunes give way to a bleak gravel plateau.

Science fiction plant

This desolate and eerie place is the setting for one of the world's strangest plants, the *Welwitschia mirabilis*. Also called the *Welwitschia bainesii*, after the painter Thomas Baines who sketched the plant after a journey to the Zambezi with Dr Livingstone, it sprawls on the floor of the gravel plain like some many-tentacled monster from another planet, its leaves probing out in all directions from a thick and woody central stem. Welwitschia is a dwarf tree, distantly related to the pine, and although it seems to have

MIRACLE IN THE DESERT Resembling the wreck of some unidentified flying object, a *Welwitschia mirabilis* plant clings to life. Though blasted into monstrous shapes by sun and wind, it can miraculously survive in its desolate garden for 1000 years.

SANDS OF TOMORROW These sand-smoothed dolerite rocks in the higher altitudes of the eastern Namib will eventually disintegrate, feeding more sand to the desert. Now they shelter a few bushes of *Arthraerua leubnitziae*. Beyond, Rössing Mountain looms.

THE DESERT QUEEN The tough *Hoodia gordonii,* known as the 'queen of the Namib', cheerfully defies wind and sand to produce clusters of exotic flowers. Its stems are armoured with spikes, and the flesh of its petals is utterly indigestible to animals.

many leaves there are in fact only two. About 2 m long when fully grown, they die at the tips and split lengthwise into frayed ribbons.

In a land that can be waterless for years on end, welwitschia lives, like the other plants of the gravel plain, on droplets of water condensed from the fog that blankets the land every morning.

One theory is that these droplets are absorbed by the tough leaves. Another is that they are simply collected by the leaves, and drop off, seeping into the ground to be gathered later. The plant sends down a taproot that can be as long as 20 m, to probe for subterranean water. It takes 20 years for a wel-

witschia plant to produce its first flower, but it is a plant with no need to hurry; for it lives for more than 1000 years.

East of the plateau the world becomes less sinister, although far hotter without the covering of fog. At last there are clouds instead of mist. Some rain falls, grass starts to sprout, thorn trees appear, and the desert ends.

The world is more familiar, but the memory of the desert remains in the earthy perfume of the dust-laden wind which carries its odour to distant parts – a reminder that the brooding Namib lies below the horizon, magnificent in its untamed desolation.

The savage, lunar landscape of South West Africa

Warped and twisted by incomprehensible, unpredictable changes, this tortured world has survived a long beating from the elements. It is a tough, resilient land, which has received scant tenderness from nature.

THE MOODY CANYON At sunset and dawn the 160 km Fish River Canyon, 500 m deep, presents a dazzling array of colours. At night it is a place of moody solitude, cloaked in mysterious shadows. The river is still gouging its canyon deeper, year by year.

87

*No quarter for life, in an
eerie, relentless world of canyons,
sand and sun-drenched rock*

ONLY A MAN from the moon would find the landscape of South West Africa familiar. Vast plains of sand and rock, drenched in the relentless light of strangely bronze-coloured sunshine. Barren mountain ranges, sharply etched against a washed-out sky. Hot days, cold nights. Deep canyons gashed into the ground as though nature, in a paroxysm of rage, had set out to torture an obstinate part of the world. An atmosphere of brooding stillness and solitude. Memories, mainly unpleasant and best forgotten, of ancient mysteries and a barbarous past of incessant human conflict. No clouds, no rain for eight months of the year.

And yet, in this harsh setting, many strange and beautiful things: wonderful gemstones; malachite mountains; underground jewellery boxes of dazzling colour; hardy vegetation, nearly all armoured with thorns; weird insects that invariably sting; savage animals definitely not to be touched; some men still living in the Stone Age, others in the age of iron, others in the age of plastics with, between them, a cultural gap of thousands of years of suspicion and incomprehension.

South West Africa, covering an area of 824 269 square kilometres, has never had a satisfactory name acceptable to all its diverse people. The *Namib* (waterless place) lying along the west coast is the least inhabited of the whole thinly populated area. Bushmen and Europeans are scattered over the whole territory. Hottentots live in the south, Herero in the centre, Ovambo in the north, and the strange Bergdamas in isolated pockets in the central mountains. Each ethnic group has its own language and culture, each its own appreciation of and attachment to the rugged environment where it makes its home.

Geologists find South West Africa a fascinating and varied study. Everything seems to have happened there and, denuded of any dense covering of vegetation, it is all so beautifully exposed. It is a land where gemstones take the place of flowers; where chemicals colour the mountain slopes more vividly than any vegetation; where a landslide down the face of a precipice leaves a scar of pure quartz which has the appearance of a rose-coloured waterfall tumbling down where running water is hardly ever known.

It is a classic geologist's textbook of a country, with ready-made illustrations of all manner of sediments, eruptions, erosions and examples of the effects of wind, sudden changes of climate, and the extreme alternations of ice ages, wet periods (or pluvials) and baking heat.

The oldest datable rock constituents of South West Africa consist of a variety of lavas and sediments deposited beneath water about 2000 million years ago. About 300 million years after this basic deposit, a mass of molten matter from the core of the earth forced its way into this top covering and, cooling, formed such structures as the Fransfontein granites which still remain on the surface, having survived 1700 million years of change.

Clues from the dawn of creation

From the time of their appearance, there was a long period during which many changes must have taken place, but what the surface of South West Africa looked like at this remote period it is very difficult

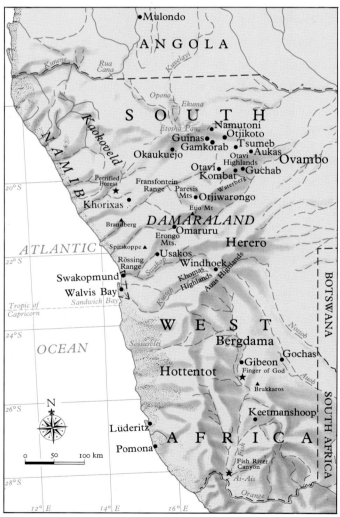

GARDEN OF GEMS South West Africa is a land of barren mountains and bare canyons, where gemstones take the place of flowers.

even to imagine. A geologist, probing the mysteries of the past, has to be a Sherlock Holmes, diligently searching the garbage dumps of creation for fragmentary clues. He is faced with the task of assembling whole landscapes from fragments which survive as tantalising relics of the total wreck of mountain ranges, vanished seas, swamps and deserts which have time and again, perhaps, totally replaced one another.

About 600 million years ago what geologists call the Damara System was created, when a variety of quartzites, mica schists and marble was laid down beneath a long-vanished sea. This system remains in the Auas Mountains, the Khomas Highlands and the Otavi Highlands. It adds to the face of modern South West Africa some particularly rugged areas of rock wilderness.

Following the laying down of these sedimentary rocks, there came a period of instability. It was as though the earth were suffering from indiges-

tion. There was a time of stomach rumbling, belching, burping and metamorphosis. Shale was transformed into shist; sandstone to quartzite and even into granite by the application of prodigious heat. It was during this time of change that rich mineralisation occurred, with the appearance of rocks called pegmatites carrying uranium, tin, copper, lithium minerals, gemstones and many other minerals and metals of considerable interest to man. They are mined today in such places as Tsumeb, Kombat, Berg Aukas and Brandberg West.

Then came an ice age. The southern part of the territory was worn down to a flat surface and submerged beneath the waters of the sea. Into this water was deposited a 1500 m thick layer of sediments known as the Nama System, and composed of a richly fossilised succession of quartzite, limestone and shale.

For the following 200 million years things were relatively quiet. It was a time of good rainfall.

GOD'S FINGER A steep cone of schist, topped with a massive pillar of rock, seems to point to the heavens. Hottentots believed that this extraordinary structure, near Asab, had supernatural powers. And so they named it *Mukurob* (the finger of God).

Natural erosion steadily levelled the country, leaving elevated ground only at Windhoek and Otavi. Primitive life flourished in conditions which were temperate and agreeable.

Then the climate became colder and, 280 million years ago, ice covered the face of the land and life fled to warmer areas. Striated pebbles, smooth, almost polished rock floors, known as Dwyka Tillite, all remain from this inhospitable period, especially in the Kaokoveld.

Why such extreme variations of climate occur is difficult to explain. Fortunately, they come to different zones of the earth at different times. Life has generally survived by migrating or developing elsewhere. Those creatures who could not move simply died, and their evolutionary chains reached a disconcerting end.

This ice age continued for 60 million years. Then the climate warmed, the ice melted and vast swamps and lakes were formed. Into these were deposited the shales and sandstones of Auob and Nossob. Vegetation flourished. Huge forests produced the beds of coal found in Ovamboland and in the Gochas area, and left the petrified forest west of Welwitschia.

This was the age of the reptiles. Their footprints and skeletons tell the story of how they once ruled the earth. But they vanished from the area, along with the forests, when the climate changed again. The rains dwindled. Red shales and sandstone were formed in the swamps and lakes, full of fossil remnants of plants and dinosaurs. The relentless dwindling of the habitat of swampland and lake continued until desert conditions came with aeolian (windblown) sandstones. Dunes covering the surface are still to be seen in the Etjo and Waterberg mountain ranges.

Eruption from the depths

Another time of instability came. The core of the earth experienced another spell of indigestion. Molten dolerite was squeezed into the sediments to form sills and dykes. Basaltic lavas erupted from the depths and poured out on the surface through the throats of the volcanoes, finally choking them, as though nature had had enough of the epoch of fire, and was deliberately plugging off the holes and vents.

The volcanic cones have long eroded away. The granite cores which choked their throats remain as such notable landmarks as the Brandberg, Erongo, Spitskoppe and Paresis mountains. This choking of the volcanoes took place about 190 million years ago, at about the same time as the breaking up of what is known as Gondwanaland, and the formation into identifiable shapes of the continents of today from one original land mass.

About 100 million years ago there was a further spasm of volcanic activity. A batch of volcanic throats or pipes were blown up to the surface and these were filled with the soft material known as kimberlite, which often contains diamonds. Near Gibeon and the volcanic massif of Brukkaros, several of these pipes were blown up to the surface, and there is some speculation that they brought with them from the depths the diamonds subsequently found scattered along the skeleton coast of the Namib.

A time of good rains returned, but the wet spells seem to have alternated sharply with short dry spells. This hindered the growth of vegetation and left the land ill-protected against sudden floods. Rivers alternated from periods of violent floods to periods of aridity.

The floods, when they came, knifed their way through the naked earth and cut the sharp canyons of the Kuiseb and the Fish River, creating in these areas, in relatively short periods, the enormous scenic spectacles of today. The Fish River Canyon is the second largest on earth, and the Kuiseb is one of the most savage and primeval scenes imaginable, in a setting of total aridity.

The wet spells gradually dwindled. The dry spells became longer and eventually merged to form the arid period of today. The Namib Desert was created along the coast. The rivers dried and their courses were choked with sand. The Kunene River in the north still brought water down from the highlands of Angola, but the sand clogged its lower course. The vast swamps it had formed in Ovamboland started to dry. Etosha was left as a pan only temporarily filled at times of floods, with the river changing its course away from the sand and direct to the Atlantic Ocean.

South West Africa today is a scantily inhabited, rocky, arid island in a sea of sand. East, west and south of its highlands lies pure desert. North of it is the wilderness of southern Angola. Warped and twisted by continuous, unpredictable, incomprehensible changes, it survives as a tortured world unto itself. It has survived a long beating from all the elements. This is a tough, resilient land which has received scant tenderness from nature and offers no

CANYON OF FIRE The rugged canyon of the Kuiseb River cuts a jagged wound through barren terrain, ablaze with sand that glows from pink to purple in the rays of a setting sun. The canyon shimmers in torrid summer temperatures, discouraging tourists and even the hardiest wildlife.

BEAUTY'S STING The bright, soft, sweetly scented spring blossoms of *Acacia nebrownii*, protected by its tough, savage thorns. This hardy tree is dangerous, although alluring. Its thorns are an effective deterrent to browsing animals.

quarter to any form of life struggling to establish itself there. All it can offer is the strange comfort of a part of the world which makes no effort to dissemble, confuse or disguise its essential harshness.

Thorns from paradise

The vegetation which makes a home in this setting is understandably tough and stubborn, with some very peculiar species which, finding South West Africa to their liking, would feel out of place in any more kindly environment. The Bushmen, in fact, have a legend. They say that the god Thora, gardening in paradise, found a number of trees which he thought ugly. He pulled them out and they pricked him with their thorns. In a rage he tossed them over the wall of paradise. They crashed to earth in South West Africa, many of them roots uppermost and with their branches buried in the sand.

Some of the trees died. Others, such as *Moringa ovalifolia*, were indifferent. They simply continued to grow upside-down, forming a weird forest, 30 km west of Okaukuejo at what is known to Europeans as *Sprokieswoud* (wood of ghosts), an area held in considerable awe by the Bushmen.

In his weeding-out of paradise, Thora made a thorough job of thorns and spikes and distorted shapes. For, surprisingly, some 3500 species of plants are found in South West Africa. In the four-month rainy season, parts of the country where moisture falls and is not immediately evaporated have a pleasant greenness. About one-tenth of these plants are water-conservers or succulents, storing moisture for lengthy periods of drought and, by their prudence, making life possible for many creatures which would otherwise find the desert inhospitable.

The coastal belt of sand dunes has its species of mesembryanthemums, anacampseros, huernia, hoodia, stapelia, and other resolute little plants. Where underground water can be tapped by long, probing roots, the leafless Nara plants grow, as well as many surprisingly handsome trees, especially acacia species such as the Ana trees, which yield edible seed pods. On these pods, and the melons of the Nara plants, the Topnaar Hottentot people base their lives in the valley of the Kuiseb River.

From its source on the central plateau, the Kuiseb carves its way down the escarpment through a spectacular canyon and then, reaching the coastal desert, flows underground for its last 150 km to the sea. Periodically, heavy rains on the plateau send flash floods storming down the river course. These scour out the sand and push back the desert which has insidiously worked its way up the river by wind action during the dry spells.

To live in this valley, the Topnaar Hottentots need at least 10 km of riverine forest for each family. Their goats live on the seed pods; they live on the goats' milk and meat. Both man and goat relish the Nara melons. There are only 200 Topnaar Hottentots and their lives are hard. It might be suggested that these people would do much better elsewhere, but they love the place. To them, the howling voice of the wind sings of home as it blows the sand up between the gaunt cliffs of the canyon.

The southern part of the central plateau starts from

pure desert near the Orange River and then is gradually covered in grass as rainfall increases to the north. Notable in these parts is the *kokerboom* (quiver tree), whose proper name is *Aloe dichotoma*. A whole forest of them grows near Keetmanshoop. The popular name comes because the Bushmen use the fibrous core to make a pincushion type of quiver for their arrows. They are slow-growing, stately trees, with the hardiness to withstand long periods of total drought.

In the Fish River Canyon

Some fine specimens of kokerboom grow so close to the edge of the Fish River Canyon that they seem to be watching the view. The spectacle of this gigantic canyon from dawn to dusk each day is indeed spellbinding. The Fish River, like the Kuiseb, has its source in the better-watered highlands. Instead of flowing due west to the sea, it flows south. After 500 km it reaches the head of its canyon, a vast mishap to the landscape which was carved out in the course of probably four wet spells during the last million years.

The canyon is still being deepened today, but at a far reduced rate, for conditions are drier. It is 500 m deep and 160 km long. Through it, the river twists and zigzags with some classic examples of meander-

UPSIDE-DOWN WOOD Early Bushmen believed that these *Moringa ovalifolia* trees were flung out from Paradise and landed upside-down, but continued to grow. This weird forest, 30 km west of Okaukuejo, is named *Sprokieswoud* (fairy wood).

93

ing. Huge detached buttresses stand waiting like condemned prisoners to be carried off by the next floods. There are crumbling precipices, and a succession of deep pools, well populated with fish.

Temperatures on the floor of the canyon are formidable – over 45°C in daylight and seldom below 35°C at night. Several sulphur and hot springs come to the surface in the canyon. One of them, at a place aptly named by the Nama Hottentots *Ai-Ais* (very hot), is a spa with elaborate amenities, even though it lies in a setting so rugged and barren that Moses and his followers would have felt at home (and found delight in picking up the gemstones which lie amongst the rubble on the canyon floor).

The Fish River eventually flows into the Orange. Walking up the full length of the canyon is a feat of endurance which has been performed several times. The most rugged part lies immediately above the hot springs at Ai-Ais, where a huge rock, split into four sections and known as the Four Sisters, marks the beginning of the deepest length of the canyon. Relentless heat, masses of gnats and flies, sand and rocks impede the way. Date palms flourish, some planted, it is said, by Germans who hid there during the First and Second World Wars; some by an occasional hermit; and some by a man with cancer who made his way into the deep canyon to seek a cure in the mineral waters and the heat.

Troops of zebra, baboons, some kudu, several snakes, many scorpions and a few other odd creatures find a home there. Twenty days of hard walking are needed to travel the full length of the canyon. When night falls, the place seems to be the lair of utter darkness. Only a thin ribbon of stars lies overhead. The walls of the canyon seem to press ever closer. Complete silence prevails. The hours are long and lonely, and the dawn something which the sun has forgotten.

From the source of the Fish River northwards and along its own upper valley, the vegetation is fascinating. Thorn trees such as the driedoring, the box thorn and feed shrubs such as the *Justicia* species appear in great numbers. The Ana trees revel in the increased moisture. There are huge specimens, with trunks 10 m thick, growing in the watercourses, dropping their twisted pods for game and domestic animals to eat and distribute the seeds through their own droppings.

White thorn trees line the river banks and stand around the dry pans, patiently hoping for them to fill again another day. Hakiesdorings provide a tangle of thorny brushwood, while, most characteristic of all in

LOVE'S PLANT The wild cucumber, *Cucumis africanus*, is a tasty vegetable prized as an aphrodisiac. Protected by thorns, like many desert plants, it flourishes in areas where some moisture can be found, particularly in the sand-filled watercourses.

this half-desert landscape, the majestic kameeldorings offer all life in this tough environment the kindness of shade beneath their umbrella-like canopies of branches. These same trees provide superb firewood that gives a subtle flavour to cooking. There is an aroma to the smoke which is redolent with invitations and memories of countless campfires sat around by hunters and explorers; by itinerant traders; by raiding warriors; by wandering missionaries; and by all the other restless people who have found their way through the African wilderness.

All of these acacia specimens are at their best in spring. Without waiting for the rains they anticipate the wet seasons by covering themselves with white and yellow blossoms, saturating the air with an almost overpowering perfume. Like the rainbow at the end of a storm, these blossoms sing a message of faith. They are making a propitiation to nature in their way, asking for an end to drought and the drab, dry, bronze-brown of winter – pleading for the coming of clouds and a transformation to four months of green vegetation and flowing water.

When the rains come

With the coming of the first rains the whole landscape puts on a new costume. All manner of busy little plants push up through the softened soil, shoulder pebbles aside and stretch eager leaves for a share of sunshine, moisture and life. The ground becomes thickly covered with the golden-coloured flowers of massed dubbeltjies, beautiful to see, but a curse when their seeds develop as sharp-thorned pods. These seem cynically designed to imbed themselves in the hooves and feet of beast and man, and to be carried on to some new area before the victims manage to free themselves from the ingenious encumbrance.

Kinder by far are masses of lilies: the white-coloured nerine, the dainty *Boophane disticha*; the white and yellow creepers which wind up trees and rocks; the *Grewia* species covered in white and yellow blossoms; the *Crotalaria* species with flowers seemingly made of gold; the *Tephrosia* in red; the *Leonotis* in orange; and the *Sesamus* in purple.

Of great delight to the Bushmen and Hottentots are the edible plants known as *veldkos* (veld food), which flourish at this time and make these four months a period of feasting. Mushrooms appear, especially at the foot of ant heaps, and provide a real delicacy. In the south-east region there are truffles of the *Terfezia* species which would excite a gourmet, and mushrooms, called the ejova by the Herero, which flourish on termite heaps and make a marvel-lous dish, especially with venison.

The bulbous tubers of the *Cyperus* species, the *Ceropegia pygmaea* and the various *Brachystelma* species all grow in the sand country of the north and are nutritious and delicious. The *Walleria nutans* has a taste similar to that of a potato. The wild date palm has a luscious fruit. So has the palm apple, with its sweet-tasting fibrous pulp, its edible fruit, and the decorative fan-shape of its boughs – altogether a useful and elegant plant.

To those knowledgeable in veld lore, there is an excellent living in the wilderness, at least during the wet season. Even the thorniest plants produce tasty fruits, hoping to tempt some creature, repelled from eating the plant itself, to nibble carefully at the fruits and then distribute the seeds in exchange for the meal. Others offer liquid as the inducement for living things to consume them and scatter the seeds. Tsamma melons are the principal suppliers of water in the sand areas. The Nara melon, its fruit tasting like a cucumber, has edible seeds which are considered to be aphrodisiac in effect and are exported to several countries.

The *Fockea* and *Raphionacme* species of tubers also produce water, while the marula tree yields an aromatic fruit, fine for jellies and juices and, when it is allowed to ferment, a good producer of alcohol. Game animals, men and even birds, find the marula season to be a jolly time. Even bull elephants are reported as being on the tipsy side during the silly season in the wilderness.

The northern part of South West Africa is a vast, flat sea of sand, but with a good cover of trees. This is the land of gigantic wild figs, of the manketti trees, whose fruit is one of the principal foods of the Bushmen; and of the baobab, one of the grandest and most useful of all trees.

Monarch of the trees

If the god Thora threw this tree over the walls of the garden of paradise, then he gave to the wilderness one of its best assets. North of the Tropic of Capricorn, throughout Southern Africa, the baobab is the undisputed monarch of all trees and plants. Wherever it grows it dominates the surroundings, not only by sheer bulk, but also by the weird appearance of oddly shaped branches. They do indeed look like the roots

MEETING OF THE SEAS (*Overleaf*). A sea of sand sweeps into the cold waters of South West Africa's coast at Sandwich Harbour. And a flock of flamingos swoops over fetid, algae-infested mud islands that create a haven for many bird species.

95

of an upside-down tree, groping blindly into the sky, while deep underground there is another tangle of what would seem to have been the original branches.

If its appearance is slightly overwhelming, the baobab is nevertheless a most kindly giant, and one, moreover, quite free of thorns. Every part of the tree is useful. The spongy wood can be macerated into rope or paper. The leaves can be boiled and eaten as a vegetable. The pollen of the flowers yields an excellent glue. The seeds are pleasant to suck, slightly acid in taste and refreshing; they can be ground and roasted to make coffee. The fruit pod contains tartaric acid, and because of this the baobab is often called the cream of tartar tree.

The bulbous trunk of the baobab is formed of layers of fibrous matter, each layer about 6 mm thick and taking a year to grow. An average mature baobab with a diameter of 7 m has taken 600 years to reach this size. They live for perhaps 1000 years. When they decide to die they do it very thoroughly. Few dead things look deader than a dead baobab. They simply collapse, from a noble giant to a pile of pulp which disintegrates in a surprisingly short time. Baby baobabs look so different from their parents, just nondescript little shrubs, that even the observant Bushmen have a legend that baobabs do not grow. They come fully grown, presumably still being thrown out by the industrious gardener, and the dull thumps of their crashings to earth are said to be often heard.

The northern frontier of South West Africa is the river known as the Kunene. Within South West Africa itself there is not one stream capable of defying drought through the year. The Fish River, deep in its canyon, has pools which never dry, but the river is quite dormant for most of the year. Only on the southern frontier, where the Orange flows, and the northern frontier on the Kunene, is there constantly flowing water.

The Kunene has a dramatic course. Originating in the highlands of Angola it flows southwards, enters the Kgalagadi sand country near Mulondo and then forms a flood plain, with a very sluggish flow, as far as Olushandja, where its impossible southwards course into the desert is abandoned. Like a defeated army disengaging, the Kunene suddenly veers westwards, speeds up and tumbles headlong over the 135 m

SPRING OF LIFE (*Preceding page*) In the sun-baked wasteland of Etosha Pan, a herd of oryx (gemsbok) take their turn at one of the few springs, flavoured by various mineral salts. *Etosha* (place of mirages) is a sanctuary for all game animals.

waterfall known to Europeans as the Rua Cana, a corruption of the Ovambo name, *Oruva Ha Kana* (hurrying waters). From there it forces its way through 150 km of rocky gorges with a series of rapids and, on both its banks, as wild a stretch of country as can be seen anywhere in Africa. The Ovambo know the river simply as *Omulonga* (the river). The name *Kunene* (the right side) they apply to the northern banks, while *Kaoko* (the left side) is applied to the southern banks.

The badlands
The Kaokoveld, as it is known to Europeans, is a wilderness complete, a hard, rocky, ruthless landscape lying as an intermediate terrace between the Namib and the interior. Along its coastal belt, the sands of the desert incessantly drift northwards. Where rivers force their way seawards they erode their way into the rock landscape, creating the most appalling badlands.

Reaching the desert, they are in eternal conflict with the sands. In the dry seasons, the dunes wander across the beds of the non-flowing rivers and choke them. When floods come, the water has to almost blast a way out through the obstructions. In a famous 1934 flood, the Swakop River, after five years of drought, pushed so much sand out to sea that, carried northwards by the Benguela Current and washed on to the beach, it rebuilt the shoreline for 2 km into the sea, and at the old harbour of Swakopmund left the original jetty built by the Germans standing disconsolately 1,5 km inland.

The Kunene River, being perennial, is in constant combat with this drifting sand. A 45 km wide belt of high dunes presses into the lower reaches of the river, and the Kunene carries the sand down to the sea. The Benguela Current then carries the sand north of the river, where the waves dump it on the beach once again and the coastal promenade is resumed.

By a cruel contradiction, the Kaokoveld is often the scene of floods. Its annual rainfall is only around 100 mm, but this tends to fall in a very short period. Some of the valleys, where enough soil has been held, contain the water and support tropical vegetation. Other valleys just cannot cope with sudden storms. The water simply washes everything before it, and races downwards. Within a day the land is as dry as it was before the rains.

In the canyons these flash floods are a menace. They crash their way through obstructions, undermining whole lengths of the canyon sides. The piecemeal collapse that follows creates the jagged, dangerously crumbly badlands of the Kaokoveld and the rest of the western escarpment of South West Africa.

The Kunene escapes from the sand by swinging sharp west. Several other rivers draining the highlands of Angola persist in a southern course and, in trying conclusions with the desert, simply lose themselves. One such ill-advised stream is the Kuvelayi. During its brief flood season, from February to April, it manages to push southwards, filling up a few shallow lakelets such as Opono and Ekuma, and then, at the end of its resources, pouring a thick ooze of slush into the vast 90 km by 50 km depression known as *Etosha* (place of mirages). For a short period, Etosha is at most 1 m deep in slush, and in this rather nasty liquid flamingos in vast quantities, and other water fowl, feed on algae and other items.

With the end of the flood season the slush dries out into a powdery dust overlying a soft, greenish-coloured clay, strewn with fragments of sandstone of a purple tint. The half-dead lake is haunted by mirages and dust devils wandering over its flat surface. Springs of brackish water reach the surface around the verges of Etosha, and trees grow around the shores in profusion.

Big-game animals have always found the area to their liking. Grazing is excellent and vast herds of zebra, wildebeest and springbok roam around the verge, together with numerous kudu, hartebeest, oryx, eland, giraffe, elephant and a few rhino. The herds are followed by numerous predators – lions, leopards and cheetahs.

Fort in the wilderness

The brackish water of most of the springs of South West Africa is very palatable to game animals. On the south-eastern verge of the Etosha pan there is one famous and ancient watering place of this kind. A salty spring bubbles up in a swampy, reed-grown morass in the centre of a limestone basin. Well-trodden game paths wander into the area from the surrounding wilderness. To the Ovambos this spring is known as *Omutjamatunda*. Travellers used it as a regular staging point, and Europeans distorted the name into the *Namutoni* of today.

It was there that the Germans established an outpost and Customs post, building in 1903 a fort complete with battlemented walls and towers. This was destroyed in a siege and a fight with Ovambo warriors, but a new fort, built on the site in 1905, still stands. Gleaming white in both sunlight and moonlight, this lovely building keeps guard over the

Social weaver (*Philetairus socius*)

Bird that builds a sunshade

Every living creature that burrows, crawls, walks or flies in the oven heat of the Kgalagadi faces a desperate problem: how to keep cool during the heat of the day.

Many animals solve this problem by burying themselves in the sand by day and coming out to hunt at night. Scorpions are able to survive where other creatures would shrivel in the fierce heat because a thin layer of wax makes their shells impervious, so that hardly any water is lost by evaporation. There are rodents which are able, in some way that is not yet fully understood, to manufacture water inside their own bodies from the material they find in dry plants.

But one of the most ingenious ways of finding shade and so conserving moisture, is that of the diminutive social weaver. With others of its kind it builds a sunshade, forming the roof of what must be the world's most remarkable bird's nest.

The weavers – grey, with chestnut backs and black-streaked heads – gather in small flocks, select a suitable tree and build a roof of strong twigs high above the ground. It looks as though a thatched roof has been dropped on to the tree. Beneath the roof each pair builds a nest chamber of grasses and straw, reached by a tunnel.

Chicks are raised safe from most predators except for tree-climbing snakes and honey badgers.

As many as 150 social weavers – and occasional rosy-faced lovebirds and scaly feathered finches – may share a single nest. In a sense, the birds are misnamed, for the only social thing about them is the common roof that they build to their nests. When flocks fly off to feed, on insects and grass seeds, far from being social they are extremely quarrelsome, filling the air with their noisy *klok-klok* calls.

CLOTHED . . . The candelabra euphorbia (*Euphorbia ingens*) is one of the most widely distributed trees of the African wilderness.

. . . AND BARE The mighty baobab tree stretches its naked, spectre-like boughs and powerful trunk toward a grey winter sky.

ancient watering place. Elephants pass close to its walls. In the moonlight the lions and the leopards see its reflection mirrored on the water they drink.

South of Etosha, the sandy plain is underlain with limestone or dolomite. In a setting that lacks surface water, there occur at places such as Otjikoto, Guinas and Gamkorab, sinkhole lakes, caused when under-ground water has dissolved the limestone to form a cool reservoir and the roof has collapsed.

C. J. Andersson, one of the pioneer explorers of the last century, in his book *Lake Ngami*, has left a good description of Otjikoto as seen by the first Europeans to discover it.

'After a day and a half travel, we suddenly found

DEATH DANCE A few writhing twigs of vegetation lurch toward the sky, like some parched creature dying of thirst. This watercourse, Sossusvlei, on the edge of the Namib Desert, receives only an occasional flood of chocolate-coloured water.

THE WEAVERS' HOME A communal nest of the sociable weaver. Vast numbers of these excitable, busy little birds find a home in one such nest. Occasionally, a snake will also take up residence in the nest and feed on eggs and fledglings.

ourselves on the brink of Otjikoto, the most extraordinary chasm it was ever my fortune to see. It is scooped, so to say, out of the solid limestone rock; and though on a thousand times larger scale, not unlike the Elv-Gryta one so commonly meets in Scandinavia. The form of Otjikoto is cylindrical; its diameter upwards of 400 ft (122 m), and its depth, as we ascertained by the lead-line, 215 ft (66 m), that is

at the sides, for we had no means of plumbing the middle, but had reason to believe the depth to be pretty uniform throughout. To about 30 ft (9 m) of the brink, it is filled with water.'

The level of the water was reputed to remain constant. Only one steep and slippery path reached it from the ground level. Andersson and his companion in his travels, Sir Francis Galton, dived in for a swim,

TSUMEB, HILL OF MAGIC METAL

One of the great steps forward in mankind's story came with the discovery of metal-working about 8000 years ago, somewhere in the area that is now called Asia Minor. Nobody knows whether the knowledge was carried south of the Equator by wandering smiths or whether, many centuries later, the secret was independently rediscovered by groups of Stone Age hunters thousands of kilometres away. The second version seems likelier, for there must have been countless occasions when men used gorgeously coloured stones – shaded blue, purple, green or red by the copper salts they contained – in their pottery furnaces.

Eventually, somebody must have noticed how a golden-red liquid was drawn out of the stones by the fierce heat; how, when it cooled, it became solid again, keeping the shape of whatever had contained it; how it could be hammered thin and flat, or ground to a sharp cutting edge.

Copper, because it is so easy to extract, was probably the earliest metal ever worked by man. The name comes from the Latin, *cuprum*, meaning Cyprus metal, for the Romans found mines being worked on the island of Cyprus well before the time of Christ.

In Africa, surface outcrops were mined long before the coming of the white man. Present-day Katanga, Zambia, Zimbabwe, the northern part of the Transvaal, Namaqualand, Angola and South West Africa all yielded rich lodes of copper from easily worked surface depots.

Copper ore commands attention from prospectors, for its brilliant colours make it immediately apparent. Its sulphides produce the purplish-brown of bornite, the dark grey of chalcite, yellow chalcopyrite, and the blue of covellite. Native copper, which sometimes occurs in almost pure forms, is red. Its oxidised minerals range from the beautiful peacock blue of azurite to the green of brochanite, chrysocolla and malachite. The red of cuprite and yellowish-green colours are produced in the arsenates.

Crystal clusters of astonishing colours form at Tsumeb, a veritable hill of oxidic copper ores near Otjikoto in South West Africa. It was first mined, centuries ago, by the Bergdama tribesmen – or rather by their womenfolk, for women and children did all the labour. A male skeleton has still to be found in any shaft where falls of rock killed the workers.

The men, however, kept the smelting to themselves. Certain clans and families specialised in the work, which was surrounded by an aura of magic. During the dry season, when the water table was at its lowest, shafts, adits and trenches were dug out to about the 12 m level before they flooded.

Malachite ore from Tsumeb was carried to smelting sites where water and anthills were available for the building of furnaces. Once moistened, an anthill was easily hollowed out to the required shape, and the material, cemented by ants' saliva, baked hard. Clusters of furnaces were built near a supply of water, each some 700 mm high by 350 mm in diameter.

Goatskin bellows were used to blow in air through pipes made of clay. Alternate layers of ore and charcoal were banked inside the furnace.

The master smelter and his assistants then indulged in rituals to aid the smelt. Magic ingredients were placed in the furnaces and the fires were lit. Ritual dancing and singing continued throughout the period of smelting. When the smelt was over, the furnaces were broken open and the copper removed. This was then re-smelted, refined and poured into moulds to form ingots, generally of a cruciform pattern. These were the standard items of trade. From them were made spear-heads, hoes and other implements, jewellery and ornaments.

A master smelter was both honoured and feared, for he was regarded as possessing knowledge of the black art. Women were totally excluded from such knowledge. They dumped their heavy loads of ore next to the furnaces and retreated respectfully, back to their holes in the ground to dig for more.

somewhat to the consternation of the local tribesmen who had some belief that whoever entered the pool would surely perish. The water was cold and limpid. Incredibly, in a reservoir of water quite isolated from any streams, it was full of fish, small but very tasty to eat. Enormous flocks of doves resorted to the place to drink, the woods resounding with their cooing.

The pure if hard water in the sinkhole of Otjikoto made it another well-known staging place for travellers. Andersson and his party met there a number of Bushmen and Ovambos carrying copper ore. The mines were further south. The ore was packed in baskets made of palm leaves and equipped with wooden handles. Each basket contained about 40 kg of copper ore, with the porters travelling stages of about 25 km each day for ten days to reach their destination. In so thirsty a climate, the water at Otjikoto was one of the few pleasures on a toilsome journey.

The copper came from one of several mines. About 18 km from Otjikoto there was a veritable hill of vividly coloured oxide ore rising above the bush.

This great hill of malachite was named by the Hereros *Otjisumo* (the place of frogs). The name was corrupted to Sumeb by the Nama, and to Tsumeb by the Europeans. In continuous production from prehistoric times, this mine, since Europeans worked it and kept records, has yielded over 700 000 tons of copper, 2 million tons of lead, 800 000 tons of zinc, and smaller quantities of cadmium, germanium and silver. There is no foreseeable end to its profitable life, and Tsumeb is world famous for its great variety of crystallised oxide ores.

An astonishing total of over 100 different minerals is found in this one-man-band of a mine, and a full collection of samples is quite dazzling. This prodigious concentration is found in a pipe-like body 185 m by 75 m and reaching downwards to a known depth of at least 1400 m.

A dream that failed

Tourmaline, a lovely gemstone with a vast variety of colours, mainly green and blue, is found near Usakos. Amethyst, deep violet in colour, is found in the Otjiwarongo and Omaruru districts. There is blue chalcedony at Otjisondu and red chalcedony in the Kaokoveld. Agates may be found on the beaches, especially at Luderitz. Rose quartz is found in the Rössing Range, where manganese stains it varying shades of pink and red.

Zinc, copper, lithium, manganese, tin and wolfram are in deposits scattered from the valley of the Orange River to the Kunene. Some of the deposits are in areas so remote, arid and rugged that their profitable working, at least for the present, is impossible. In some places, man has tried, and his experiences have been bitter. In the bleak valley of the Khan River, a German company established a substantial copper mine in 1908, but the green-blue stains of malachite in the rocks were just mirages of wealth. The Germans left at the time of the First World War. The British took over but after 21 years of struggle against the impossible the mine closed. On the walls of the manager's house somebody scrawled a message which long remained as a piece of warning graffiti.

'No rain, no wealth,
We abandon ye therefore to the sun,
the sand and the flies.'

On the other hand, in equally impossible situations, man sometimes experiences a miracle. The Skeleton Coast from the Ugeb River to the Kunene River fringes the Namib, and that is surely one of the harshest landscapes in the world. A bleakly cold sea to the west; a barren wilderness of sand to the east. The area is swept by the cruel winds, with vicious sand storms. Dense fogs last days on end, moistening the sand with clammy mist, corroding metals in a landscape of death seemingly abandoned by God. But one day in April 1908 a labourer shovelling sand off the railway dropped his spade and carried to his foreman, August Stauch, what he called a 'pretty stone'. Stauch tested the stone on the glass of his wristwatch and found it was a diamond.

As in Namaqualand, suddenly diamonds were found all over the wilderness as though they had rained there overnight. Stauch and a Dr Scheibe went prospecting in the Pomona area of the coast. While Stauch plotted their position on a map, he told his servants to look for diamonds. One of them simply went down on his knees and filled both hands with diamonds, even stuffing some into his mouth. They lay on the ground as thick 'as plums under a plum tree'. Dr Scheibe stared at the scene in amazement and simply repeated over and over again *'Ein Märchen . . . ein Märchen* (A fairy tale . . . a fairy tale).

It was more than that. Between 1908 and 1914, some 5 million carats of diamonds were recovered from the desert of South West Africa. Many more millions of carats have been recovered since then. If the trees of South West Africa were thrown there as weeds over the walls of paradise, then perhaps the diamonds were the tears of the blessed damozel who leaned out from the gold bar of heaven.

The Karoo, a land that time has worn away

*This is a landscape of moods,
sometimes sinister, sometimes placid,
which seems to sweep on
for ever. The horizon could well be
the end of a flat earth.*

OCEAN OF COLOUR A rainbow pierces the storm-pregnant sky above the prairieland near Zastron, in the Eastern Free State. This typical South African landscape is dominated by a koppie, whose hard roof has resisted millions of years of erosion.

*Thirstland of the Karoo,
where little more can be
heard than the whisper of winds*

SOUTH AFRICA's classic South African scene, the real scenic emblem of the country, is the vast prairieland of the veld, sweeping away to a flat-topped koppie that stands on its own, like a sentinel keeping watch on the utmost rim of the earth. Such a spacious landscape essentially belongs to the high central plateau, especially to the more southerly portion

known to the Hottentot tribes as the *Karoo* (a thirst-land).

It is there that the flat-topped koppies are lords of an enchanted world where the springboks *pronk* with their strange, stiff-legged springs high into the air; where sunsets and dawns look as though the sky has caught fire; where the jackals sing to the moon, and the flocks of sheep wander incessantly over vast ranges of grazing land; where stillness can be felt and little more can be heard than the whisper of winds and the sound of a solitary wind pump quietly creaking, as though talking to itself in solace for its loneliness.

The Karoo gives its name to the largest geological

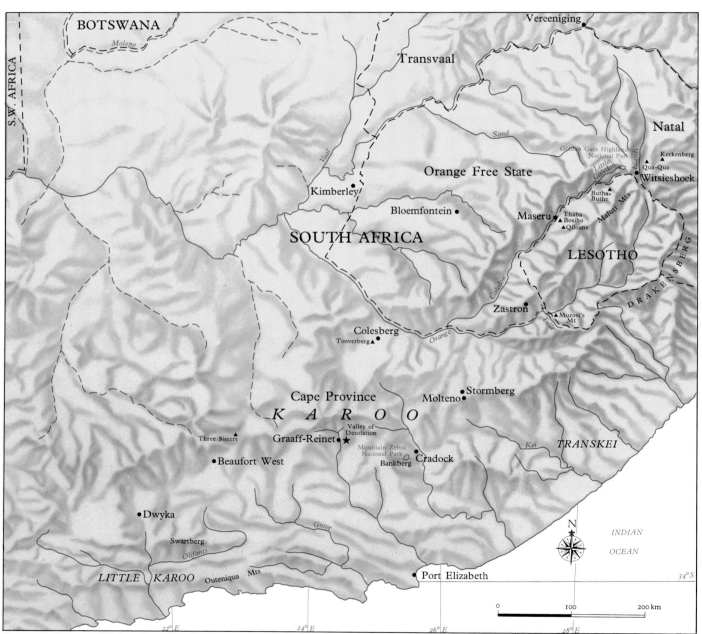

TOMB OF FORESTS Mighty forests were buried in the Karoo during a massive laying down of sediments between 150 and 250 million years ago. The flat-topped koppies of the area have resisted erosion well, and indicate the height once reached by the entire Karoo.

system in Southern Africa. It is a system which provides fully two-thirds of the surface of Southern Africa with an immensely thick deposit of sediments. In reduced thickness it is found in many parts of Africa south of the Sahara, and also appears in other Southern Hemisphere continents. No part of this system was ever under the sea: the fossil remains with which it is richly littered all belong to freshwater and terrestrial types of life.

A prodigious amount of material went into the making of the Karoo System, and where it all came from is something of a mystery. Some ancient landscape, complete with mountain ranges, volcanoes, hills and valleys, must have come totally to grief to provide the shales, silts and sandstones, washed by rainwater into vast bogs and marshes, steadily rising higher in successive layers until the system reached the staggering thickness of about 7000 m.

What seems to have occurred is that after the creation of the Cape System something happened to the earth. Either it was tilted by some extraneous force, or affected by a shifting of the weight of the continents. The Northern Hemisphere became warm, while the Southern Hemisphere was covered in ice. The Northern Hemisphere entered the Carboniferous Age and received its deposits of coal from dense forests. The Southern Hemisphere shivered for many bleak years, with all life dead or gone to warmer areas.

Then, about 250 million years ago, another profound change took place. The Southern Hemisphere became warm. The ice melted, life returned. Small, swimming reptiles flourished in the slush and mud created by the melted ice. Their fossils are very numerous and well preserved among the layer of ice-marked rocks, known as Dwyka Tillite, which covered the land surface. These rocks are made of mudstone, bluish-grey in colour and containing numerous pebbles and boulders scratched by ice.

When the ice retreated

Forests grew as the ice vanished and, in an atmosphere of steamy, humid heat, the age of the dinosaurs commenced and lasted for 125 million years. During this long period the sediments of the Karoo System were laid down in three sequences, each influenced by some special conditions of climate or other circumstances.

First to be laid down was the Ecca Series, rich in plant fossils and containing most of the coal deposits of Southern Africa. The deposit reached a thickness of 2000 m, and consisted of dark-coloured shales and sandstones, with carbonaceous shale. It was obviously the burial ground for dense vegetation and many mighty forests, and the remnants are so well preserved that near Vereeniging in the Transvaal, tree stumps have been excavated in their original growing position.

Above the Ecca Series lies the Beaufort Series, a deposit which in places reaches an extraordinary thickness of over 3000 m. The sediments in the Beaufort Series are slightly more colourful sandstones and mudstones, with numerous vertebrate-fossil dinosaur and amphibian remains, as well as anthracite coal in Zululand and the Eastern Transvaal.

On top of the Beaufort Series of the Karoo System there was deposited still another layer of sediments, known as the Stormberg Series. The remnants of this deposit loom up like an island in the midst of the grass-covered surface of the Beaufort Series, and provide the foundation for the mountain country of Lesotho and the Drakensberg.

The Beaufort Series is exposed as the surface of the modern landscape extending over the arid Karoo area of the Cape Province, the Orange Free State, Eastern Cape Province, Transkei, parts of Natal and the Transvaal. With rainfall varying considerably over this area, the covering of grass and other vegetation changes. Different parts have different appearances but, beneath the covering, like Kipling's Colonel's lady and Judy O'Grady, they are sisters under the skin.

The veld of South Africa, then, is essentially the surface of the Beaufort Series, worn and weathered down by time. The flat-topped koppies scattered over this surface have resisted erosion better than the surrounding land, and so give an indication of the level once reached by the entire Karoo. At some stage, a considerable volcanic disturbance occurred. Into the thick deposit of sediment there was intruded a mass of molten matter known as dolerite. This material was forced up from the molten core of the earth and into the sediments, where it cooled and hardened into strange forms. There are long, vertical dykes, some of them exposed on the surface like prehistoric walls. Horizontal sills and sheets of dolerite are also common, and the whole complicated intrusion has had a variety of effects.

Dolerite is an extremely hard rock and the intrusion provides the soft sediments with something like a stiffening skeleton. The movement of water is contained and directed by the presence of these natural walls and floors. Miners are frustrated if the coal seam they are following is intersected by dolerite.

The intrusive rock is extremely hard to penetrate and, in any case, usually transmutes such soft things as coal seams into some quite different material.

The flat-topped koppies are the products of these dolerite sills. In the arid Karoo areas of the Beaufort Series, the land surface is almost unprotected by vegetation. Many violent rainstorms do occur, in spite of the general aridity, and these play havoc. The land surface is simply carried away piecemeal by the powerful run-off. The flat-topped koppies remain through the chance possession of an 'umbrella' consisting of a dolerite sill – a dark-coloured layer of rock about 2 m thick and covering the top of the koppie. It defies the efforts of the rain to remove it. The length and width of the koppie depends entirely on the extent of the sill. Some koppies are table shaped; others have the appearance of stools; others, known as rhino horns, have only a tip of dolerite protecting a sharply pointed summit.

Even the toughest dolerite cover, however, will eventually disintegrate. When it does, the hillock beneath it soon collapses. The sediments are rapidly carried away, leaving another curious sight on the Karoo. With the sediments of the hills completely removed, the dolerite fragments remain on the level of the plain, so neatly dumped together that many of the piles seem to be the work of giant housemaids. Sent to clean up the countryside, these industrious creatures have swept all the debris into neat piles and then gone off for tea. Presently they will return with dustpans to collect the piles of dolerite, and nothing will remain of a vanished hill. The rain will then start another erosion into the unprotected surface, encounter another sill of dolerite, and another flat-topped koppie will slowly be revealed as the unprotected sediments around it are carried away.

The last of the Cape lions

Many of these dolerite-protected koppies are notable landmarks. The Three Sisters, north of Beaufort West, are three strangely similar stool-shaped hillocks, familiar to most travellers along the main rail and road routes from Cape Town to the north. Overlooking the old frontier town of Colesberg there is a particularly symmetrical koppie, discernible for a deceptively long distance and presenting exactly the same aspect from all directions. Known to pioneer

LAND OF FREEDOM A herd of blesbok roam across the veld, lush in its summer garb. Thunderclouds gather above the looming mountains of Lesotho, which provide a dramatic backdrop to some of the most breathtaking scenery in Southern Africa.

LONE SENTINEL As though standing guard over its barren kingdom, the *Tooverberg* (magic mountain) soars skywards. Two wind-pumps, drawing water from deep below the ground, signify man's will to wrest a living from this arid landscape.

travellers as *Tooverberg* (magic mountain), this stool-shaped mass of sediment reaches a height of 1 907 m. At its foot lies a celebrated watering place, once frequented by huge herds of game animals, and this area became a great resort of hunters. In the vicinity of this koppie the last of the *kwaggas*, a form of zebra, were killed towards the end of the 19th century; the last Cape lion was shot in 1836; and the last of the blue buck about the same time.

Many magnificent examples of these flat-topped hillocks, table-topped, stool-topped, pointed tops, all uniform in height above the prevailing level of the plain, occur north of Cradock. The Mountain Zebra National Park, high on the slopes of the Bankberg range, is in the centre of a classic expanse of this Karoo country. There is an awe-inspiring panorama of a landscape which seems to sweep on for ever. The horizon could well be the end of a flat earth.

Light, atmospheric moisture and haze cause subtle changes almost hourly. The horizon sometimes seems nearer, at other times it recedes. Unfamiliar hillocks appear in the distance, resembling the vanguard of an invading army. Search for them a few hours later, and they have retreated and are utterly lost; the furthest horizon is obscured by a shimmering haze. It is a landscape of moods, sometimes threatening and

sinister, sometimes placid and inviting, offering a traveller the prospect that another world lies somewhere far away, a place where hope is young, not jaded, and the taxman never heard of.

The Mountain Zebra National Park is a sanctuary for survivors of the great herds of plains game which once wandered over the Karoo. When Europeans first explored the central plains they found such astonishing numbers of zebras and antelope, principally gnus, hartebeests, blesboks and springboks that they considered the supply of game to be inexhaustible. A mass slaughter promptly commenced, but is was not only the guns of the professional hunters which destroyed the game. Settlers introduced flocks of sheep; watering places were occupied by man and his livestock; and in all the vast spaces of the veld there was just no room for wild animals.

Sir John Fraser, son of the Reverend Colin Fraser, pastor of Beaufort West in the centre of the Karoo, has left a notable description of the year of the great drought of 1849.

'One day,' he wrote, 'a travelling *smous* (pedlar) came to Beaufort West and brought the tidings that thousands of *trekbokken* (migrating antelope) were coming from the north, devouring everything before them. About a week after the *smous* had left Beaufort

West, we were awakened one morning by a sound as of a strong wind before a thunderstorm, followed by the trampling of thousands of all kinds of game – wildebeest, blesbok, springboks, kwaggas, elands, antelopes of all kinds – which filled the streets and gardens and, as far as one could see, covered the whole country, grazing off everything eatable before them, drinking up the waters in the furrows, fountains and dams wherever they could get at them; and, as the creatures were all in a more or less impoverished condition, the people killed them in numbers in their gardens. It took about three days before the whole of the *trekbokken* had passed, and it left our country as if a fire had raged over it. It was indeed a wonderful sight.'

Only remnants of the former herds of antelope survive in the Karoo. The mountain zebra is carefully protected in the Mountain Zebra National Park, but there are only about 150 of these sure-footed animals left. Gnus, springboks, elands and hartebeests are more numerous and at least safe from extinction. To see a herd of springboks wandering over the Karoo, especially at sunset, and suddenly excited, all bouncing over the prairie as though toys mounted on coiled springs, is an unforgettable experience.

The bounding or springing carries the springbok about 3 m into the air. The animal lowers its head, fully extends its legs and bunches its hoofs together, arching its back in the process and throwing the haunches down. The white dorsal crest is fanned out along its back in a strikingly handsome manner. In this strangely elegant arched shape, the animal suddenly seems to spurn the earth. It simply shoots straight up into the air. For a breathtaking instant, like Nijinsky at the height of his gravity-defying leaps in ballet, the animal seems to be weightless in the air. Then it drops, but hardly seems to touch the ground before it is up in the air again, sometimes at a sharp angle to one side, then to the other, then straight up again, then forward. Then suddenly it will stay on the ground, lower its dorsal fan and, with neck extended, ears and horns laid back, nose pointing forward, it will race ahead with tremendous stride and pace.

The springbok is a gazelle, and most graceful in build. It is the national and sporting emblem of South Africa and its natural home is the vast open plains of the Karoo. It requires very little water and its famous migrations, when springbok swarmed in millions, were occasioned by searches for fresh grazing fields. Normally they are almost silent, but when on migration they make a peculiar half whistle, half snort. The sound, especially at night, when thousands of them make this noise, is uncanny. Another animal at home in the prairielands of the Karoo is the *meerkat,* or suricate. This jolly and beautifully marked little animal is a mongoose-like creature which lives in colonies. Meerkats are great lovers of the sun. They spend the days lolling about around their burrow entrances, soaking up sunshine, lying on their backs to warm their bellies, then on their bellies with their legs spread out so that they are absolutely flat on the ground. After a chilly winter night, they rush out to greet the sun and saturate themselves with warmth-making ecstatic crooning and muttering noises. When aroused they sit up on their hind legs, view the surroundings and then pop down into the safety of their burrows. Almost immediately, however, they peep out again with avid curiosity to watch anything approach or pass. They are real children of the sunny veld.

The gnu: a bundle of oddities

The *gnu*, so well known for generally occupying the 'g' space in children's picture-alphabet books, is another creature peculiar to the high plateau of the Karoo. This is, in fact, a very peculiar animal indeed. The Bushmen gave it the name of gnu from the odd noise it makes, a bellowing snort with a metallic ring. It is a medium-size antelope, the bulls about 1,5 m high. Although known as the black wildebeest, it is dark brown in colour with a handsome buff-coloured mane and tail. For the rest, it is a very mixed-up animal, with the body of a Shetland pony, the horns of a cow, the tail of a horse, the beard of a goat and a standard of behaviour best described as skittish. There is a constant tossing of heads (they are subject to maggots in the nostrils), and a great deal of cavorting and barging. When alarmed they storm off in a fine stampede, then in the midst of retreat two bulls, presumably with lurking animosity or simply over-excited, will suddenly stop and commence a furious fight, butting and goring at each other. Just as suddenly they will dart off again, then stop so abruptly that they half tumble over, turn and glare fixedly at whatever has disturbed them, and make a disapproving blubbering noise.

The herds of plains game of past years and the flocks of sheep of today flourish on the nondescript but extremely nourishing shrubs which cover the

LAND OF GIANTS *(Overleaf)* Like a battalion of giants, the pinnacles of ancient rock formations rear above the Valley of Desolation, near Graaff-Reinet, in the Great Karoo. In the centre is Spandau Kop. The Sundays River flows eastwards on the right.

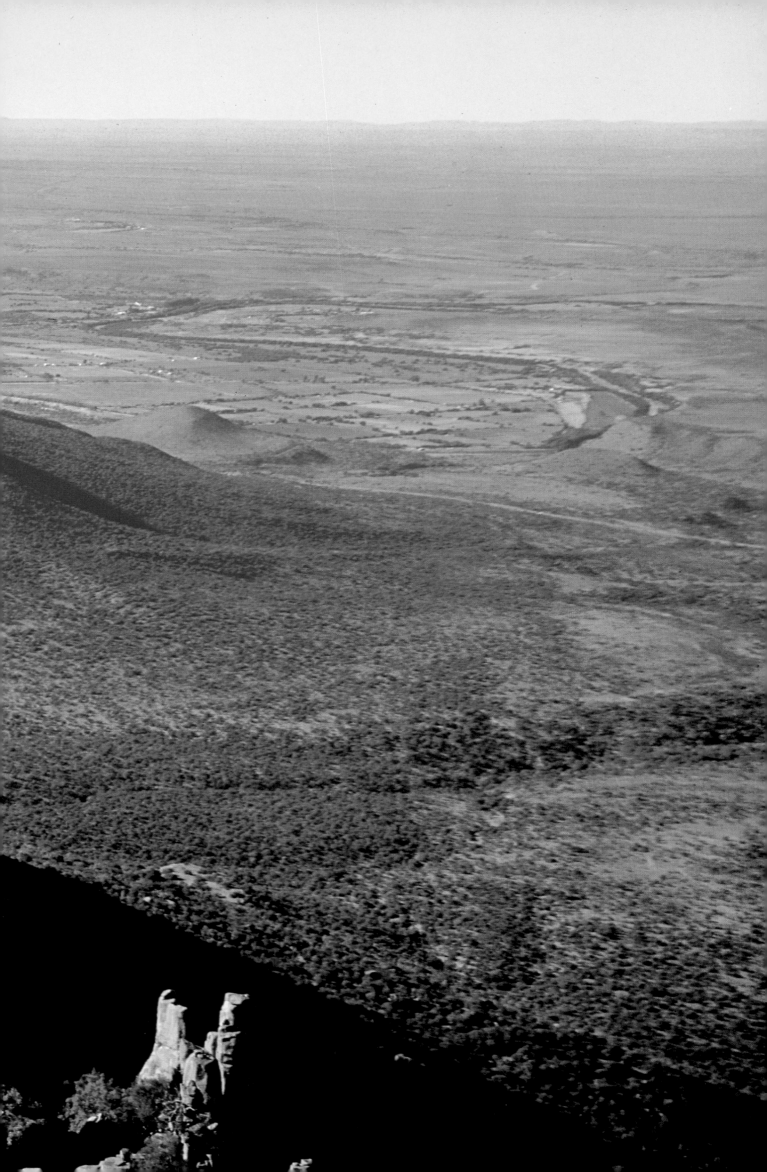

SUMMER MAGIC Plants and trees find the Karoo a hostile land in winter. But in summer, nourished by periodic rains, plants which have been dormant burst into bloom. This coral aloe, one of many flowering aloes of the Karoo, enjoys only a brief reign.

Karoo, and the grass which grows in the more northerly areas where there is better rainfall. The springboks are adept, too, at using their hooves to dig out bulbs and roots, much like Bushmen scavenging for *veldkos* (food of the field).

Many of the plants of the Karoo are succulents, and the moisture they store supplies the antelope with most of their water. Few trees grow in the area, but those that do, such as *Acacia karroo,* the sweet thorn tree, provide nutritious and palatable eating from their leaves and seed-pods. They grow mainly on the banks of watercourses, and their yellow blossoms

perfume the dry air with a sweet odour. In a favourable season there are also spectacular displays of flowers. They appear and disappear so suddenly that they could well be a floral-patterned carpet, rolled out by the gardener of the Karoo to welcome special guests and then rolled up again as soon as the visitors have departed. Mesembryanthemums are particularly numerous, their spring flowers so dense and vividly coloured that they seem to glow with an inner fluorescence.

In what is known as the Little Karoo, the plain between the Swartberg and Outeniqua ranges, such prodigious numbers of *Ganna* plants flourish that the area is often called Ganna Land. Ganna is the Hottentot-Bushman name for the eland, and this species of antelope had a particular taste for the plant. Ostriches also flourish on these plants and

SANDSTONE WONDERLAND (*Preceding page*) The sandstone landscape of the Eastern Free State is a wonderland of weird formations. Clusters of clouds dance over this peaceful region of orange-coloured rocks, willow-lined streams and grassy valleys.

other food plentiful in or peculiar to this long plain between the mountains. Although ostriches are widespread throughout Africa, this area is their particular paradise. Everything suits them. Their feathers grow to perfection and they have proliferated in an environment free of parasites, with a warm, dry climate but well watered by the mountain streams. Man hunted the birds from early times, and then domesticated them. The result was a landscape which has no comparison anywhere else. Flocks of thousands of domesticated ostriches graze in the fields of lucerne grown to feed them. There is a strange old-world elegance to the area. The big birds have a stately grace to their walk and behaviour, while their courtship involves a display of feathers and a strange ritual of dancing and bowing.

Plants of the highveld

North of the Orange River the surface of the Central Plateau is richly grassed. Although it is essentially the same sedimentary deposit of the Beaufort Series, the higher rainfall stimulates a different vegetation. It remains an open, rolling prairie type of country, the grassveld or highveld of Southern Africa, pleasantly green in summer but dead and frostbitten in winter. The grasses are segregated into sour and sweet veld areas. A considerable variety of grasses grow in both areas, with such genera as *Cymbopogon* and *Themeda* in the sweet areas, and *Themeda triandra* in the sourveld. There is a distinct difference in the taste of the grasses.

Trees do not like the highveld. But *Acacia karroo* grows in the hollows, where it finds some protection from the winter wind. And along the river banks the graceful Natal willow *(Salix woodii)* finds a home, safely sleeping through the winter months with leafless boughs swaying gently in the icy air of the long nights.

There are not many species of flowering plants, but wild daisies and poppies are common, as well as several species of *Convolvulaceae* such as the morning glory. On the rocky hillocks, and especially in the protection of the kloofs, there are many flowering aloes; lovely members of the *Amaryllis* family; yellow arum lilies *(Zantedeschia pentlandii)*, proteas *(Protea caffra)*, and the pretty *Leucospermum gerrardii*.

Before man tamed the veld, the rich grazing of the grassveld supported huge herds of antelope, principally zebra, wildebeest, eland, springbok and blesbok. With the approach of winter these animals migrated to warmer areas, especially in Natal. They found the easiest routes down the escarpment, and

Ostrich *(Struthio camelus)*

Bird of myth

The dry, open scrubland of the Karoo is ideal country for the flightless, long-striding ostrich. This largest of living birds will eat almost anything that moves and many things that do not – mammals, lizards, insects, other birds, fruit, plants, even stones and pieces of metal, that lie in its gizzard as an aid to digestion. With a 4 m racing stride, the ostrich can reach speeds of more than 60 km an hour. Its height helps it to spot enemies at a distance, but if one gets too close, the ostrich has powerful legs, and claws capable of ripping open a lion. Ostriches do not bury their heads in the sand in moments of danger, as the legend says, but there is still some basis for the myth. For the chicks, instead of running away, will often stretch out flat, feigning death.

the trails blazed by their hooves were followed by the Bushmen hunters, the roving bands of Iron Age warrior tribes, and by European hunters and explorers.

The spectacle of these prodigious herds of migrating plains game must have been staggering. They were counted in millions. Their golden age was before the coming of the Iron Age tribes. The Bushmen, with their bows and arrows, did them little harm. They simply played their part with the lions and other natural predators in maintaining a balance in nature. For the Bushmen, nature had created in this area a real heaven.

At the bottom of the Stormberg Series, on which the mountains of Lesotho are based, lie what are known as the Molteno Beds. They are composed of shale and sandstone which, made of quartz grains with crystal faces, has a fine glitter. Fossil plants are found in these Molteno Beds, and above them lie the Red Beds, composed of red sandstone, shale and mudstone, rich in the fossils of dinosaurs.

It is above these two beds that there lies one of the most beautiful of all geological formations, the Cave Sandstone. While the two earlier deposits were laid down in water, this sandstone was deposited by wind. The grains of sand are fine, rounded and brilliantly coloured by iron oxides into spectacular shades of red, orange and yellow. This deposit contributes to the scenery of Southern Africa a landscape of singular grace and beauty.

Sandstone is easily worked by water, eroding into deep valleys and gorges flanked by towering precipices. Vivid colours and bizarre formations make these sandstone valleys tremendously spectacular. A superb example is the upper valley of the Little Caledon River in the Eastern Orange Free State, the area of the Golden Gate Highlands National Park.

The Golden Gate itself is a majestic sandstone cliff towering over the right-hand bank of the river near its headwaters. The natural colours of the sandstone are themselves brilliant, but the cliff is so situated as to catch the rays of the setting sun, and the massive pile glows as though with an inner radiance.

The whole length of the Little Caledon River leads through a sandstone landscape of remarkable charm. It is a golden countryside. There are fields of wheat and maize; orchards of yellow peaches; willow and poplar trees, their leaves aflame with colour in the fall; meandering streams; snug little farmhouses made of sandstone blocks; towering cliffs and detached hills, modelled by the weather into odd shapes; balancing rocks, vast caverns and innumerable rock shelters scolloped out by water and providing homes for the Bushmen.

The sweet grass has a gold-red colour, especially when in seed. Game and domestic animals fatten on it, and it is pleasant to see at least some remnants of

NATURE'S KALEIDOSCOPE The thunderstorm has passed over the sandstone country. The rumbles and crashes fade in the distance. Now the lustrous Golden Gate shimmers in sunlight, enhanced by the rare spectacle of a majestic double rainbow.

VALE OF ECHOES The sounds of man and game echo eerily in this lush region of soaring sandstone cliffs and valleys in the Eastern Free State. The wealth of beauty is enriched by the dazzling array of colours of the rock strata, trees and plants.

the former herds of antelope still roaming over the area. Arum lilies, watsonias, fire lilies and red-hot pokers ornament the green-and-gold setting. On the high ledges nest the lammergeyers, the great vultures with wingspans of nearly 3 m. With silent ease they glide down the long valleys between the sandstone precipices, and the whistle of the wind in their wings is sometimes the only sound to echo back from the golden rocks.

A Bushman's idyll

To the Bushmen, this setting was idyllic. It provided ample food, water and firewood, and comfortable, commodious shelter. They lived well and had the leisure to perfect their culture. They sang and danced, and the walls of the sandstone caves made excellent galleries for their artists. A variety of subtle earth colours was also available to provide paint. These colours were mixed with albuminoid binders made of animal blood and applied to the rock face with brush-like instruments. The artists must have thoroughly enjoyed their work. Their pictures are lively and full of humour. It is easy to imagine them working on the pictures, watched by an admiring group of spectators. A good combination – a dinner of venison washed down with fermented honey, appreciative spectators, and workmanship so meticulous that very few accidental splashes, smudges or examples of faulty drawing have ever been found, although the primitive artists had no way of erasing mistakes.

Flat-topped hills are numerous in the sandstone country. Several of them have played significant parts in the story of Southern Africa. Like the flat-topped hills in the Beaufort Series of the Karoo, the sandstone hills are uniform in height and are the isolated remnants of a former higher plain. Many of the sandstone flat-tops are of considerable size, and make formidable natural strongholds. Their summits are well grassed and, at least during the rainy season,

THE MASSACRE A painting by Thomas Baines of the 1860 antelope slaughter.

One of the most destructive hunts in history

To the pioneers, it seemed inconceivable that the herds of plains game could ever be destroyed. They stretched for kilometre after endless kilometre across the Karoo, out-numbering it seemed the stars of the Milky Way. But where something can be had for nothing, man can lose control of his own reason. He can become the most destructive of all animals, justifying what he does by the reasoning that somebody else will do it if he does not.

contain water in pools and marshes. The steep slopes and final precipitous rock faces generally have only one or two practical approaches and, with these paths barricaded, any attackers were confronted by obstacles which could prove insurmountable. The flat-tops, in fact, played the same role as the medieval castles in Europe. An Iron Age chief so fortunate as to have in his possession a commodious, flat-topped hill had a very secure stronghold.

In the vicinity of the Golden Gate there are some fine specimens of these flat-tops. The upper valley of the Elands River is dominated by a most majestic natural fortress known to the Bushmen as *Qwa-Qwa* (whiter than white), from the colour of the droppings of the vultures which have used its ledges as resting places from time immemorial. This massive pile of sandstone provided the Bushmen with good caves, and then became the stronghold of a regular robber-baron named Whêtse and a group of Kgolokwe tribespeople. Driven away in 1856, when his rustling became intolerable, Whêtse made a daring escape through a great cavern and was seen in those parts no more. Kwena and Tlokwa tribespeople displaced his followers, and today this rugged valley in the foothills of the Maluti range is the homeland of the *baSotho ba Borwa* (Sotho people of the south). Their country is an independent Bantu homeland, which they call Qwa-Qwa. It will be interesting to see what the outside world makes of such a peculiar national name in the United Nations, and in popular songs.

Not very far from Qwa-Qwa hill soars another table-top celebrated in the story of South Africa. This stately pile was named *Kerkenberg* (Church Mountain) by the Voortrekkers. With its level summit reaching a height of 2083 m, it is a notable landmark, dominating a fine expanse of undulating veld, thickly grassed, well watered and brilliant each Easter with the colours of massed cosmos flowers.

In the lee of this mountain, in 1837, Pieter Retief, the Voortrekker leader, made a base camp with 54

The slaughter of the great antelope herds of the central plateau was unparalleled, even in the plains of America where the buffalo was practically wiped out. A classic example was a vast hunt organised in 1860 as an entertainment for the visiting Prince Alfred, second son of Queen Victoria. An account of this hunt, staged at Hartebeestehoek, near Bloemfontein, was published in the form of a commemoration of his royal highness's visit.

'Next morning early, preparations were made for a magnificent hunt, such as the Royal Prince had surely never shared in or seen before. On the right in this valley we saw drawn up, in a long line, from eight hundred to one thousand baRolong, under the command of the son of their Chief, Moroko. They had also with them, a small distance in the rear, about three hundred pack oxen drawn up in line, with pack-saddles on them all prepared for loading up the game.

For some time we saw no more of the baRolong, who, separating into two equal parties, had ridden off to the right and left in lines, keeping as much as possible under the cover of the hills in the direction of the plains, dropping a man every hundred or two hundred yards as they went along, until they had reached out for a distance of perhaps three or four miles into the plain, when each party turning inwards until they met, they thus formed a large continuous curved line of men, which enclosed immense masses of game.

The quantity of game shut in by the baRolong was estimated at from twenty to thirty thousand. The herds of animals could be seen rushing in wild confusion at full gallop along the living cordon which enclosed them. The several kinds of game – ostriches, Burchell's zebras, wildebeests, bonteboks, springboks – kept generally each kind in separate herds or droves, crossing and recrossing one another in the greatest confusion and terror as they careered along the line seeking for a point through which they might break. The clouds of dust which they raised, as they galloped onward, and in which they were enveloped, heightened the confusion. Every now and again some large mass of game, consisting of several thousand head, would in desperation make a rush at some apparently weak point in the living fence. Presently, at another point, a drove of wildebeests, fierce with terror, would make a wild rush at another point of the line, and – amidst clouds of dust, the falling of the dying ones, the tumbling of those living over those who were slain, the roar caused by the trampling of so many galloping feet over the ground, the bellowing of the wounded wildebeests, the shouts and cries of the baRolong, the continued popping of guns and rifles – would resolutely break through the line, and madly career off into the apparently boundless plain.

Fiercer and more determined rushes were made by the maddened animals upon the line – more and more of them were shot down or killed by assegais – but no baRolong stopped to lift what he had killed. Flocks of vultures, delighting in slaughter, hovered round, and sometimes pitched on the ground quite close to the hunters. Thus swept on this great moving mass of life. As the circle still contracted, the droves of game formed into larger masses, and, at last, reckless apparently of death and wounds, broke through the drivers in numerous bodies, so that when the whole mass swept past Mr Baines' house in the narrow valley down which we had ridden to the farm, probably not more than three thousand head of game of all kinds remained enclosed by the hunters.'

wagons and then, with a scouting party, set out to reach Port Natal. Close to Kerkenberg, the high plateau ends. There is a sudden, spectacular drop, with a vast panorama of the high Drakensberg and so sweeping a view of Natal that Retief named the place *Blijde Vooruitzicht* (the joyful prospect). From there, Retief descended the escarpment. Behind him, over 1000 wagons steadily concentrated at Kerkenberg, their journey apparently ended by the precipice, while the Voortrekkers waited to hear details of Retief's reconnaissance. When he returned with news that they could descend into Natal, the great camps exploded with joy and the rock precipices of Kerkenberg must have echoed and re-echoed with the sounds of their celebrations. Their descent of the escarpment, down the paths blazed by migrating game, must have been a grand spectacle. Many of them were descending to death in violent confrontation with the Zulu army, and nowadays Kerkenberg is the scene of an annual gathering in memory of those years of bloodshed.

The most famous of all the flat-topped hills is *Thaba Bosiho* (the mountain of the night). This is the national stronghold of the Sotho people, and it is revered by them as the saviour of their kind. Without it, they would have been totally annihilated.

The massive sandstone pile of Thaba Bosiho dominates as wild and rugged a piece of country as could be seen anywhere. Behind it looms the long range of the Maluti Mountains, actually the western side of the pile of basalt which forms the roof of Southern Africa, and, on the eastern side, is known as the Drakensberg. Below the 2000 m contour of these mountains, the basalt is replaced by cave sandstone. Tremendous natural erosion has carved this sandstone base into complex valleys and plains, littered with rock fragments, flat-topped segments remaining from higher levels, and an extraordinary collection of strangely shaped pinnacles and boulders. Through this rock wilderness, the Caledon River makes its way to join the Orange.

How the Sothos were saved

Total chaos came to the whole area in the 1820s. On the east coast, Shaka was building his Zulu nation and there was a vast human disturbance. Refugee tribes and raiding warrior-bands spread out over the

RIVER OF MOODS One of the great rivers of Africa, the Orange is a river of constantly changing moods: warm, enigmatic, lazy for much of the time, yet suddenly violent as it drowns the countryside with frighteningly powerful floods.

veld like the shock-waves from the centre of an earthquake. The Sotho tribal groups living in the valley of the Caledon found themselves under heavy attack. Their established way of life was shattered. Many of them were killed, others fled into the mountains and turned cannibal to tide themselves over what was called the *Difaqwane* (period of migratory wars). Among the survivors was the young chief, Moshesh, of the Kwena people. He possessed a flat-topped mountain named *Butha-Buthe,* but it was insecure and too small for his followers. He was told of a far better flat-top further south. He sent a scouting party to find this place. According to legend they first saw it from the distance as night fell. It seemed quite insignificant, and they were disappointed. From a distance it does, indeed, look puny. The scouts went on in the dark, and then camped close to the flat-top. When dawn came they were astounded. The flat-topped mass of sandstone loomed over them with tremendous power. They named it *Thaba Bosiho* (the mountain of the night), for it seemed to have grown during the dark hours.

They returned hot-foot to their chief and told him of the wonders of Thaba Bosiho. Its top was commodious, there was water, and the cliff faces were

unscalable. There were only a few paths to the summit, and these were easy to block or defend. Provided the defence was resolute, Thaba Bosiho was impregnable to ground attack, and certainly one of the world's most formidable natural strongholds.

Moshesh was delighted. He led his people to their new home. On the way they ran the gauntlet of packs of cannibals and even Moshesh's grandfather, Peete, ended up in a cooking pot. The survivors, however, reached Thaba Bosiho, and its summit became their refuge. Many violent attacks were made on this stronghold. Raiding warriors such as the Ngwaneni, the Koranna Hottentots, the dreaded maTebele, all tried to subdue Thaba Bosiho and were driven back, their officers tearing off the plumes from the warriors' heads in mortification when they refused to try one more attack. Units of the Zulu army swept the length of the valley and examined Thaba Bosiho with interest, but Moshesh in his wisdom kept them away by paying tribute of girls, skins, feathers, and fine beer brewed for their proud colonels and captains.

Moshesh became known as the chief of the mountain, and to him for protection came many destitute refugees. From the 2000 followers he had originally led to Thaba Bosiho, he found himself at the head of a tribe which was destined to become the nucleus of the Sotho nation. Without Thaba Bosiho, these people would have been lost, and they grew to love the pile of sandstone with a reverent affection. Moshesh himself would never leave it. He had his home in a sandstone building on the summit, and through the long years of peril it is said that before each dawn he went to the doorway and eagerly watched to see the sun climb over the jagged peaks of the Maluti. As the first glittering diamond sparkled over the dark basalt heights he would say: 'I have again seen the light.'

Europeans came to the central plains and Moshesh received them in his stronghold, feeding them standard fare of tea, coffee and sponge cake, baked by his wives from a recipe given to them by the wife of a German trader. Quarrels occurred over stock theft and boundary disputes. Twice the Boers attempted to take Thaba Bosiho by storm and were driven back with galling loss. Twice, also, the British tried to subdue this stubborn chief and his mountain. It was invincible. Its cliffs rebuffed the most resolute attack, and simply echoed back the sounds of cannonading.

RIVER OF DREAMS The hazy, dreamlike course of the Caledon River, the boundary between South Africa and Lesotho. The Caledon is known to the Sotho as *Mohokare,* meaning river of willow trees – groves of which cluster along its winding banks.

MONSTERS' PLAYGROUND Once the haunt of dinosaurs, now only strange rock formations remain of Lesotho's ancient landscape. In the centre is the famed *Qiloane* (the pinnacle). In the background are the sandstone cliffs of *Thaba Bosiho* (the mountain of the night).

Thaba Bosiho remained unconquered. Basutoland (now Lesotho) became a British Protectorate in 1868, and Moshesh died on his stronghold two years later. He is buried on the summit. It is said that his spirit remains in a strange dune of red-coloured sand. The dune wanders about, blown by seasonal winds. But, like Moshesh, it never leaves the summit. If it reaches the edge, upcurrents of wind blow it back. If sand is carried away it will, somehow or other, if legend is to be believed, find its way back to this remarkable stronghold, a place with an atmosphere today of total peace, strength and serenity.

The summit of Thaba Bosiho is 1769 m high. Next to it, like a sentry or guard, there stands an extraordinary peak known as *Qiloane* (the pinnacle). All down the length of the valley of the Caledon River there are other fortress piles of sandstone, each with some legend or story attached to it, and each with its own atmosphere. Murosi's Mountain, overlooking the Orange River, is a grim, sullen-looking stronghold looming steeply over the river like a highwayman waiting by the roadside to prey on passing traffic. Murosi, in fact, was a veritable prince of rustlers. He was the chief of the Phuthi people and, with a very mixed following, he turned this flat-topped height into a real robbers' roost.

Twice the mountain was attacked by forces of the Cape Government trying to bring retribution for numerous raids and outrages. Both attacks were beaten back with heavy loss. Soft-leaded bullets caused grievous wounds on the attackers. Bushmen allies of Murosi used bows and poisoned arrows. All through the icy winter of 1879, snipers picked off victims as government forces laid siege to the stronghold. It was a bitter story of feud, vengeance, murder and stubborn courage. Each night saw raids and counter-raids; men killed; prisoners taken, with Murosi personally decapitating one European patrol-man on the summit edge of the mountain in full view of the besiegers.

The setting was perfect for such a drama. Murosi's Mountain stands in the heart of a wilderness of rocks and peaks. Such rivers as the Orange and the Telle flow silently out from the basalt roof of Southern Africa. Dark-coloured mountains loom up as far as the eye can see. The Telle valley is stunningly beautiful, a piece of scenic daring in a way, for the river has washed a valley deep into the underwear of the basalt heights, revealing the cave-sandstone under-garments with all their rills, frills and colours, con-trasting with the sombre shades of the higher lavas.

Zigzag bridle-paths find complex ways over the ranges. There are lost valleys and secret caves, their walls covered with paintings and many of their en-trances scarred with bullet marks. Rustlers, robbers, outlaws, renegades, cannibals, all used this wilderness as a lair and each had his favourite stronghold. The story of Murosi's Mountain is perfectly understand-able in a setting so primeval.

When spring came in 1879, 400 regulars of the tough Cape Mounted Rifles were marshalled for an attack, supported by volunteers and African levies. They were a crowd of adventurers as mixed as the men of the French Foreign Legion: remittance men, hard cases, mercenaries, all bound together in a mili-tary unit renowned for rugged courage and comrade-ship. To spur the men on, rewards were offered for Murosi and his son Dodo, dead or alive, and to the first man to reach the summit.

For four days before the grand attack, artillery lobbed one shell every ten minutes at the mountain. Then, at 10 p.m. on November 19, 1879, the troop-ers paraded in dark clothes, with blacking on their guns and bayonets. At midnight the bombardment suddenly ended, and three gaudy skyrockets cut the air above the mountain and died with a shower of hissing stars in the dark waters of the Orange River.

All through the dark hours the men fought their way upwards. The false dawn was already lighting the sky when the scaling ladders were placed against the final cliff, at a place on the eastern slopes known as Bourne's Crack.

Up the first ladder climbed Lieutenant Springer. He was near the top when one of Murosi's men looked over the edge into his face.

'Don't come up here boss,' said the man consider-ately in English. 'I'll shoot you.'

'Go to hell!' replied Springer. Raising his revolver he shot the man dead, the body hurtling down into the darkness past the ladder. All round the mountain there was a great clamour of combat as different approaches were tried.

Springer clambered to the top, followed by his men. Forming into a line, they swept the summit. For a few minutes it was hand to hand, but the defenders were cut down or shot where they stood. Some dived directly over the precipices. The few who escaped did so by a miracle of rolling down the slopes, and diving into the waters of the Orange.

End of the affray

The mountain summit was a shambles, littered with the bodies of 200 of Murosi's men and most of their women. Murosi's body was found among the dead. Captain Jonas, a renowned sniper, was also found with 14 bullets in his body, but his rifle still gripped in his hands. At 5.30 a.m. Murosi's head was set up on top of the self-same pole which had carried the remains of the unfortunate patrolman.

Dodo had vanished, but he was found later in a cave beyond the Orange, dying of wounds and with a thigh broken in his wild escape.

On the summit, Murosi's gunpowder storehouse containing 7 tons of ammunition was exploded and the fortifications partly destroyed. Then the troopers went away. Forty-three Europeans had been killed and 84 wounded in the attack. Three Victoria Crosses were awarded for gallantry. Five hundred of Murosi's men, the cream of his rustlers and all his sons, had died.

Only the brooding old mountain is left, with its slopes still littered with cartridge cases and the bric-à-brac of battle. Beneath it, the great river sweeps silently past on its way to the sea. In their nature, this river and the rugged old mountain are characteristic of Southern Africa itself, every inch richly storied with legends and tradition, and over the whole an atmosphere of almost tangible romance.

The Drakensberg: roof of South Africa, and mother of rivers

The birth of the Drakensberg range took the form of a prodigious fireworks display. Volcanic fissure after fissure erupted and poured out its lava until at last a large area of Southern Africa was covered to a depth of about 1500 m.

THE BARRIER A towering wall of rock and ice, the *abaMponjwana* (place of little horns) ridge of the Drakensberg seems designed to bar intruders. On the right is Cathedral Peak. Next to it is the Bell, with the Outer Horn and Inner Horn in the centre.

*Thunder rolls and echoes
among peaks that were
born in fire*

IN THE CENTRE of Southern Africa, like a dark island in a sea of grass-covered plains, there lies a gaunt, steep-sided mass of basalt, the country's principal watershed and its rainy roof.

The coming of this basalt was in comparatively recent geological times, about 150 million years ago. It was as though nature suddenly became a little bored, after taking so many long millions of years to lay down the sedimentary rocks of the Karoo Systems. A change was indicated – something really spectacular to mark the ending of the age of monstrous reptiles, swamps and interminable rains.

Rivers of fire

The change took the form of a prodigious fireworks display. Volcanic fissure after fissure erupted, pouring out lava until at last a large area of Southern Africa was covered to a thickness of about 1500 m. This mass of basalt, known as the Drakensberg Volcanics, flowed from ruptures in the earth's mantle like rivers of fire. One flow cooled, and was followed by another, producing distinct layers varying in thickness from 1 m to over 50 m and of considerable difference in hardness and character.

These basalts are interesting rocks to examine. In the molten state they were full of bubbles of gas. As the basalt cooled, the gas bubbles filled with minerals which crystallised into the cavities. A lump of basalt resembles a dark-coloured fruit cake. Imprisoned in the rock are agates; rose-pink amethysts; calcite; chalcedony; quartz; zeolites of lovely green shades; a great variety of agate pebbles formed in steam holes in the upper levels; and pencil-like pipe amygdales which formed in the lower levels, in escape tunnels made by gas rising from below.

The basalt is soft and crumbly. To provide it with some backbone, nature thoughtfully squeezed up from the depths a succession of intrusive flows of hard dolerite. This rock worked its way between the basalt layers to form horizontal sills, or up the original feeder channels of the basalt flows, solidifying in them to form supporting skeletons of dolerite dykes.

This whole mass of basalt was then left by nature to the weather. Clouds blown in from the warm Moçambique Current in the east brought rain to this high roof. The run-off of water was a cutting tool that carved a masterpiece. Deep valleys, ravines and gorges were cut, full of rapids, cascades, waterfalls, caves and pools. The face of the rock island was worn back, leaving spectacular pinnacles, buttresses and precipices. Landslides littered the approaches with giant boulders; wild valleys were deeply eroded into the roof of the basalt island.

As it remains today, this mass of basalt covers practically the whole of Lesotho, an area of 30 344 square km. On all sides, its aspect is of a range of gaunt mountains, known to the Zulus on the eastern

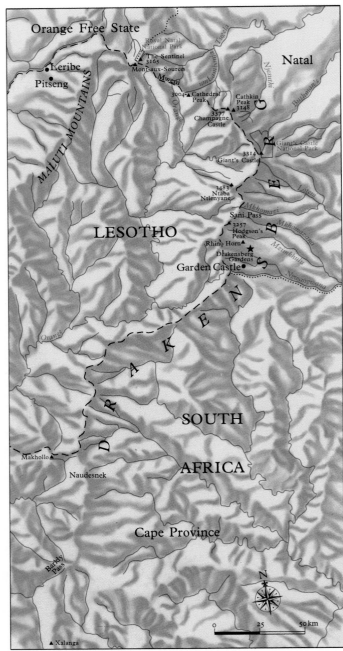

MOUNTAIN OF THE DRAGON The Drakensberg, dominating Natal, gets its name from a legend that dragons once lived there.

THE BADLANDS This area of the Drakensberg, near Garden Castle, was a haunt of rustlers and Bushmen who raided farmlands of southern Natal. The fast-flowing streams provide pure drinking water. The wall of the Drakensberg is hidden by clouds.

side as *Ukathlamba* (the barrier); to the Sothos as *Maluti* (the heights), or, when they talk of the eastern precipices, as *Dilomo tsa Natala* (the cliffs of Natal). Europeans refer to these same eastern cliffs, and the whole escarpment of South Africa, as the *Drakensberg* (mountains of the dragon), from an old legend of the sighting there of monstrous flying lizards, breathing fire.

The Sothos' greeting

The highest point on the Drakensberg is the incongruously named *Ntaba Ntlenyane* (nice little mountain), which reaches a height of 3483 m. The whole summit of the basalt island is a jumble of spongy, water-soaked bogs, complex, zigzagging valleys, springs, waterfalls, streams, rivers, mist, snow and clouds, all inextricably mixed into a gigantic scenic symphony perfectly described by the greetings exchanged by the Sotho horsemen when they meet one another on the bridle paths which seem to reach almost to the stars: '*Khotso*' (peace); and '*Pula*' (rain).

The most spectacular length of the Drakensberg looks down on Natal, Griqualand East and the north-eastern portion of the Cape. For 350 km the Drakensberg presents a high wall of basalt precipices. There are no easy ways over this mass of rock. The few passes are steep, zigzag routes following watercourses. Bridle paths, wilderness trails and tracks follow the contours along the lower slopes, but it takes a mountaineer to find a way to the summit of most of the peaks. In some areas mountain hotels and holiday resorts have been established. Other areas remain completely wild and difficult of access, and demand no little endurance from those with the energy to explore them.

Snow can fall along the Drakensberg in any month of the year, but winter usually sees the heaviest falls. The summer months are marked by some of the noisiest and most spectacular thunderstorms occurring anywhere on earth. From November to May these violent storms break in two days out of three.

Clouds start to close in for the brawl at about 11 a.m. Preliminaries commence at about 1 p.m. with a few bangs and buffets. By 2 p.m. there is general uproar. To a climber caught in such a storm the experience is something like trying to shelter in a box

THE AMPHITHEATRE In the background looms the Mont-aux-Sources Amphitheatre, birthplace of the Thukela River, which leaps down to the Natal lowlands. In the foreground, like petrified theatregoers, are the remnants of a sandstone ridge.

THE OUTLIERS As though guarding the main wall of the Drakensberg, the Pyramid and the Column thrust above the horizon. Both present stern challenges to mountaineers. Only the most skilled and resolute have scaled these summits.

SANCTUARY The Royal Natal National Park, nourished by the young Thukela River, nestles at the foot of the Mont-aux-Sources Amphitheatre. To the right of the Amphitheatre towers The Sentinel, marking the northern end of the high range in Natal.

of fireworks after somebody else has thrown in a match. Tremendous flashes of lightning seem to tear the sky to pieces. Thunder rumbles, explodes and echoes in an incessant uproar. Rain streaks down at over 50 km an hour, usually turning into hail at some stage, with lumps of ice the size of pigeons' eggs.

Even more abruptly than they started, these mountain thunderstorms end. The clouds suddenly lift, there is a real flaming sunset and by evening all the stars are out, quite dazzling in the well-washed, pollution-free sky. Storms of longer duration, accompanied by days of clammy mist, also set in at times and bring an average rainfall of 2000 mm, the water

soaking into the basalt and then oozing out to feed the rivers.

Scars on the slopes

The vegetation on the slopes, a thick covering of grass and a few shrubs, is sufficiently hardy to be able to shrug off these storms – not, however, without many scars. Slopes with a southern aspect – the

KINGDOM OF THE DRAGONS (*Overleaf*) Night beckons. The last of the sun's rays flicker eerily on the peaks. It is now somehow less difficult to believe Bushmen's tales that dragons once lurked here. The tales gave the Drakensberg its name.

THUNDER MOUNTAINS The section of the Drakensberg which is dominated by the *Ndumeni* (place of thunder) dome. Violent thunderstorms, many among the wildest on earth, fracture the sky here for two days out of three during the summer.

coldest slopes – are particularly marked by such storm scars. Bare, crescent-shaped terraces pattern the slopes in thousands. Each of these neat little terraces is about 1 m wide and up to 10 m in length. They appear to be caused mainly by melted water from snow and frost. This icy water saturates the soil, causing it to sag and form these strange-looking scars, rather reminiscent of the incisions made on the faces of certain primitive tribespeople.

The north-eastern end of the basalt 'island' is fittingly marked by an outstanding, fang-shaped peak known as The Sentinel. It is 3165 m high and a dominant landmark, visible from Natal and the Orange Free State. Behind it lies a high, boggy plateau overlooked by a gently rising height known as *Mont-aux-Sources* (the mountain of springs), around whose slopes dozens of springs bubble up and combine their clear waters to form several of the major rivers of South Africa flowing east and west.

This great watershed has a notable atmosphere. Surrounded by clouds, often with a summer thunderstorm exploding below the level of its summit, it seems to be a small world of its own, lost in space. Jagged peaks menace it on all sides. Snow blankets it thickly in the winter, while the summer months see its bogs decorated with many flowering plants, notably red-hot pokers and various species of erica which flourish happily in alpine conditions of incessant rain, hail, snow and powerful winds.

To the east, the plateau falls away in some of the most majestic precipices of the whole Drakensberg.

THE ANGRY PEAK The Zulu tongue is full of poetry, and to the Zulus Giant's Castle, in the distance, is known as *iNtabayikonjwa* (the mountain at which one must not point). They believed that if anyone pointed at the mountain it would cause bad weather.

HEAVEN'S DOORWAY Like a doorway from the heavens, a cleft in the Mont-aux-Sources plateau offers a breathtaking view over Natal. This spot can be reached by scaling relatively easy mountain routes on the northern side of the Drakensberg.

Crescent shaped, these precipices form the Mont-aux-Sources Amphitheatre. The Tugela Waterfall leaps down this high face and then, like a glistening snake, the river twists off through the foothill country with, on both sides of its banks, the Royal Natal National Park.

Some of the best climbing in the Drakensberg is to be found along the Mont-aux-Sources Amphitheatre. The Sotho tribespeople know the area as *Phofung* (place of the eland), for the foothills were always favourite grazing grounds for these, as well as several other species of antelope.

The Mont-aux-Sources area is easy of access, but south of it, for 35 km, the face of the Drakensberg is approachable only with difficulty. In the foothills of this area live the members of the Ngwaneni tribe. The basalt mass looking down on their homeland has been eroded into so many spires and pinnacles that part of it is known as *Mweni* (the place of fingers), and by many this is considered to be the most spectacular part of the whole Drakensberg. In the marshes immediately behind these pinnacles the Orange River has its source, commencing a long journey to the sea through a valley so complex that it is known as the 'zigzag'.

Projecting eastwards from the main wall of the Drakensberg there is a high ridge, so jagged in its outline that the tribespeople call it *abaMponjwana* (the place of little horns). On this ridge stand Cathedral Peak (3004 m), the unmistakably shaped Bell (2930 m) and an assembly of other peaks whose jagged summits, the Outer and Inner Horn, the Chessmen, and others, all contribute to the impression made on the tribespeople that the ridge consists of a mass of horns.

South of this ridge, the umLambonja River has its source and flows through a rugged valley. This is another great climbing area. The highest point is the dome known as *Ndumeni* (place of thunder), 3200 m high. A path follows the contours at the foot of the main wall of the Drakensberg. For 45 km this path finds an involved way through most difficult country, providing access to the foot of many climbs to such heights as the almost unscalable Column (2926 m) and Pyramid (2914 m), or to relatively easy passes such as the Organ Pipes.

Where Bushmen hunted

The umLambonja River draws its waters from at least 100 separate springs. The foothill country through which it flows is richly grassed, and attracted from earliest times vast herds of antelope. These antelope,

Lammergeyer or bearded vulture (*Gypaetus barbatus*)

The timid giant

Few birds are more impressive in flight than the lammergeyer, or bearded vulture. Opening its wings to their full spread of nearly 3 m, it soars majestically and effortlessly on thermals – rising bubbles of warm air whose complex internal currents provide a constant updraught. Circling high above the mountains, the bearded vulture quarters large tracts of territory at gliding speeds of up to 130 km per hour. It is the largest of all the vultures, and is easily identified by its diamond-shaped tail. On the ground, a 'beard' of black feathers on either side of the bill makes it unmistakable. Across its eyes is a sinister-looking black mask.

It nests on remote cliffs, where it lays its eggs. According to folklore, the bearded vulture has carried off human beings. It is much maligned by these tales. Its weak toes and claws are probably inadequate weapons for the killing of game of any kind.

Despite its size, the bearded vulture is in fact a gentle, timid bird – a factor making for survival in a creature which lives by scavenging. It feeds on carrion and offal, and is able to digest bones. Often its food comprises bones picked clean by other scavengers. When confronted with a large bone, the vulture drops it from a great height onto rocks. Then it circles down to scoop out the marrow with its gouge-shaped tongue.

But cautiousness and a degree of intelligence are not sufficient when times change. The bird's numbers are dwindling with the reduction in wild animals and their replacement by domestic cattle, which are not normally left on the veld to decompose. Man has to step in, and efforts are being made in the Drakensberg to ensure the survival of this magnificent creature.

LOWLANDS OF TRANQUILLITY Vanishing storm clouds race onward, and sunlight floods the saturated approaches to the southern Drakensberg. The grasslands eventually give way to the cave-sandstone foothills. On the extreme right soars the Rhino Horn.

in turn, attracted Bushmen hunters who found this area to be something of a paradise. Not only was there a plentiful food supply, but the many tributary valleys of the umLambonja were well wooded, and erosion had carved out from the sandstone below the basalt a magnificent series of caves and rock shelters. In one valley alone, that of the Ndidima River, there were 17 of these natural rock shelters. On their walls the Bushmen left nearly 4000 separate rock paintings, most of them highly colourful and many reaching a superb standard of artistry. These are probably the most beautiful prehistoric art galleries so far found in any caves. One cave alone, Sebayeni, has 1146 of these remarkable pictures.

The area drained by the umLambonja River ends

at one of the most dominant of the Drakensberg summits, the 3182 m high Cathkin Peak, aptly known to the Zulu-speaking tribespeople as *Mdedelele* (make room for him), because of its overpowering presence in the range. This great mountain acts as one of the main cornerstones of the Drakensberg, swinging the range around more to the south and, in the process, being well exposed itself. A difficult 'E' grade, and a frustrating mountain to climb, it stands near a ridge of jagged-looking peaks, including one weird-looking height known as *Ntunja* (the eye), with a great hole bored by nature immediately beneath its summit. It glares out over the surrounding countryside like a one-eyed giant.

Behind Cathkin Peak stands a sinister-looking peak

SNOW IN SANI PASS Blanketed with snow, the *Sani* (pass of the Bushmen) winds its way towards the roof of Southern Africa. This white landscape of crisp, clear air, solitude and silence has seen many a skirmish between farmer and cattle rustlers.

known from its shape as the Monk's Cowl. It towers 3234 m high and has an evil reputation amongst climbers. It rears up steep and dark against the main wall, which here reaches a height of 3377 m on the summit of what is known as Champagne Castle.

For the next 45 km, the Drakensberg maintains a remarkably steady height of around 3150 m. There are no gaps or easy passes to the summit. The impression of a precipitous island is complete, with an undulating sea of grass-covered foothills sweeping in upon it from the east. Two rivers, with their complex of tributaries, have their sources along these slopes, the quaintly named *Njesuthi* (well-fed dog), and the Bushman's River. The name of Njesuthi particularly suits this rushing torrent. Fed by numerous

tributaries, it gains in size and power, bounds happily down rapids and waterfalls and eventually joins the Tugela as though off to hunt with a whole pack of hounds.

The Bushman's River has its source on top of the escarpment, immediately behind the 3314 m high mountain known to Europeans as Giant's Castle, but to Africans as *iNtabayikonjwa* (the mountain at which one must not point). The name reflects a superstition common along the Drakensberg, with several variants. It is said that pointing at the mountain implies disrespect, and bad weather will inevitably follow. Another mountain near Cathedral Peak also has this name. It is tabu to women. If they point at it, they will surely marry somebody living on its

slopes. The residents on the slopes are said to be unprepossessing.

Giant's Castle looks down on the Giant's Castle Game Reserve, a wilderness area preserved as a home for herds of mountain eland, hartebeest and other antelope. The valley of the Bushman's River was also a home of Bushmen, and their caves are preserved, having many galleries of paintings on the rock walls.

Giant's Castle, like Cathkin Peak, is particularly prominent, for it acts as another cornerstone, swinging the escarpment sharply south-westwards and leaving itself exposed in the process. It is a great gatherer of clouds, and many violent storms have their origins around its cliff faces.

South of Giant's Castle there looms another high wall of basalt. Rivers such as the Loteni and the Mkhomazi tumble down from the summit in lovely sequences of cascades and falls. Trout live in the pools and there is an atmosphere of solitude and wildness, with crisp air and crystal-clear water.

In the Sani Pass

Up the valley of the Mkhomazana River, the classic pass from Natal to the summit of the basalt island finds its way. This pass, known as *Sani* (pass of the Bushmen), was used from early times. It climbs through singularly wild country, full of memories of rustlers, renegades, and many vicious fights when vengeance-seeking tribesmen and farmers encountered bands of the wiry little Bushmen cattle thieves. Long files of pack mules and donkeys still make their weary way up this pass, while Sotho horsemen in their blankets and straw hats ride their hardy ponies to the most improbable heights.

South of the Sani Pass stand the twin Hodgson's Peaks, 3257 m high, named after a farmer accidentally killed there while on a punitive raid against Bushmen rustlers. They act as reminders of past days of hard riding and misadventure.

The Drakensberg continues southwards, its unbroken line of cliffs looking down on a sweeping stretch of farming country. The foothills are a pattern of maize fields, sheep and cattle pastures, while rivers such as the Mzimkhulu and the Ngwangwana have their sources on the heights, rush down through many a gorge, fatten from their tributaries and feed deep pools where trout lurk and the mountains ad-

mire their own reflections, on surfaces like glass.

Beyond the Cape border, the Drakensberg swings south-westwards again. For another 300 km the wall of cliffs continues without a break. There are no holiday resorts and little development. Farms make a patchwork of the downlands, but the foothills and the main wall of the basalt island remain inviolate. It was in this part of the range that the legend of the dragon had its origin. It must have been easy to believe such tales in such an area. The wall of mountains seems remote and aloof. To the Zulu tribespeople they were *uluNdi* (the heights), another world of snow and rains, while they lived in the warm and fertile lowlands. What manner of creatures – mammal or reptile – lived beyond the edge of the escarpment only legend could describe. Even today there are dark valleys, caves and rustlers' hideaways where few men ever walk.

As the mountain wall continues southwards it slowly loses height. Farmlands crowd closer to the foothills. The highest road pass in Southern Africa, Naudes Nek, climbs to the 2500 m level and then manages, with a last wriggle, to clear the summit. The route is dramatic and spectacular, with heavy snow in winter, masses of red-hot-poker flowers staining the slopes like pools of blood in March, and near by, the bulky peak of *Makhollo* (great mother), looming up to an altitude of 3000 m.

'Place of the vultures'

Still further south there is another pass, Barkly Pass, which penetrates the Drakensberg through a red-coloured sandstone valley. The range, by this point, has lost both height and bulk. Its sandstone foundation is more apparent, and the giant cliffs of basalt have vanished. Sheep by the hundreds of thousands graze along the slopes; but the Drakensberg still retains its beauty and its wildness, with farmers and rustlers waging an interminable war.

Then, abruptly and fittingly, this noble range comes to its southern end at a last towering mass of cliffs known as *Xalanga* (place of the vultures). From The Sentinel in the north to Xalanga in the south, the wall of basalt has provided South Africa with a mountain backbone 450 km in length. North of The Sentinel, the name of the Drakensberg is applied to the escarpment of the central South African plateau, and this continues for another 600 km with, especially in the north-eastern Transvaal, some majestic scenery. But the 'mountains of the dragon' proper are the eastern edge of the basalt island, the rainy roof and the greatest heights of Southern Africa.

THE BRASH BULLY The Zulus christened Cathkin Peak *mDedelele* (make room for him) – the descriptive name they give to a bully. This flat-topped mountain, one of the dominant peaks of the Drakensberg, indeed seems to shoulder aside all lesser peaks in the range.

Pans: scenic wonders where animals can slake their thirst

Some pans are started off by creatures as insignificant as ants. They bring lime to the surface, forming salt licks for big game which churn up the ground, so creating a muddy hollow that will develop into a pan.

THE OASIS Like an oasis in the desert, a pan means the difference between life and death for wild creatures. This pan, in the Etosha area of South West Africa, is largely dried up, but there is still water to attract wildebeest and zebra.

In an otherwise barren land, the shallow, water-filled hollows called pans rank among the natural wonders of the world.

It can be said that the opposite of a waterfall is a pan. Water likes to go somewhere: up through evaporation; down through gravity. In a waterfall it is going somewhere in a hurry, and the consequence is one of the most enjoyable of all scenic spectacles.

Moving water is the most powerful erosive tool of nature. Set to work on a landscape, like the broom in the tale of the sorcerer's apprentice, it has to be sharply watched and tightly controlled by nature, otherwise its ceaseless labours will result in the ultimate of erosion, the production of what is known as a *peneplain* (almost a plain). In this gently rolling almost flat landscape, the water is made captive by its own exertions and is unable to go anywhere at all other than straight up or down. Sideways, it just flounders, for there is no run-off on a level landscape.

In such a peneplain, rainwater will collect in any hollow and wait to evaporate or soak down into the earth. If the hollow is large, then a lake will be formed. But lakes are more generally geological accidents caused by landfalls or other obstructions blocking the flow of a river. On a peneplain, the rainwater is more likely to find its way into shallow depressions, and pans are formed – seldom more than 1 m deep and of varying shapes and sizes ranging from a few metres across to several kilometres.

In the internal drainage area of the Kgalagadi there are something over 9000 pans. Another prolific area is a belt, 150 km wide, of arid low-relief country running north-north-east for nearly 1000 km from Calvinia in the Cape across the Karoo to the Transvaal. Few of these pans contain permanent water. For most of the time they are dry, their floors level, hard, encrusted with odd salts washed into them, shimmering with heat, glaringly white, and full of mirages.

There are some famous pans in this belt. *Verneuk* (deception) Pan was used by Sir Malcolm Campbell as a speed track for his record-breaking *Bluebird* in the 1930s; and several others would serve admirably as motor-racing circuits if they were not so remote from centres of habitation.

Other well-known pans are found in the Eastern Transvaal. Most of these have a different origin from the pans of the more arid areas. They seem to be relics of a former drainage system. This area is a watershed, with the Vaal River draining it to the west and the uSuthu to the east. The Vaal eventually so eroded into the watershed that it captured some of the headwaters of the uSuthu. The upper course of the uSuthu and several of its tributaries almost ran dry. In only a gently graded landscape, the broad, shallow former courses of the river and streams were converted into chains of pools, pans and a few expanses of water so considerable as to justify the title of lakes.

One of these is Lake Banagher and another is Lake Chrissie. Both dry out completely at times, but in years of good rainfall they are handsome sheets of water. Lake Chrissie, the larger of these lakes, is some 20 km in circumference and up to 3 m deep.

Lake Chrissie lies in the typical pan setting of a shallow depression in the veld. It has no cliffs and no shore. It simply spreads, rises and falls according to the rains. From the air it looks as though some careless artist has accidentally dropped a blue paint pot onto a scene carefully coloured green. The biggest splash is Lake Chrissie, the second biggest is Lake Banagher, while all around are the little blobs and splashes of about 30 smaller pans and lakes.

An added pleasure to the scene is the presence of vast herds of blesbok. This was always the home for these antelope, whose flesh yields some of the finest of all venison. Today they are almost domesticated and farmers conserve and breed them in these parts. Their light brown coats blending harmoniously with the colours of the landscape, they feed and laze on the green grass surrounding the pans, and are distinguished by the white blaze on their foreheads which

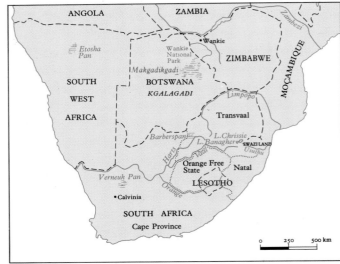

WHERE WATER IS TRAPPED Shaded areas show major pans – places where water cannot drain away, though it often evaporates.

Three stages in the formation of a pan

Stage One A small, salty pool appears in a shallow depression. Game animals use it for drinking and wallowing.

Stage Two Heavy rains swell small pools into larger pans as the animals wallow and carry away mud.

Stage Three Some pans, like this one at Wankie, become small lakes, seldom more than a few metres deep. Note the ant-heap under the tree. Lime brought up by such an ant-heap was probably the beginning of this pan.

gives these graceful creatures their name.

Another type of pan is created when a suitable hollow occurs close to the course of a river meandering across an area of low relief. When the river is in flood it spills out over the surrounding plain and fills the hollow. There is a fine example of such a pan at Barberspan in the Western Transvaal. Known to the local tribespeople as *Leghadighadi* (the deep water hole), it is fed by flood spill from the Harts River and, with an extent of 25 square km, is the size of a small lake. It has the usual hard, flat bottom contain-

ing as much as 8 m of water, depending on the floods of the river. The water in this great pan is permanent and full of fish, particularly of barbel which give the place its Afrikaans name of *Barber*. Carp, yellowfish, and mudfish also live there, while a vast colony of birds, including flamingos, regard it as home.

The origin and development of pans is strangely varied and makes a fascinating study. In the pan belt of the Karoo, for instance, pans and dust devils are inseparable, if incongruous, companions. The pans start off as chance hollows in the plain. Water collects

Lesser flamingo (*Phoeniconaias minor*)

The mysterious flamingo

There are still plenty of unsolved mysteries in the world of birds, and one of them is to account for the comings and goings of flamingos. Flocks of them will turn up at any time anywhere in Southern Africa where there is water of the right depth. Even where many of them breed is a mystery. So meticulous are their requirements that it is only rarely that suitable conditions are found. The water has to be at the right level – shallow enough for them to walk on the bottom, on stilt-like legs, but not so shallow that it is in danger of drying up in the fierce African sun. It has to have the right mineral content; and it has to be rich in the nutrients on which the birds feed. Even then, a rainstorm may flood out the nests and end breeding for that season.

Flamingos are the only birds to feed with the head upside-down. The bill, when inverted, becomes a scoop which is moved from side to side. The water passes through, while minute organisms are trapped in a filtering device.

Usually, this strange process is combined with an absurd paddling of the legs, which stirs up the sediment and increases the amount of food passing through the bill. They sometimes swim where the water is deeper, and even up-end, like ducks.

There are two species of flamingo in Southern Africa. The lesser, with a dark red bill, and the greater, which has a bill that is black at the end then pink further along. The lesser flamingo has a deeper, more red-pink colouring than the greater, but either can turn the sky pink when, in great flocks, they take wing. It is one of the most gorgeous sights in nature.

in the rainy season and soaks into the mud it creates in the floor of the hollows. In the dry season the water vanishes and the mud dries into dust, whitened by mineral salts. The air above the dazzling white pans becomes superheated and starts to rise, spiralling as it does so, picking up the dust and wandering off across the plain as a dust devil.

The dust will eventually be dumped when the dust devil loses its strength and collapses. Some of the dust will be carried back into the hollows by water run, but most of it will remain elsewhere. Thus, the hollows tend to be deepened and expanded, with the dust devils as both their offspring and their creators.

Even more remarkable are the pans which owe their origin to creatures as insignificant as ants. The Wankie National Park of Zimbabwe has some magnicent examples of such pans. Without doubt, they rank among the natural wonders of the world in the spectacle they present of the drama and beauty of big-game watering places.

An understanding of these pans begins with the knowledge that animals crave such salts as sodium and lime. Wherever such elements appear on the surface, wild animals, especially browsers such as the elephant, eland, oryx, kudu, giraffe and rhino, will be attracted to what are known as salt licks.

In the area of the wind-blown sands of the Kgalagadi which extends over the Wankie National Park, there are deposits of lime just beneath the surface. At Wankie they inhibit the growth of vegetation and create open glades.

Ants and moles play a vital part in bringing some of this lime to the surface. Ants are the principal agents, for they work deep and produce substantial ant-heaps above ground. The wild animals are attracted to the ant-heaps and eat the soil in order to get the lime. They trample the surrounding soil into dust and this is blown away by the winds. A hollow forms. When the rains come, water gathers in the hollow. This water carries lime into the pan from the surrounding surface. The animals like the taste. They drink the water, wallow in the mud and, by tramping or puddling the floor of the pan, they firm it into a leak-proof seal.

Ted Davison, who was first warden of the Wankie National Park, explains in his book *Wankie* how, once started, a pan is widened and extended by large animals, able to move as much earth as an army of navvies:

'When the water in them is getting low and is much puddled by game, samples have shown that well over 10 per cent of it was matter in suspension;

THE QUIET LAND Earth, sky and water all play their part in creating this symphony of stillness in Griqualand East. On the horizon, beyond the pans and beyond the foothills, stretches the great range of the Drakensberg.

so that an elephant drinking 250 ℓ of water would be carrying away in its stomach 25 kg of soil. In the course of only one year a single elephant might remove from pans some 5 tons of soil in this manner alone, quite apart from the quantity carried away on its feet and body after a mud bath.'

Buffalo also remove vast quantities of material from the pans. A herd of several hundred animals in one visit can significantly affect the size of a pan. The more lime in the water, the greater the attraction for animals. Pure water is of no interest if they can find a supply of lime and sodium mixed with their drink.

With the pans formed, the next stage in their growth is for life to develop in them. Game animals and birds leave dung and droppings in the water. This produces bacteria and plankton. Numerous insects are attracted, and mosquitoes breed with facility. Frogs and toads soon arrive on the scene. Fish, such as barbel, which flourish in muddy water, also appear, especially if the pan has any connection with the overflow of a river. But even without such a connection they manage to pass over dry land, or are carried there in the form of eggs which somehow survive the digestive systems of birds.

Then come crocodiles to feed on the fish. A good-sized pan in the driest setting can still be home to a crocodile. Where they come from is often a mystery. Possibly the smell of water draws them across many kilometres of arid country. On the other hand it may be that a strain of crocodile has adapted itself to living on dry land, leading a nomadic life exploring the pans, feeding on the bigger fish, and then either wandering off or aestivating in some hideaway in order to survive a dry season. It is notable that these pan-dwelling crocodiles are on the small side. They are not much danger to the game animals, although they take a few birds and perhaps an occasional small antelope; and they have been found trampled to death, possibly having been so unwise as to try a bite on an elephant's trunk.

In all the world, there is no spectacle more wonderful than a lime-rich pan situated in the haunts of big game. By day and night the wild animals come to drink and there is endless entertainment and drama, far more engrossing than anything to be seen in a cinema. In the book *Trail of the Copper King*, based on the diary of Orlando Baragwanath the great prospector, there is a record of an evening at one such pan in the sand country of the Kgalagadi.

Baragwanath was on his way north in 1899 on a journey which resulted in the discovery of the copper belt of Zambia. He and his companions had become aware that they were being tracked by a party of Bushmen. In order to discover the reason for this furtive pursuit, Baragwanath and a half-breed Bushman in his employ hid themselves in a tree overlooking a pan where the Bushmen would have to drink, as it was the only available watering place in a vast area of arid wilderness.

When Orlando and his companion commenced their vigil there were five giraffes loitering around the pool. They had already had their drink at sunset, but were in no hurry to depart. It was pleasant at the

SHARING A DIMINISHING SUPPLY A mixed group of kudu, springbok and guinea fowl slake their thirst at what is left of a rapidly drying pan. In the rainy season, a pan can be a vast sheet of water, but in dry weather many become, at best, mere puddles.

waterhole. The flaming brilliance of the desert sunset had just died away from the still, reflecting surface of the pool, like a fire being washed away by sparkling drops of stars. All was quiet.

Suddenly the elephants came. A hundred or more of the great creatures walked out of the surrounding bush. The giraffes scattered, and the elephants took over full rights to the waterhole. They waded into the water with great splashing and animation, the big bulls shouldering their way in front and then stretching their trunks in a long, long stretch, hoping to find cooler water where it was deeper.

There was tremendous drinking. The rising moon silhouetted their dark shapes against the rippling light on the waters. Then they finished. In a concerted movement they turned for the shore. The sound was like the rushing of a rapid, with all those mighty feet wading towards the edge. And as they reached the water's edge a curious thing happened. A cloud obscured the moon. There came a sudden, startling silence. It was as though the whole herd had vanished at the end of an African dream.

But the moonlight came again, and found them on the edge of the pool. On padded feet they had left the water together as the shadow came. On land an elephant can be a silent thing, and their dark forms had merged with the night. They stood beside the waterhole and gossiped together about the day.

A second, smaller herd approached. They were obviously on friendly terms. The animals greeted one another with the strange stomach-rumbling sounds elephants use to express pleasure. The calves ran forward to greet old playmates. The newcomers took their turn at the water. The calves played together while a few little bulls with scores to settle squared up to each other, ears standing out, flicking their trunks at each other in challenge.

Then, by some silent signal, the first herd moved off. There was a great bustle among the cows sorting out their calves. Little elephants chose the wrong mothers, and there was a deal of hooting, honking, squealing and racing about when they found their mistake. Orlando saw one irate cow fetch her calf a good box on the ear with her trunk when she was forced to return to find him. Then it was all over, and stillness returned to the pool.

Presently four giraffes came down to the water. They stooped like camera tripods on the far side of the pool and had their fill. To join them, four battle-scarred old buffalo bulls trooped down in file, real hard cases, long since retired from their herds after surviving innumerable fights, often among themselves, all for the love of a few hundred females. Now they were taking life very easy.

It was while he watched them that Orlando sensed, rather than saw, the new arrival. Below him, in the deepest shadows of the trees, Orlando saw a leopard, audacious and bold. The animal slipped down to the water's edge. He took his drink and sat for a while in silence, watching the reflections and the dark shapes of the buffaloes, while a cheeky little plover bird who seemed to think he owned the water-rights swooped low over the heads of leopard and buffalo alike, scolding noisily at the intrusion.

The leopard arose from his dreaming. His night was just beginning. Ignoring the plover with fine contempt, he walked silently towards Orlando's tree. From below he looked up long and searchingly, without quite knowing the reason for his own suspicion. Then he moved off, dodging the moonbeams, as one who preferred the shadows, until he reached a dead tree 50 m away, standing like a tombstone over its own grave. There the leopard paused, staring intently ahead, his tail switching slowly.

There was a cough-like snarl. A lion hurtled out of the darkness. The startled leopard sprang for the dead tree. From a branch it spat its hate down, while from the ground the lion, a young male, looked up with its yellow eyes warning that this waterhole was its chosen hunting ground for the night, and the leopard was superfluous company. Having made its point the lion went off a little distance. It lay down in the dark shadow of a tree, assuming a cloak of invisibility.

The centre of interest was now the pool. Orlando knew that the lion's eyes were fixed on it as eagerly as his own. The four buffaloes were still mooning around, but no lion in his right senses would tackle them. For a quarter of an hour, all was still. Once the leopard made a tentative move to descend from his tree, but a throaty snarl from the lion sent him back to his perch.

Down to the pool came three eland – big, gentle creatures, always very wary for, notwithstanding their size, flight is almost their sole means of defence. The lion flattened himself in the grass, his eyes steadily regarding the eland. The eland were on the far side, beyond the lion's reach. They were joined by a giraffe. Then a fourth eland came down. He was not on speaking terms with the other three of his kind. He walked around the pool edge, closer to the lion.

A brush with death

Orlando saw the lion's ears twitch slightly. He must have been praying to some strange god for good fortune. The fourth eland came closer. Then he stopped, found a place where he fancied that the water was sweeter, and drank his fill. All was silent. The eland finished his drink. Even the twitch in the lion's ears froze as he waited to see which way the eland would move; towards death waiting for him in the shadows, or towards life in the moonlight.

The eland turned towards death. Orlando held his breath, waiting for the kill. Then the buffaloes moved. They walked in leisurely single file around the dark pool. The eland paused irresolutely. The buffaloes walked between him and the shadows. Unaware of his brush with death, he tossed his head in annoyance, and turned in his tracks.

The lion must have cursed. He tore out of the grass like a battering ram. There was uproar at the pool. The eland and the giraffe vanished. In momentary surprise even the buffaloes started to run. The lion, obviously inexperienced, forgot himself. He saw the buffaloes running, and he chased them.

One old buffalo recovered his wits and glanced over his shoulder. What he saw soon had his dander up. One lion chasing four old warriors, and a young lion at that! He whirled in his tracks, and his companions joined him. The lion applied brakes. The buffaloes put their heads down and went for him, but the lion did not stop to argue. He disappeared at speed with the buffaloes in full pursuit behind him. From the dead tree trunk Orlando heard a curious sound. It was very much like a leopard chuckling.

Where an 'island' of water is swallowed up by a 'sea' of sand

By establishing harmony between themselves and the wilderness, the Bushmen found strange comfort in its very harshness; discovered companionship in its loneliness; learnt a patient resignation from its ruthlessness.

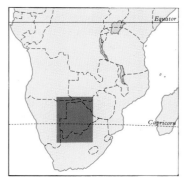

THE SURVIVORS Two Bushmen, etched against the sky, explore the Kgalagadi (Kalahari). The only other sign of life: a gnarled tree, scantily clad with foliage. Both tree and men have learnt the lesson of the wilderness: how to survive.

161

From the flood-waters
of Okavango to the
red sands of the Kalahari

THE KALAHARI may be many things to many people but, strangely enough considering its reputation, it is not a desert. In the language of the people who live there *Kgalagadi* means a wilderness, and this is precisely what it is. Europeans have corrupted the name to Kalahari and spread the notion that it is a desert but, compared to the grim Namib of South West Africa, the Kgalagadi, well covered in trees and plants and with an average summer rainfall of 250 mm, is a savanna parkland. It is inhabited by a dense population of wild animals, and it is a happy hunting ground for the nomadic Bushmen, as well as being the home for several Tswana tribes and tribal groups of mixed origin who know themselves as the *ba-Kgalagadi* (people of the wilderness).

To anybody moving south from the huge, elevated central continental plateau of Africa, the Kgalagadi is a cul-de-sac, a topographical dead end. The cul-de-sac, blocked by the arms of a horseshoe-shaped highland, is like a tilted saucer, with the southern and eastern parts higher than the north or west. It lies in the centre of the southern part of the continent, where rain from the east coast has almost petered out and no rain at all comes from the desert west coast. What does reach it from the east is greedily soaked up as fast as it falls. There is nothing to run off, and the rivers flowing southwards from areas of better rain in the north find themselves caught in a trap. They simply spread out and lose themselves on the floor of the cul-de-sac. They form shallow lakes and marshes, make despairing efforts each flood season to refill the deepest parts of the depression, such as the Makgadikgadi Pan, and then vanish below the ground or evaporate into the hot air.

The floor of this great cul-de-sac is covered in aeolian, or wind-blown, sand, eroded from the surrounding highlands and from mountain ranges which used to dominate this area. These ranges have now either vanished, or are so buried in sand that only their summits emerge as ridges of hills. The sand mantle covers an area of 1,2 million square km and is the world's largest continuous sand surface. It varies considerably in depth. In some parts it is shallow; in others it is over 100 m deep. The grains are often coated with iron oxide, which gives them a vivid red

colour, especially in areas of great aridity. The more water, the paler the colour, with yellowish and even pure white sand where springs or other supplies of moisture bleach out the oxide.

To the economic geologist this sand cover is exasperating. Buried beneath it must be all manner of interesting things, but prospecting through deep sand is difficult even with the most sensitive instruments. Nevertheless, much has been learnt, and enough treasures discovered to provide the economic spur for modern geologists and prospectors to devise complex techniques of study, search and analysis.

Where the hard surface below the sand has been exposed in watercourses, it is seen to consist of elements of the familiar igneous and sedimentary rocks which make up the rest of Southern Africa, and therefore can be expected to contain a similar mixture of metals, minerals and precious stones.

Gold was in fact found by prehistoric man along the course of the Tati River which flows erratically on the south-eastern verge of the Kgalagadi. In 1867 a young German geologist, Karl Mauch, was shown

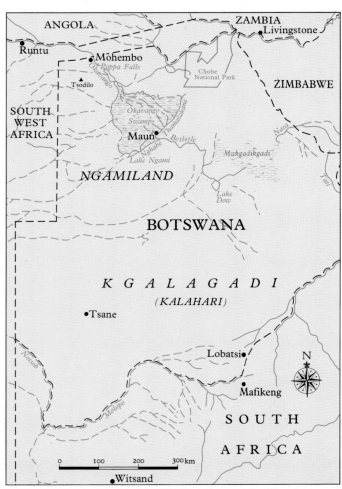

HAPPY HUNTING GROUND The Kgalagadi, nourished by rivers and swamplands, is inhabited by a dense population of wild animals.

THE WATCHER Ever-watchful, a springbok ram stands gracefully, its image glistening in a clear stream. Full of life, springbok face many natural enemies. But in places, the Kgalagadi, despite its reputation, is a refuge that offers ample food and water.

these ancient workings by the renowned hunter, Henry Hartley. Mauch described them to the newspapers, in glowing tones, as King Solomon's mines rediscovered; and so, for the first time, the attention of the world was attracted to the prospects of gold in Southern Africa. Nothing very profitable was ever recovered by the later diggers on this old field, but the small rush to it was a prelude of things to come on the Rand.

Trees of the Kgalagadi

Botanically, the Kgalagadi is a savanna-like thornveld. There is an excellent cover of sweet grass on which game and domestic animals thrive, while the numerous species of acacia trees are also nutritious, with leaves and seed pods which are very palatable to all browsing animals. Perhaps the most typical tree is the *Acacia erioloba*. The world of sand particularly suits these trees, and their elegant, sunshade-shaped canopies make them prominent in a landscape of plains and vast, straight horizons.

Numerous species of aloes and lilies provide patches of colour in the parkland, while the northern portion of the Kgalagadi is vividly green. Here, rainfall increases, and rivers such as the Okavango pour vast quantities of seasonal floodwater into the flat sand country, as though under the delusion that the Kgalagadi is the sea.

GIVER OF LIFE The nutritious seed pods of an *Acacia haematoxylon* are scattered on the Kgalagadi's red sands. The pods are eaten by antelope, which in turn scatter the seeds in their droppings. Thus, in a forbidding wilderness, the cycle of life is carried on.

'DESERT' RICHES The grass-and-tree-covered thornveld of the Kgalagadi provides rich grazing land for game and domesticated animals. The area offers evidence that the Kgalagadi, despite its name and fearsome reputation, is not a true desert.

The Okavango is one of the major rivers of Africa. From its headwaters in Angola it draws massive supplies of clear, pollution-free water. In the beginning its course is purposeful if misguided. It flows strongly southwards, over a series of rapids and one handsome waterfall, the Popa Falls. Then it crosses the frontier of Botswana at Mohembo and finds itself confronted by the Kgalagadi. The river experiences complete disarray. The water spreads out into a delta-like maze of channels, lakelets, lagoons and swamps – 16 000 square km of concentrated blue water, dense beds of reeds and papyrus, and innumerable tree-covered islands.

The amount of annual inundation depends on the rainfall in Angola. This can vary from 800 mm to 2500 mm and is unpredictable, especially to anyone in the Kgalagadi. In the month of June the first of the new season's floodwaters reach the sand country. First the pools and lagoons in the delta proper are topped up. Trickles start to make their way down dried-up channels. At first they snake along at far less than walking pace, greedily soaked up by the sand as they travel. Steadily, however, they are pushed on by

THE DEVIL'S BLOOMS (Overleaf) After the spring rains the devil thorns bloom in the Kgalagadi. But this flowering carpet is deceptive. Many animals – and barefooted Bushmen – tread warily here. The seed pods are covered with triple-pronged thorns.

the weight of rainwater pouring in from the north.

These slow trickles can be dangerously deceptive. Overnight they can suddenly develop into substantial rivers. Some blockage in the rear, a drift of sand or a pile of papyrus, has given way, perhaps, or a larger flood has reinforced the first tentative effort. Walls of water can sweep down a channel as though intent on

Namaqua sandgrouse (*Pterocles namaqua*)

Pigeon of the desert

As the sun begins to climb over the arid wastes of the Kgalagadi, vast flocks of small, mottled-brown birds set out for the waterholes. They are Namaqua sandgrouse which, despite their name, have nothing to do with grouse and look more like their close relatives the pigeons.

Apart from the resemblance, sandgrouse and pigeons drink alike, keeping their heads down and gulping until satisfied. They are the only birds able to suck up water. All others have to lift up their beaks to let the water trickle down their throats.

Some authorities believe that this desert dweller has perfected a unique method of supplying water to its chicks; that when drinking it soaks its breast, then flies rapidly home, so that the young can drink from its moistened feathers. Doubts were raised by an ornithologist who bred sandgrouse in captivity, and observed that the parents carried water in their crops, then regurgitated it into the mouths of their young. Supporters of the 'wet feathers' theory point out that captivity can alter the behaviour patterns of birds.

Sandgrouse will fly long distances to waterholes, but at other times they prefer to remain on the ground in large groups – often numbering in the hundreds – feeding on seeds and vegetable shoots.

Normally extremely cautious and creatures of strict habit, sandgrouse occasionally fly off on unexplained mass-suicide excursions. They fly far beyond their normal ranges. Although a few survive to breed in such places as Denmark, most inevitably perish.

totally inundating everything ahead. But the resilient sand provides increasing resistance the further southwards the floods persist.

There are many surprises in this inundation. A dry channel can become a strongly flowing river. The water penetrates to some persistent blockage and the channel deepens, breaks its banks, perhaps forms a lagoon, or floods the surrounding countryside. Perhaps another meandering channel also fills up, joins it, and the superior head of water pushes the stream in the first channel into reverse. The current promptly starts to flow in the opposite direction from its original course. Sometimes it is as though the whole flood is in retreat. But what is happening is that the water mass of the Angolan floods is finding its balance for the season against the mass of the Kgalagadi. It is a fascinating tussle with endless permutations in patterns. The vast delta is a changing labyrinth of watercourses which can have no permanent arrangement.

Just as surprising and confusing is the inundation of the plains around, and particularly south of the delta channels. As the floods wax, so more of the level landscape is covered. The depth of the water is seldom more than 450 mm and in most parts only about 150 mm, but from one horizon to the other it is all a vast lake, dotted with trees and thousands of strange 'islands' formed from termite and ant heaps.

How termites survive the flood

The termites seem quite indifferent to the advancing waters. Their mounds are so expertly sealed that they remain perfectly snug. With the queen and most of her community well below water level, the termites and ants live on their food stores until the floods subside and they can resume their usual foraging. Many of these termite mounds are so large that trees grow on them. Wild animals and birds use them as resting places, while the sodden grass provides luxuriant grazing.

The delta of the Okavango can perhaps be best described by a complete contradiction. It is an 'island of water in a sea of sand'. It is an island, moreover, which is densely inhabited. Fish life is prolific. Countless fish fry hatch out at the time of the floods. The water is rich in food, and every clump of half-submerged grass seems to shelter shoals of tiny fish. Different species of bream, tigerfish and barbel are the most common.

Feeding on the fish are numerous crocodiles and aquatic birds, notably fish eagles, kingfishers in considerable variety, and a vast number of waders. There

REJECTED BY MAN Camels, brought to the Kgalagadi by settlers, were finally abandoned. Their numbers are now increasing.

MELON HARVEST Tsamma melons flourish in even the most arid parts of the Kgalagadi, and sustain man and animals alike.

are pelicans, geese, ducks, storks, avocets, stilts, and practically every other species in the African community of birds which find their living by grubbing around in shallow water.

Hippos feed on the grass-covered islands and in the reed beds. Their 'harrumphing' is the most characteristic sound of the delta, especially at night when the birds sleep and the water world is eerie in its atmosphere of total stillness.

Antelope are very numerous. The richly marked and elusive Chobe bushbuck lurk in the thickets on the islands. The larger sitatunga, rather similar in appearance to the bushbuck, makes its home in the dense beds of reeds and papyrus. This is one of the shyest of all game animals. Water is its ideal element, and sitatungas are excellent swimmers. When disturbed they sink quietly into the water, submerging until only their nostrils remain above the surface. In

WHERE WATER IS A MEMORY Ostriches congregate in the dry course of an intermittent Kgalagadi river. In the rainy season a trickle will flow along this bed, at first being absorbed by the thirsty sand, but eventually developing into a swift-flowing torrent.

the reeds and shallower water their elongated hooves allow them excellent mobility. Only direst necessity ever drives them from the water world for, on hard, dry land, they are awkward and slow.

Red lechwe, another species of water-loving antelope, also inhabit the Okavango delta, wading into the water in order to feed on the aquatic plants. Not as shy as the sitatunga, they emerge onto the open flood plains to feed on the grass, and they like to be, at least for part of their lives, on the dry ground which the sitatunga find so abhorrent.

These water-loving antelope seem to have little fear of crocodiles. Some are probably eaten, but the flavour and scent of their meat, like that of the

The singing sands of Witsand

One of the strangest phenomena in all the vastness of the Kgalagadi is that of the singing sands. Their story is told in T. V. Bulpin's book *Discovering Southern Africa*. On the verges of the sand wilderness proper, near the Orange River, there is a particularly fine and noisy example of this peculiarity of sand dunes. At a place known as *Witsand* (white sand) there stretches out, surrounded by the usual red-coloured sands, a tongue of pure white sand about 9 km long and 2 km wide.

These white dunes consist of the usual aeolian, or wind-blown, sands which apparently were blown over a supply of water. The water, reaching the surface under pressure, bleached out the iron oxides in the sand and thus removed its red colour. This relief from coatings of foreign matter, the moistureless atmosphere, and the smoothness and uniformity of size of the sand grains as a result of ceaseless wear, produce the effect of roaring or singing.

The smooth surface of the grains allows a large contact area during movement. Friction, normally subdued or lubricated only by moisture, then sets up vibrations which produce the strange sound. The uniform grain sizes have a similar harmonic frequency, and this controls the pitch of sound.

The dunes are also notable for fulgurites, probably caused by flashes of lightning fusing the sands. The fulgurites consist of strings of fused sand, glazed and mirrored in parts, and up to 3 m long.

When it rains, the singing sands are saturated with too much water, and the sound is suppressed until dry weather returns. Visitors to the dunes, hoping to hear the sound, are advised to go only during months which have an 'R' in them.

The southerly face of the dunes is the noisiest. The sound consists of a definite roar when the sands are violently agitated, and a singing hum when they are poured or gently moved. A man sliding down a dune can be heard 100 m away. Even moving the fingers backwards and forwards through the sand produces a roar. A strong, dry wind produces an eerie, moaning noise from the dunes.

Some visitors to the dunes take pairs of empty preserved-fruit bottles, welded lid to lid. A small hole is drilled through the lids. One jar is filled with sand. The two jars are then screwed together like a large-scale egg-timer. Allowing the sand to run from one jar into the other creates a good roar or hum. Provided that the sand is kept hermetically sealed in the jars it can be carried away, even to moist climates, and will continue making its sound until moisture eventually leaks in and mutes it.

LAND OF GOLD A lone fisherman on the Okavango River paddles a tree-trunk canoe for home. The region is rich in bird life . . . and breathtaking golden sunsets. The nearby Okavango delta attracts game animals in enormous numbers.

turpentine-scented waterbuck, possibly provide them with some natural protection by being un-appetising to crocodiles.

These antelope, however, are not unattractive to lions, leopards or cheetahs. Such predators haunt the whole area. Lions swim to the inner recesses of the delta, and there is no island beyond their hunting range. Only the densest reed beds provide complete sanctuary for the antelope. Lions even clamber aboard the floating islands of papyrus.

Crocodiles, incidentally, find lions perfectly to their taste. Some tremendous battles royal take place in this water world. Many lion claws have been found in the stomachs of crocodiles shot for their skins – evidence of some titanic struggle between two of the most fearsome predators on earth.

In a really good flood year the waters of the Okavango can penetrate to some strange places. Lying 150 km south of the delta is Lake Ngami. The name *Ngami* means 'the big waters', and when Europeans first saw it on August 1, 1849, David Livingstone, who was one of the party with W. C. Oswell and M. Murray, recorded of the lake that: 'It is of such magnitude that we could not see the farther shore, and could only guess its size from the reports of the natives that it took them three days to go round it.' (See box, pp. 176–77.)

The lake must then have been about 150 km in circumference and nearly 2 m deep. It was a year of good floods in Angola and vast amounts of water were flowing in the various channels.

Many other early travellers visited Ngami. Their descriptions varied so much that it was almost as though they were describing a mirage. Ngami could go through the full range, from a spacious lake, to a pond surrounded by dense reeds, to a totally dried-out skeleton of a place with a hard floor littered with the carcasses of the game and cattle that died there when the water vanished. All manner of reasons were given for this wide variation. Travellers sometimes just doubted the veracity of earlier descriptions. It must have been very disconcerting to travel 1000 km across the wilderness to reach the fabled lake, and then find nothing better than a dusty depression with a few Bushmen digging holes in the hope of finding underground water.

No one realised in those years that Ngami was

THE SANDS AWASH (*Overleaf*) The rainy season is over. The downfalls have been heavy. Streams have swollen into raging rivers, and at Gadixwe Lagoon, the floodwaters of the Okavango delta wash over the Kgalagadi, forming a vast sea of lakes.

LONE BEAUTY The wonders of the Kgalagadi are both great and small. A water lily, *Nymphosia lotus*, blooms in solitary glory on the Okavango swamplands. Soon the swamps will begin to dry up. Rivers and streams will once again be choked by sand.

completely dependent on the extent of the rain in far-off Angola. The local tribespeople only knew that the water came from the Okavango. Some of them in fact blamed the drying of the lake on Europeans. (See box.)

The unpredictable Lake Ngami is not the furthest place reached by the waters of the Okavango. Some of the canals and watercourses attain the status of fine rivers, their banks lined with tall trees, their quieter pools covered in lovely waterlilies. Such an extension of the delta is the Thamalakane River on whose banks stands Maun, the lonely but picturesque little administrative capital of what is known as Ngami-land.

About 20 km south of Maun this waterway reaches a fork. One branch swings eastwards as the Botletle River, another branch turns westwards as the Nghabe River and this is one of the main supply channels for Lake Ngami. The area through which it flows was always a great resort for elephants and giraffes. Travellers with the good fortune to see it in a flood season were delighted to find such a splendid stream in so desolate a wilderness. William Baldwin, who hunted there in 1858, found it in superb condition.

'This river appears of great breadth,' he wrote in his book *African Hunting and Adventure*. 'Nor do I see any possible way of crossing it, as I do not know where the stream runs to, and as far as the eye can

BIRD PARADISE A host of birds – ibis, cormorants, herons and egrets – roost in a dead acacia tree in the Savuti Marsh of Chobe National Park. This emerald-green wilderness is a paradise for birds, and game animals in immense numbers feed here.

reach there is nothing to be seen but reeds, so tall and thick that it is impossible to force your way through them. There is safe harbour here for all the game and wild animals in South Africa. I never saw anything like it, and my Hottentots say it is all the same all the way to Lake Ngami, about thirteen days from here in a wagon.'

Lechwe, kudu, waterbuck, zebra, eland, wildebeest, roan, sable, springbok, duiker, oryx, buffalo, elephant, giraffe, ducks and flamingos . . . myriads of mosquitoes, buzzing tsetse flies and the water alive with fish . . . mice and gerbils in countless numbers, living in colonies in the sand and a great danger with their plague-bearing fleas . . . jackals, hyenas, lions and leopards . . . the list of wildlife was, and still is, a matter of wonder to any naturalist.

Fish that breathe air

Particularly remarkable is the adaptability of all these wild creatures to the erratic succession of floods and droughts. Some of the fish, such as the barbel, seem to regard Lake Ngami as a special paradise.

Its waters are so rich in plankton that, even when instinct warns the barbel of a decline in the water, they will not retreat to safer areas. For such contingencies they have developed a bronchial organ which allows them to breathe dry air. They bury themselves in mud, and carry with them in pouches enough water to provide their bodies with moisture for very lengthy periods. If they sense the presence of water in other pools they are quite capable of wriggling their way over the mud to a new home.

The Botletle River, in a good season, feeds the waters of the Okavango in a meandering route eastwards for 300 km. It fills up numerous shallow pans, then ends its task by pouring what is left of its flow into an enormous and strangely uncanny depression in the wilderness known as *Makgadikgadi* to the Tswanas, and as Lake Makarikari to Europeans.

Makgadikgadi is over 1000 km in circumference, and 100 km across at its widest point. It is a great place for mirages, and the depression is itself so deceptive as to be at least as disconcerting to travellers as is Ngami. At the height of the flood season, Makgadikgadi receives water from the Okavango, and also from the Nata River flowing in from Zimbabwe in the east. For both rivers this is the end of a long journey. Makgadikgadi is less a sea than a nemesis for them. The combined flow manages to fill it up with perhaps 150 to 250 mm of water, thickened to a sludge by mixture with the soda, salt, plankton and assorted chemicals picked up from the level floor.

Animals in tremendous numbers gather in and around the verges of this almost supernatural inland sea. Flamingos come in such numbers that flocks of them cover 15 km of sludge in a single patch. Wildebeest are particularly partial to the taste of the sludge. They migrate to Makgadikgadi in thousands, along with zebra, springbok, hartebeest and other game.

Fish appear in the lake with the water. Barbel buried in the dry mud are immediately reactivated, while other fish and aquatic creatures simply swim in with the floods. The depth of the sludge is ideal for pelicans, ducks, geese, vast numbers of waders and, of course, the flamingos. They fly in happily, splash down and sink their heads into the nutritious goo. The squawkings, splashings and callings make a weird symphony, especially in the evening.

The vanishing waters of Ngami

When David Livingstone reached the shores of Lake Ngami in 1849, there stretched before his eyes a sheet of water so vast that he could not see across to the other side. Yet other travellers were to come back with a different story. Instead of a lake, they found a dry sun-baked depression with no evidence that there was any water nearer than the Okavango Swamp, 150 km to the north.

To travellers, the way in which the waters of Ngami came and went was a mystery. To the tribespeople living around the shores of the lake it was a matter of life or death. The true explanation of the mystery is that the amount of water in Lake Ngami depends on the amount of rain that falls in Angola, 1000 km away. In a good year, the waters of the Okavango delta will be topped up to the point that they overflow into Ngami. In a dry year the supply to Ngami is switched off, as if from a tap.

The tribespeople, faced with a succession of dry years in the 1920s, sought for an explanation that was closer to home than the hills of Angola. In doing so they missed the real cause, but hit upon a profound truth: that when man interferes with the balance of nature he produces results that are totally unexpected.

The story is told in *The Ivory Trail*, by T. V. Bulpin, an account of the life of the hunter and adventurer S. C. Barnard. One night, Barnard was joined at his camp fire by a wandering Zulu herbalist named Mgwazi, who had lived

At night, a clammy mist often rises from the lake. In the daytime this mist forms a haze, with a watery, copper-coloured sun peering through it. Thick bubbles constantly form in the green slime on the floor of the lake, rise to the surface of the water and remain there, giving the lake the singular appearance of having bumps or boils. Optical effects are weird. Isolated blocks of limestone are exaggerated until they look like hills. Ostriches, for some reason, often wade far out into the lake, and are so distorted optically as to look like large-sized elephants. The flamingo flocks seem to be feeding in the sky more often than standing in the water.

The entire run-off from the Okavango delta and the Nata is evaporated from the Makgadikgadi. Within a short while of the ending of the seasonal inundation, everything is gone. The hard, level floor of the depression is bone dry. A few outlying pans manage to retain water for at least a little while longer. But Makgadikgadi is lifeless – just a vast, white, soda-salt-covered skeleton of a lake on which nothing moves save mirages and dust devils whirling aimlessly about.

The only part of the Kgalagadi which is pure desert in the classic sense of the word is the south-western end. This is a world of red sand dunes, but even here rivers occasionally flow and then, sinking into the sand to escape the heat, leave moisture which man can tap from shallow wells. Even in the driest parts, there grow the courageous little tsamma melons. With two fruiting seasons each year, they support life with generous supplies of rather

---

n the vicinity of the contrary lake. According to Mgwazi, he desiccation of Ngami started with the advent of European traders who bartered guns to the tribespeople for skins nd ivory.

'Now you must know,' stated Mgwazi, 'that in those imes the Okavango was indeed a mighty river and Ngami vas a sheet of water like unto the sea. There were hippos in ll the waterways in numbers beyond count, and they gave is much trouble in the lands.

'When the corn was ripening we had to beat drums all night to drive the hippos away, while the women spent all lay fighting off the birds. Between the birds and hippos, the people had no rest until the crops were reaped and safely tored away.

'Now these hippos were cunning. We dug deep pits to atch them, but seldom did they fall in. Then the white men ame with their guns which could kill hippos. They shot one f them, to show us how easy it was with their weapons, and o make us anxious to possess these wonderful things, no matter how high the price.

'So our people bought all the guns for which they had attle or ivory or goods; and each gun was only bought if the vhite man proved it by shooting one hippo.'

When life was good

Then, when spring came, the white men went off with their vagons full of our things, driving our cattle before them, nd leaving us with the guns.

'Now life was very good. The white men had shown us now to make sledges and break in oxen with neck-yokes, so hat the women no longer had to carry everything.

'We shot the hippos and killed much game. Our crops vere good and even the dogs were sleek and fat from easting on the venison. But then we noticed that each year he reeds were growing bigger. Soon they covered the river;

and when the floods came, vast masses were washed down, like floating islands, and these blocked up all the narrow passages. You see, there were no longer any hippos to eat the reeds, or to force new passages through them.

'Then one morning after the rains had started the women went to fetch water. They came running back, calling the men to come and see the river. It was in flood, and in its waters there came down countless numbers of floating reed islands.

'Where the water entered Ngami the reeds jammed up into a solid barrier, and season after season this barrier choked up tighter and tighter. The barrier of reeds was like a wall. We were driven from our lands when the water was pushed back and flooded beyond its ancient banks.

'So it lasted for many seasons. Then, far away the weight of the water forced a new passage for the river and it flowed in a new direction.

'We tried to destroy the barrier of reeds by firing it, but we could not succeed. The river flowed elsewhere. Each year the country changed. It became drier and drier. Droughts came upon us, where before there was plenty. The desert crept into our gardens and stole our crops, and there were no drums we could beat to drive it away.

'Instead of the misty rains we had enjoyed of old, there now came only sandstorms and thirst. The land became a wilderness, with dead stumps instead of green forests; and Ngami, instead of a sea, became a bowl of dust. All this was because you white men taught us the mystery of guns and how to kill the hippos who, for all the forgotten years, had kept the rivers open; and although we did not know it and hated them as thieves, they were more truly our friends than those accursed guns which have brought more sadness to the world than good. May those who first made them be despised by all the spirits.'

GARDEN OF LILIES Delicately textured lilies ride the gentle ripples of the clear-water Monachira Channel of the Okavango River. The channel feeds the Okavango delta – an evergreen feeding ground for abundant bird and animal life, and for man.

178

DUSTBOWL The hard, salt-encrusted floor of the Makgadikgadi Pan. In the rainy season the pan is covered in slush, providing rich food for aquatic birds. But at other times it is a desolate dustbowl. Vegetation clings to life until the following season.

bitter-tasting but refreshing liquid, and pulp and seeds which are nutritious.

Dew also falls throughout the Kgalagadi and keeps the vegetation moist, even in the dry seasons. When the summer rains come (November to April) there are powerful thunderstorms. These noisy tumultuous affairs flood portions of the wilderness, burying roads and paths under water.

People of the wilderness

Man, like the wild animals, has to be hardy and resolute to survive. In the whole area of the Kgalagadi there are only 650 000 people, 80 per cent of whom live along the eastern verges. Of the people who live in the wilderness proper, perhaps 10 000 are nomadic Bushmen and, with South West Africa, this is their last sanctuary. It is here, in the Kgalagadi, that their culture of the Late Stone Age still survives. The hunters using bows and poisoned arrows, and the women incessantly searching for *veldkos* (wild bulbs, insects, fruits and tubers), make only isolated attempts, stimulated by European example, at agriculture or animal husbandry.

The Bushmen of the Kgalagadi are of the same stock as the people who once inhabited the whole of Southern Africa. In the harsh conditions of the wilderness these Bush people never reached the cultural heights of their vanished relatives in more congenial areas, such as the Drakensberg and Zimbabwe. On the few stone surfaces available to them in the waste of sand, they did try the art of painting. In the rock shelters of the Hill of Vultures north of Lobatsi, and in the quartzite Tsodilla Hills in the north-western extremity of Botswana, they created galleries of interesting pictures. But these paintings are far inferior in technique to those in areas where availability of colouring material, suitable rock faces and relative ease of living made it possible for the Bushmen artists to produce their masterpieces.

The sand wilderness of the Kgalagadi, with its vast solitudes, was too severe an environment to stimulate art. At least, however, the wilderness offered sanctuary to a people who would otherwise have entirely vanished. By establishing harmony between themselves and the Kgalagadi, the Bushmen found strange comfort in its very harshness; discovered companionship in its loneliness; learnt a patient resignation from its ruthlessness. Where others were repelled by the fear of thirst and death, they were offered hope, and the chance of continued life when all the rest of the land they once called their own was denied them.

An underground wonderland, sculpted by nature

There are enchanted lakes, where seldom a ripple ever disturbs the mirror surface; pits deep enough to imprison monsters; and shadows darker than the extremes of outer space

THE MONSTER OF SUDWALA This massive column of dripstone, in the Sudwala Caves of the Eastern Transvaal, is named the Screaming Monster. It stands 6 m high, and is still in the process of formation. Prehistoric man may have worshipped it.

Caves: a grotesque
and enchanted world, created
by drops of water

IN HIS SEARCH for mineral wealth, man probes to enormous depths in the mantle of the earth. But nature has her own entrances to the underworld: great caverns, scooped out of solid rock by the action of water. Their dark passageways lead to many surprising things.

There are glittering caves, so packed with crystals, stalactites and stalagmites that the discoverer feels as though he has found his way into a treasure house. There are caverns filled with weird rocks, twisted shadows, and patterns on the walls which make them galleries of art – grotesque, absurd, horrifying, beautiful, repellent. Man's art, whether abstract, impressionist or naturalistic, does not surpass these subterranean exhibitions.

There are enchanted lakes, where seldom a ripple ever disturbs the mirror surface; pits deep enough to imprison monsters; and shadows darker even than the extremes of outer space. In places, the caverns seem to be part of the womb of creation. They are workshops, filled with debris, bric-à-brac, rejects, skeletons, fossils and other traces of the earliest discernible forms of life. It is impossible to enter such places without an awareness of the presence of something intangible, indefinable, neither hostile nor friendly, indifferent to intrusion and totally elusive!

Caves occur in all types of rock, and water is the tool nature uses in creating them. Their size and existence is entirely dependent on the chance confrontation of their parent rock with a flow of water which, in the nature of that mischievous and energetic element, finds a weakness and worries it into a passage beneath the surface.

Decorations – by man and by nature

The sandstone formations at the base of the Drakensberg have been particularly exposed to powerful water action from the mountain streams. Innumerable caves and shelters have been scalloped out of the rock, and such places, many of them very commodious, provided shelter for primitive men, notably of the Late Stone Age from 2000 to 9000 years ago. They were dry, protected from the wind, and conveniently situated next to streams where water and firewood could be obtained. And they had smooth walls, to tempt artists into exercising their talents.

Such sandstone caves were decorated by man alone, for nature had not on hand the essential means. It was only where water scalloped out similar caves in limestone that the sequence of natural decoration could take place. The Cango Caves are a spectacular product of such a sequence. They lie on the lower slopes of the *Swartberg* range in the Cape Province. This range, notwithstanding its name (black mountain), is made of sandstone containing vivid red-orange colours. At the base of this sandstone mass there lies a deposit of dark limestone. Where the caves occur today, this limestone was faulted or cracked along an erratic zone sometimes reaching 100 m in width. Nature set out to reseal this subterranean fissure with a deposit of a crystallised form of chalk known as calcite. Water also found its way into the fissure and dissolved, rather than washed away, huge cavities. It was an unhurried process, for the water had little movement. It drained rather than ran away, carrying its spoil of dissolved calcite and limestone.

The final draining came when the water dissolved for itself an exit somewhere in the lower levels. With this plug removed, the subterranean lakelets disappeared, leaving behind a chain of connected empty chambers, extending westwards for about 3000 m and with a rise and fall of less than 20 m.

Then began the second stage in the sequence. The workmen had moved out and the interior decorators arrived. Rainwater percolated through the ground

ENTRANCES TO ANOTHER WORLD Water, working on rock, has given Southern Africa some spectacular caves.

above the caverns. As it did so it acquired a high content of carbon dioxide from the respiration of plant roots and the bacterial decay of humus. Soaking through the calcite-filled crevice, this carbon dioxide-rich water dissolved from the limestone quantities of calcium carbonate – a substance which will not dissolve at all in pure water. Carbon dioxide is essential to its solution.

It was the fortuitous presence above the cave of a suitable covering of soil and vegetation that allowed the percolating rainwater the ideal opportunity to collect carbon dioxide. And this, added to water, produced a weak solution of carbonic acid, capable of dissolving calcium carbonate, or chalk.

Once the dripping water had carried the dissolved calcium carbonate through the ceiling of the cavern, it encountered air containing far less carbon dioxide. In an effort to balance matters, nature transferred carbon dioxide from the water. This left a superfluity of calcium carbonate which the dripping water had to shed. It is this process of shedding calcium carbonate that produces the whole wonderful decoration of caves.

How stalactites are formed

As each drop of water finds its way through the ceiling, provided its movement is not too rapid, it sheds its load of calcium carbonate where it reaches the air and a stalactite is slowly formed, with the water trickling down, each drop adding its minute contribution.

Where the drops are too rapid, or there is too much calcium carbonate to be shed immediately, the water carries it down to the floor of the cave. A second deposition then starts to grow upwards as a stalagmite, very often with a saucer-shaped depression known as a splash-cap at its point. Stalactites, therefore, come first. Stalagmites follow, or do not grow at all if the water sheds all of its calcium carbonate before reaching the ground. A stalactite and a stalagmite can both mature to the point that they join together and become a column which steadily grows fatter and can reach considerable proportions. Whole curtains of stalactites can be formed if the water drips from several adjacent points in the ceiling.

Calcium carbonate still contained in water reaching the floor of the cavern can be precipitated in several other remarkable forms. If the water is dammed up by some slight ridge and forms a shallow pool with a large surface area compared to its volume, it has the opportunity to shed its load. The calcium carbonate tends to be deposited at the edge and what is known as a rimstone dam is formed, enclosing a pool.

Flowstone is still another form of deposition, consisting of sheets of calcium carbonate covering large areas over which water has slowly moved. A very delicate deposition is known as a helictite. These are rod-like in shape, often growing in dense clusters, and twisted and warped in every direction. Minute drips coming through the ceiling cause these lovely little formations, miniature stalactites whose erratic direction is apparently the consequence of stress and warping as the fragile rods are formed.

There are several other forms of these so-called dripstone deposits, all to be found in the Cango Caves: calcite bubbles; crusts formed over the surface of pools and left behind like sheets of ice; complex needle-like crystals of aragonite or gypsum, another form of calcium carbonate formed when some sulphate is also present in the water; all are described by geologists as speleothems (cave things). Fortunately, none of these deposits is commercially valuable and provided souvenir hunters can be controlled, the caves will remain intact.

Pure calcite deposits are white. But any chemical impurities will give colour, particularly iron oxides which tone them pink to russet. Some impurities also make them fluorescent or even phosphorescent. The gaudy coloured lights which some of the modern cave promoters see fit to use for illumination do a disservice in that they saturate the natural tints of the speleothems. They give visitors the impression that caves are the products, not of the art of nature, but rather of nature suffering from indigestion.

The Cango Caves contain a vast and overwhelmingly beautiful collection of speleothems. There may be bigger caves in Southern Africa, and bigger in other countries; but these speleothems have a variety and elegance which place them amongst the finest in the world. They are a major tourist attraction.

The name *Cango* is of Hottentot origin, and means a narrow plain between the mountains. This name was properly applied to what is now called the Little Karoo. The caves happen to be in the slopes of the mountains which line the northern side of this plain. The entrance was discovered by prehistoric men, and rock paintings show that it was occupied by them in the Late Stone Age.

Inside the Cango Caves

There is no evidence in the way of paintings or bones that the early inhabitants explored the inner chambers, which darkness made impenetrable to anybody without light. For countless years they must have remained places of mystery to the people who occupied the entrance.

From the entrance, the cave floor rises gently and then descends into what has been named Van Zyl's Hall, after the local farmer who explored the caves in 1780 and is reputed to have been the first man to do so. This first cavern is 110 m long, 50 m wide and 17 m high. It contains a collection of speleothems including a stalagmite known as Cleopatra's Needle, which is just over 10 m in height and is estimated to have taken 150 000 years to build – a rate of just 1 mm every 15 years.

This first cavern leads easily into a second vast chamber known as Botha's Hall, after an early cave official. This is a gallery of beautiful, bizarre and spectacular formations. One 14 m column in this chamber is the highest in the Cango Caves. Dripstone formations of nearly every type are found in this vast collection, including rimstone pools, curtains and walls richly tinted with iron oxides. An extension of this chamber, known as the Throne Room, has the visual effect on the visitor of opening a jewellery box and being dazzled by the glittering and precious contents.

The main sequence of chambers continues westwards and leads easily into what is known as the Rainbow Room, much smaller than the first two chambers but extremely beautiful in its formations. From it, side passages branch southwards into such chambers as the Vestry, Temple, Crypt and Catacombs.

The main route again continues westwards and leads into the Bridal Chamber, where a handsome cluster of stalagmites forms the shape of a four-poster bed. From here a narrow passageway leads into a small chamber known as the Fairy Palace, crammed with another collection of speleothems and leading into the Drum Room where a curtain reverberates, when thumped, to the deep sound of a drum. This is the antechamber to the Grand Hall, a cavern 120 m long.

From here a 35 m long tunnel known as the Avenue leads, with a steep flight of stairs at the end, into the Crystal Chamber, another jewellery box of exquisite calcite formations. From here the sequence of chambers becomes decidedly more broken, with many smaller rooms such as the Crystal Palace, Crystal Forest, Ice Chamber, Devil's Workshop, Picture Gallery and Banqueting Hall. Each name provides some indication of the nature of the formations. Connecting them all, like the string in a necklace of diamonds, the passageway wanders from one to the other, with an occasional low, narrow or steep portion such as Lumbago Walk and the Devil's Chimney.

Beyond the Devil's Workshop, a new sequence, full of fantasy shapes in dripstone, was discovered in 1972. Known as Cango 2, it is about 270 m long. Even this find was eclipsed in August, 1975, when the clue of a stream that doubled back beneath the floor of Cango 2 led to the discovery of Cango 3. This is an unspoiled wonderland of beautiful and grotesque formations that stretches for 1600 m – twice as long as the Cango 1 tourist route. It is sealed by water at both ends, and so is entirely insulated from outside pollution.

Earliest forms of life

The Transvaal is particularly rich in caves. Between the Limpopo and the Vaal rivers there are portions of the country containing deposits of dolomite, a limestone rock laid down about 800 million years ago in what seems to have been a shallow sea. The calcareous material which formed the dolomite was produced partly through the agency of algae but principally from chemical precipitation. Traces of the algae found as fossils in the dolomite are the earliest identifiable forms of life in Southern Africa. The algae are known as *Stromatolites*, and may be seen in the walls of several of the caves.

Dolomite is particularly absorbent. At least 11 per cent of rainfall vanishes into this rock before it has a chance of running off. Deep crevices and underground reservoirs of water form, often feeding their water out into valleys in the form of powerful springs. Sink holes often occur when the roof of an underground reservoir collapses, while complex sequences of caves are formed as the water dissolves out subterranean crevices.

As at the Cango Caves, water dripping through the humus and vegetation-rich soil above the cave picks up a supply of carbon dioxide. This again dissolves the calcium carbonate in the dolomite, and the whole complex sequence of decorating the caverns with speleothems begins.

A fascinating example of decorated dolomite caves may be seen in the Eastern Transvaal, near Nelspruit. These are the Sudwala Caves, named after the headman of a small group of renegade Swazis who

FLUTED COLUMN Among the strange shapes formed by drip after drip o water in the Cango Caves of the Western Cape is this formation resembling the fluted columns of classical architecture. Different tints i the rock are produced by iron oxides.

fled there from their own country and used the caves as a refuge in times of war. These caves contain many beautiful dripstone formations easily viewed from a tourist route. The ceilings of the various chambers are remarkable for their fossilized algae and water-worn patterns, while beyond the normal tourist route the caves continue to an as yet undiscovered end. The 'wild' inner reaches of this cave provide a challenge to explorers – there are rock obstructions, low tunnels, mud, streams which have to be swum, and passages that call for a vast amount of wriggling and scrambling, rewarded periodically by a sudden entrance into a jewellery box of speleothems. The scramble is always refreshed by a steady current of pure air which flows through the whole complex of tunnels and caverns from some distant inlet which local legend places over 30 km away.

Home of the 'Screaming Monster'

The entrance to these caves is beautifully situated in a gorge overgrown with subtropical forest. As with the Cango Caves, prehistoric man made use of this part of the caves while prodigious numbers of bats slept in the inner recesses. Their deposits of guano attracted some commercial attention in later years, but fortunately not much damage was done in the process of recovery.

Beyond the entrance the passageway makes a sharp turn, passes a fine curtain of dripstone formations and enters the first large cavern, dominated by a speleothem of such size, power and character that a primitive culture could easily have been awed into using it as the centrepiece for some grisly sacrificial religion.

Known as the Screaming Monster, this column of dripstone has a fallen stalactite at its foot, like the recumbent form of a defeated rival. The domed ceiling above the Screaming Monster is patterned with water marks and the singular saucer-like shapes which are the fossils of colonies of algae known as *collenia*.

These algae played a major role in the chain of evolution. They flourished in warm, shallow seas at a time when the earth's atmosphere was mainly nitrogen and carbon dioxide. By the process of photosynthesis, the algae converted the carbon dioxide into oxygen and thus prepared the atmosphere for the support of higher forms of life.

TIME WITHOUT END When nature turns sculptor she has, literally, all the time in the world. This fragile sickle in Cango 2, now in its infancy, will settle down as it increases in size at a growth rate of just 30 mm every 100 years.

FANTASY IN STONE A fantastic world of stalactites and stalagmites has been created in the Sudwala Caves. The air in the caves is always fresh, and it is said that the pure air comes through a complex of passages from an inlet 30 km away.

Colonies of this ancient alga, floating on the surface of water in the caves, became embedded in the ceilings. Completely transmuted into fossils by silica, they remain as reminders of the age when life was only beginning on the ever-changing face of the earth.

Beyond the Screaming Monster the passageway enters the largest cavern so far discovered in this sequence. Named the P. R. Owen Hall after the late owner of the caves, it is more like the underground town hall of a community of troglodytes. There is a superb ceiling, decorated with collenia fossils, and complex patterns of water marks and scratches. There is a natural stage, with ample seating accommodation on the tiered approaches to the wall. The acoustics are excellent; air conditioning is impeccable; and many concerts have been staged here by visiting choirs and orchestras.

The centrepiece of this huge cavern is a massive lump of silica which must have fallen from the rear wall. Dripstone curtains and stalactites hang from the ceiling, while stalagmites stand about like statues in a gallery. High up on the one side there is another cavern, almost a smaller, more intimate, rehearsal theatre, dominated by a stalagmite known as the Red Devil and with a spectacular dyke of diapace cutting through the ceiling like a beam of rock.

The main passageway continues, as the caves, like the Russian composer Mussorgsky in his *Pictures at an Exhibition*, take the visitor on a leisurely promenade with something interesting to see at every turn. As the passage leaves the great hall, there is on the left-hand side a work of nature which puts to shame any modern abstract painting. It is really a completely filled-in passage, but its outer frame surrounds a weirdly fascinating pattern of colour and shape which it seems beyond the capacity of pure chance to have produced.

In an 'alcove' to the right stands a lovely speleothem formation, the Weeping Madonna, a stalagmite cascade with dripping water and a pool at its foot.

The guano collectors worked as far as this into the cave. Piles of rocks stacked against the walls, and dates such as 1887 and 1898 scratched into a large boulder, are probably their work.

500 million years ago

On the left-hand side of the passageway there is a dark-coloured pedestal made of a mixture of dolomite, silica, iron and manganese. Enclosed in it is a buried stalagmite. On top of this pedestal is a stalagmite formation of massive proportions. This stalagmite has been perfectly and smoothly sliced by water action to reveal a fine cross-section of its entire inside, the strata showing its manner of construction and hinting at its age. The whole elaborate pile takes the onlooker back in time for probably 500 million years.

The passageway leads on through another chamber with, on the far side, what looks to be the former entrance to an even more ancient cave, coming in obliquely but now completely blocked. The passageway, narrow and tortuous, follows the bed of a subterranean stream and this suddenly leads into the Fairyland Chamber, beautifully decorated with a variety of speleothems still being made from a ceiling of manganese dioxide and white dolomite crystals – a real chemical dreamland.

This chamber, about 500 m from the entrance, marks the end of the regular tourist route. A natural barricade of dripstone formations lies across the path. Penetrating this barrier, the passageway continues, but soon dwindles so sharply in size that it is as though the visitor had followed Alice in Wonderland and at this precise point must sample the bottle labelled 'Drink me'. Only a dwarf could comfortably walk upright here, and in the wet season the floor is the muddy bed of a shallow stream.

What is known as Corkscrew Passage soon opens up slightly into Joint Passage, so named because it is a fine example of a joint in the dolomite. It is a colourful section of the cave sequence, for here iron oxides stain the limestone red-orange, while liquid manganese dioxides have transformed parts of the dolomite into something deceptively like fossil trees.

Joint Passage opens up completely into a 30 m high

HEALING WATERS Not a ripple disturbs the tranquillity of this underground lake in the Sterkfontein Cave, near Krugersdorp in the Transvaal. Local tribespeople believed that the waters had healing powers, and could cure blindness.

FAIRY FOREST This strikingly beautiful forest in fairyland was the sight that rewarded cave explorers in 1972 when, following up the clue of a draught of air at the end of Cango I, they broke into the 'Wonder Cave' sequence of Cango 2.

subterranean cathedral, complete with numerous bats in the belfry.

The floor is littered with boulders. The builders seemingly have still to complete their work by putting in the seats. Meanwhile the passage has to find its own way through the waiting pile of material. Leaving the cathedral, the passageway enters what is called the Smoking Chamber, but would be better described as a vestry. It is a small cavern, beautifully decorated with complex calcium-carbonate crystals, some of cauliflower shape, others fragile, like little mounds of snow. These crystals form on the ceiling, decompose, drop as 'moon milk' and cover the floor like a thick hoar frost.

The walls of matt-black manganese dioxide provide a complete contrast to these crystals. There are snow-white gypsum crystals and yellow-brown dolomite crystals, all turning this pitch-black vault into a Christmas grotto. There is even a chimney, soaring up to nobody knows where and totally encrusted with pure white calcium-carbonate crystals.

The main passageway continues its subterranean route now following a bedding plane, or horizontal passage, very constricted in places. (Several sips are needed here of Alice's 'Drink me' reducing liquid, followed quickly by nibbles of 'Eat me', the enlarging snack!) The whole length of this passage is elabor-ately decorated with complex speleothems – crystals of dolomite, calcite and gypsum – providing a wide range of tints and shapes, including thin needles, symmetrically curved and twisted. Alcoves and cavities in the wall are all filled with these exquisite miniatures.

In the Arctic Chamber

The passageway opens abruptly into a large cavern which is known as Arctic Chamber, with matt-black manganese dioxide-stained walls and ceiling. This entire chamber is covered from top to bottom with a superb exhibition of white dolomite crystals. There are cauliflower shapes; dome-shaped clusters of prismatic needles; 'moon milk' piled up on the floor like drifts of snow; and many other shapes and patterns.

Passing a wall that is quite dazzling in its covering of speleothems, the passage, with a few contortions over and around fallen boulders, finds its way into what is known as the Penguin Chamber, from a small rock shaped like that quaint bird. This cavern has a wall that is pure calcite. A gorgeous pair of dolomite crystals dominate the chamber, while so many strange speleothems stand in the niches and cavities that looking into this cavern (especially from the far end) gives so complete an illusion of a coral reef that a shoal of tropical fish could swim around a corner at

STONE WATERFALL This petrified cascade is a stalagmite in the Sudwala Caves of the Eastern Transvaal. The sheen on its surface comes from droplets of water which every day add their minute deposits of rock to the ever-growing waterfall.

any moment.

The passage leaves the Penguin Chamber by means of a triangular opening 1,5 m high, and less than 1 m wide at its base. Glimmering white speleothems in flower formations have grown around this doorway and it is looking back through this that the explorer receives the best impression of being in a coral reef.

Ahead is an even grander sight. First there is a small rectangular cavern 2 m high, with its walls and ceilings completely covered with speleothems, crystals, stalactites and a whole cascade of dripstone formations. The passage wriggles a way through a barrier of stalactites and stalagmites and then enters the Crystal Chamber. This is the climax to all the caverns of the Sudwala Caves. It is a fantasy of dolomite, calcite and gypsum crystals, stalactites, stalagmites, curtains and cascades.

Strangely, in this chamber lie the completely fossilized skeletons of two small snakes. How they found a way through the long, dark tunnel and into this magic cavern it is impossible to guess. But there they died, so long ago that calcite crystals have formed in their bones.

The Crystal Chamber was discovered in 1968 by Harold Jackson, the master explorer of this cave sequence. It was his reward for arduous hours of probing ever further into the subterranean depths. Beyond this chamber, the cave sequence continues towards its as yet unreached end. The passage becomes very difficult although there are many more beautiful things to see: a stalactite shaped like a six-fingered hand; Cathedral Avenue, a vertical passage with fluted walls richly decorated with gypsum flowers; streams appearing and disappearing. And always there is the steady current of fresh, pure air promising the explorer who eventually surmounts all difficulties of obstructions, constrictions, climbs, mud, crawls and many awkward pitfalls, that at the end there will probably be an outlet back to the outside world, which seems so totally remote from the Crystal Chamber.

Major archaeological site

The caves of Southern Africa have a lengthy record of occupation by man and his ancestors.

Among the dolomite caves of the Transvaal is the Sterkfontein Cave near Krugersdorp. This cave is one of the major archaeological sites of the world, with such discoveries made there as the skull of *Australopithecus africanus*, a species of man-ape. Six large chambers are connected by a natural passageway. The Hall of Elephants chamber is 100 m long by 25 m

high and is dominated by an immense dripstone curtain, and there are many fine speleothem formations. At a depth of 50 m there is a lake which is regarded with considerable awe by the local tribespeople. Its waters are considered to have potent healing powers, especially for blindness.

Another cave of great archaeological interest is Makapaansgat, near Potgietersrus in the Northern Transvaal. This is a colossal cave, with its depths not yet completely explored. Since very early times, man has used this cave as a shelter.

Besieged in a cave

In historic times this cave was the stronghold of the chief Makhapane whose name, in corrupted form, is applied to the cave today. This chief was responsible for the massacre in 1854 of a party of 33 Europeans. Pursued by a punitive force, Makhapane and about 2000 of his followers retreated into the cave. There they were besieged, and 1500 of them died from the privations they suffered before the rest escaped or surrendered. The main entrance to this cave is 150 m high and a sinister air still lurks about the dark recesses.

Also in the Northern Transvaal are the Echo Caves, situated in a dolomite hill near Ohrigstad. There are two entrances to these caves. One provides a tourist route 400 m long which reveals some fine speleothems. The name of the caves comes from the sound produced when one of the stalactites is struck. The second entrance leads for 307 m through a sequence of dark dolomite chambers, the largest being 100 m long by 40 m high. This section is the home for several million bats.

In Zimbabwe there is a very spectacular cave system near the town of Sinoia. Known to the local tribespeople as *Tshirorodziva* (the sunken pool), it consists of a circular sink hole in the dolomite. The sink hole is full of water given a beautiful blue colour by dispersed particles of lime. Some unknown person introduced goldfish to this pool and they have flourished, living there now in considerable shoals. The surface of the water is 50 m below ground level and it goes down 95 m. A natural sloping tunnel leads to the verge of this pool, while a whole complex of underground galleries and caverns honeycombs the dolomite around it. According to legend an outlaw named Nyamakwere used this cave as a stronghold. He executed many a victim by throwing them down into the mysterious pool. The outlaw was eventually killed there himself and the pool still seems to be haunted by unhappy memories.

Earth's most ancient landscape

The land is a sea of olive-green, with blue-grey granite masses rising from it like ancient gods, turned to stone after some furious battle with the powers of creation.

MOUNTAINS OF ETERNITY Mist shrouds mountains made of rock so ancient that it dates back to the forgotten ages of the earth's beginning. On the right soar the three majestic Rondawels. Below, the Blyde River winds through the vast canyon.

Mountains loom with brooding power
over the tattered remains of
the first mantle of the earth

THE CREATION of earth's first landscape must have been one of the most stupendous spectacles since the universe itself began. As the surface slowly cooled to form a mantle or crust, it floated precariously on a central mass of superheated molten matter. It probably looked something like the skin on top of a bowl of scalding porridge. Vast outpourings of the molten inner mixture periodically surged upwards, fracturing the slender skin, spreading out on the top to form new surfaces, or cooling to leave gigantic domes and whalebacks of granite. Gas forced blow-holes upwards, and vast disturbances took place beneath the surface with molten rock forcing passages like underground rivers of fire, forming intrusive reefs and veins, dykes and leaders, or spreading out into weird lakes filled with all manner of mineral treasures.

The Primitive System

In most parts of the earth, this earliest of land surfaces has been long buried by later deposits. In Zimbabwe and the Eastern Transvaal, however, a large expanse of this Primitive System, as it has been named by geologists, is perfectly exposed. The spectacle of this most ancient landscape has to it a touch of true grandeur. Three thousand million years have passed since these great masses of granite surged upwards and then cooled, like solid, petrified, gigantic bubbles. They loom with brooding power over the tattered remains of the first mantle of the earth. A rich savanna land of trees and shrubs now covers the Primitive System. It is an undulating sea of olive-green with blue-grey granite masses rising from it like islands from a frozen sea, or like ancient gods, turned to stone after some furious battle with the power of creation.

Zimbabwe has the largest and the most awe-inspiring assembly of these colossal wrecks of a primeval landscape, whose nature was never in the memory of man. Whole ranges of them dominate the country. The surface between the Limpopo and the Zambezi rivers consists of a vast, sun-drenched, rolling parkland. West to east through it there runs a narrow backbone of high ground. This is the main watershed. The northern slopes drain to the Zambezi; the southern slopes to the Limpopo. The summit of the watershed is a temperate grassland, healthy, fertile, and always a desirable residential area for man.

Granite outcrops support and protect this high watershed. Some scarcely have their heads above the surface. Others are buried. Many surge over the parkland in total domination, and their influence on the affairs of man has been considerable.

Granite terrain such as this may be seen in several other parts of the world. Madagascar, Canada, India, Australia and Brazil all have massive piles of this type of igneous rock. Nearly everywhere, the granite is associated with a complex mineralisation. At the time of the coming of the granite, a tangle of tears, warps and cracks occurred in the mantle of the earth. Nature healed these fissures by squeezing into them a mixture of superheated igneous matter which contained an extraordinary variety of minerals and metals.

This mineralisation is highly erratic in its location and value. Southern Africa has been fortunate in that nearly everywhere the granites are found there can be reasonable expectations of associated mineral treasures. But even in Southern Africa there are some areas, such as the Western Cape, where there is granite without any sign of mineralisation. The huge domes which dominate the town of Paarl and the Berg River Valley are examples of such outcrops with no known mineralisation.

In Zimbabwe and the Eastern Transvaal the granite country of the Primitive System has been a happy hunting ground for prospectors since the first Iron

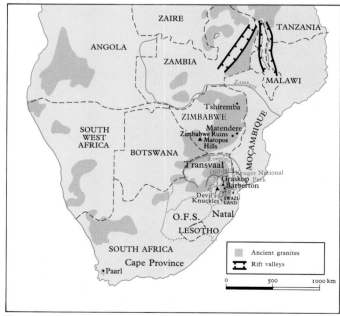

PRIMITIVE SYSTEM The oldest rocks known, the tattered remnants of the earth's first mantle, lie in the shaded areas.

GRANITE 'BUBBLES' These boulders in the amaTobo (Matopos) are part of granite which surged in a molten mass to the earth's surface 3000 million years ago. The igneous matter cooled into gigantic dome and whaleback shapes, which still defy the forces of erosion

Age men entered the area about 500 years after Christ. Antimony, arsenic, asbestos, beryllium, chrome, copper, gold, iron, lead, lithium, mica, pyrites, silver, tantalum, tin and tungsten – these are just a few of the treasures of the granite country.

Iron Age man discovered and worked gold, copper and iron. The face of the old primitive landscape became pockmarked with thousands of mine workings, each going down to the water level before being abandoned. Every surface exposure was tested and mined if found to be profitable. Modern prospectors need only to find the best of the old mines, drain them with the pumps which the primitive workers lacked, and resume profitable working.

Natural building blocks

Apart from this considerable mining industry, continuous in Zimbabwe for about 1500 years, the granites stimulated another unique activity in man – building. Granite has several peculiarities. In the process of its original cooling, natural lines of weakness and fracture appeared in the rock. For some unknown reason these lines of weakness had two subtle basic variations. In some of the granites the lines, curved in

BALANCING BOULDERS Weirdly shaped rocks are balanced precariously on one another at Tshiremba (near Salisbury), as though some angry giant had scattered them about the countryside at random The area is named after a bygone witchdoctor.

parallel layers, are on top of one another like the skins of gigantic onions. These layers peeled off under the action of weathering and formed the domes. Other masses, however, had their fractures in straight lines, branching off in sharp angles. Weathering of these granites caused them literally to fragment into shattered piles of separate rocks, with oddly assorted shapes, many of them fanciful in outline, and precariously balanced.

Men of the Late Stone Age found good shelter in these piles of rocks, for they were full of caves. Later Iron Age immigrants discovered a particular use for

the flakes peeled off from the granite domes. These flakes tended towards uniformity in thickness and they could fairly easily be dressed into suitable shapes.

The Iron Age people, who lived in the traditional mud huts of Africa, started to use the fragments to make protective walls around their settlements.

GOLDEN HONEYCOMB The Blyde River of the Eastern Transvaal scoured out these bizarre shapes – Bourkes Potholes – with the aid of loose boulders swirled about by the current. Gold was found in the river, and near by is the mine of Bourkes Luck.

When they ran out of natural fragments, they made more by expediting the normal process of nature. They noticed how the summer sun would heat the granite, a passing thunderstorm would deluge it with cold rain or hail and the consequent rapid expansion and contraction would cause the granite to crack and flake. The builders used fire to heat the granite, then threw cold water over it.

By this means they secured all the fragments they wanted, dressed them into shape, and set their women onto what must have seemed the interminable chore of carrying and then depositing one stone on top of the other to make walls. There are over 900 000 of these granite fragments in the temple walls of the Zimbabwe Ruins alone.

Throughout Zimbabwe and the Northern Transvaal, where the presence of granite made this type of architectural activity possible, there are over 8000 related examples, large and small, of similar wall building. A sigh from countless weary African women still seems to echo back from the granite domes.

Stronghold of the MaTebele

Along the south-western verge of the high backbone of Zimbabwe, for a length of 75 km, there is one particularly superb range of granite domes, whale-backs and the fragmented shapes called castle rocks. This range guarded the southern approaches of the stronghold of the MaTebele tribe.

Their renowned chief, Mzilikazi, is said to have been fascinated by this wilderness of rock. With a neat touch of humour he applied to the range the name of *amaTobo* (the bald heads). The name was remarkably apt. From the heights of the central watershed the line of domes looks like an assembly of old men, sitting in confabulation with their bald

THE STONEBREAKER A massive baobab tree has thrust its way through a stone wall at the Matendere Ruins in Zimbabwe. The ruins are typical of the ancient stone-wall buildings of the country. More than 8000 such remnants dot the countryside.

DEVIL'S DOMAIN Like a gigantic slumbering whale, the escarpment in the Eastern Transvaal looms beyond the Devil's Knuckles on Long Tom Pass. Near by are the positions where Boer forces mounted their 'Long Tom' guns during the Anglo-Boer War.

heads glistening in the sun.

There is an undeniable atmosphere of mystery in such places as this granite range. In one of the great domes, *Njerere* (the place of the hawk eagle), is a cave used as an oracle for Mwari, the all-powerful god of the Karanga tribe. To this mysterious place many supplicants have made their way and begged for the advice of Mwari. From the cave they have heard a strange booming voice answering their prayers, and then have made their departure leaving behind gifts for the god and his priests.

In many of the caves there are galleries of rock paintings, left by the long-vanished people of the Late Stone Age. Each mountain has its name and legend, and there are secret places where strange rites have been (and are still) practised. A curious natural wall of stone runs for 45 km through the range. About 12 m wide and up to 15 m high, this oddity has something of the appearance of the Great Wall of China. Geologists describe it as a dolerite dyke, left exposed by the erosion of the more fragile granite. But the tribespeople have their own explanation. To

them it was erected by a band of spirits as a wall to keep out evil powers.

River of fire
In far more recent times than the coming of the granites, there occurred in this part of Southern Africa another prodigious disturbance. About 700 million years ago, following the fracture line of the Great Rift Valley System of Africa, a gigantic crevice, 6 km wide, was torn north to south for over 450 km across the country. Through this crevice flowed a river of fire 6 km wide. In Zimbabwe, this crevice today lies exposed on the surface as a trough filled with magmatic matter of considerable mineral richness, including large deposits of high-grade chrome.

Further south, in the Transvaal, the river of fire forced its way deep underground through layers of

DRAKENSBERG'S GARDEN (*Overleaf*) Awesome in its vastness, this is the vividly coloured bushveld of the Eastern Transvaal. The Drakensberg mountains brood over a wild garden where the winds seem to whisper the stories of past adventures.

VALLEY OF PERIL Prospectors, lured to the Kaap Valley by the promise of gold, risked fever and attack by primitive tribesmen and wild animals. Though many pioneers found treasure, others found only heartbreak and disillusionment.

sediments which had been deposited on top of the Primitive System. The molten mass, carrying with it substantial quantities of platinum, chromite, nickel, iron, tin and tungsten was, in its fiery state, fluid and soft, and the established surface was quite undermined.

At the end of the flow, the river of fire spread out beneath this surface like a subterranean lake. The

OCEAN OF TREES (*Preceding page*) The escarpment of the Eastern Transvaal at Graskop sweeps down to a fertile and forested terrace, then tumbles more abruptly to the tree-covered lowveld. Beyond is the wild country of the Kruger National Park.

surface simply subsided into the undermining fluid. A huge basin was formed, with a level floor surrounded by a rim of the original higher-lying surface. Geologists describe this strange feature of the landscape as a lopolith. The magmatic fluid which caused the scenic deformity never reached the surface. With its mineral riches it cooled.

Known as the Bushveld Igneous Complex, it is famous in geological textbooks as the classic lopolith, with an extraordinary succession of rock types and ore deposits. In its centre, as something of a final touch, there is a well-preserved volcanic crater, blown up to the surface with its throat filled with a valuable

VALLEY OF PEACE The Olifants River flows lazily through its sun-soaked valley in the Kruger National Park. When European pioneers reached this river they found vast herds of elephants wandering along its banks: hence the name *Olifants* (elephants).

mud impregnated with chloride and carbonate of soda.

In the ancient landscape of the Eastern Transvaal and Swazi border country lies a valley which is scoured 1000 m deep into the crust of the earth by heavy rains and the constant run-off of streams and rivers. Looking across it, the opposite side is only dimly visible, 40 km away.

The enchanted sea
In the early mornings, mists are apt to fill the valley completely. Then it presents a unique spectacle. An alchemist has transmuted the valley into a snow-white sea, full of waves, weird forms and turbulences. The surrounding escarpment has the appearance of a circle of cliffs rising steeply from this strange sea.

This was the sight that greeted the first Europeans to penetrate the valley. To them it seemed that the cliff on which they were standing was a cape projecting into an enchanted sea. On the summit of this 'cape' was a bizarre pile of sandstone boulders – several thousand of them – arranged in odd groupings and with a variety of fanciful shapes, named the *Duiwelskantoor* (the reception office of the devil), the headland was called *De Kaap* (the cape), and the valley became known as the Valley of Death.

To countless prospectors who came later this grim valley was not misnamed. Fever haunted the area, and mosquitoes sang of blood and death throughout the long warm nights.

The great lure of the valley for prospectors was its rich mineralisation. Nature has healed the fissures torn by the cooling of molten granite millions of years earlier by squeezing into them an extraordinary variety of minerals and metals. Where these filled-up fissures will occur is totally unpredictable. Direction, depth, thickness, length, all are, to any prospector, tantalising.

To the old-time prospectors this Kaap Valley, as it is now known, was an even mixture of paradise and hell. Scenically it was a dreamland. Botanically it was quite magnificent: bushy, green, with innumerable flowering plants and elegant trees. The Barberton daisy *(Gerbera jamesonii)* grew in great patches on the valley floor and is now cultivated in gardens throughout the world. On the heights the Pride of De Kaap *(Bauhinia galpinii)* set the valley almost afire each summer with masses of red blossoms. The Christmas protea *(Protea gaguedi)* provided nectar for honey birds and wild bees, while the Paperbark acacia *(Acacia woodii)* trees growing on the floor of the valley looked as though deliberately planned by nature to provide a canopy beneath whose cool shadows a weary animal could find a sheltered resting place.

Strangely enough, to the professional prospector, the elusiveness of its mineral wealth was also one of the charms of the valley. If gold was too easy to find it would have little value. All they needed was the certain knowledge that it was there, concealed somewhere in this complex landscape. The difficulties of finding it would deter the amateurs. The traces of gold in nearly every stream were enough to goad the professionals into crawling on hands and knees over the whole valley, determined to find the source of such precious specks.

Rush for gold

The rusted fragments of thousands of prospecting pans litter the valley today, and with these simple but essential aids the professionals became so adept that in competitions they could pan their own initials,

FEVER TREES Acacia trees, such as these near Pafuri in the Kruger National Park, were regarded with foreboding by early prospectors. Because the trees grew in marsh country, the pioneers feared they might be one of the causes of malaria.

PANNING FOR GOLD In a prospector's pan lies a fine 'tail' of gold, panned near Barberton. Today, the region is littered with the rusted fragments of thousands of such pans – mute testimony to the heady days of the gold rush.

swilling the dirt around until it formed the letters of their names.

Gold was first found at the Duiwelskantoor in 1882. Thousands of men rushed to the scene and some found good alluvial nuggets, but the field was too confined to provide scope for such a throng. From the summit of De Kaap, the prospectors looked down into the valley and the temptation to explore was irresistible.

Monsieur Auguste Robert, better known as French Bob, was one of the most resolute of these prospectors. Over many months he searched through the valley, with the geological clues luring him on as though they were sirens. Testing, sampling, crushing each rock sample with a metal rod called a dolly, panning them beside some mountain stream, he found some traces of minerals nearly every time. Many other parties of prospectors were working in the valley. All were baffled at the multiplicity of clues and the frustration of never finding the parent ore bodies which must have been the mother lodes of such fragments.

In after years, French Bob confessed his own approaching despair and the frustration that was caused by the ever-present, time-consuming burden of finding food. He would have preferred starving so that he could have more time for prospecting. But this left him too weak. He had to hunt and trade skins for basic supplies, but otherwise live mainly on hope.

The samples of rock gathered by any prospector in this valley make beautiful collections. Even a modern geologist has his knowledge well exercised in identifying some of these fragments with their strange patterns, colours and odours. The old timers puzzled over them, but generally had no answers more scientific than the diggers' folklore inherited from the Californian and Australian fields where most of them had worked.

They were all looking for alluvial gold. That was the easiest gold to recover. Mining for reef gold and base metals would involve substantial development costs, and in so wild an area the thought of transporting heavy machinery and becoming involved with financiers was repellent. It is difficult to think of such things as stocks and shares in such a setting. But how marvellous a life for a man who found good alluvial gold, easy to work all by himself. Every day became an absorbing gamble, some days good, some days bad, but with at least enough to live on; and all this in a scenic setting almost beyond belief.

The search for gold

Nickel, chrome, titanium, copper, asbestos, semi-precious stones such as jasper, onyx, buddstone, veraete, verdite, stichtite, all were found in that vast valley. But gold was the real lure. For this, men wagered their lives against the mosquitoes. They searched and searched, carrying their black pans, dollies and dolly pots, and the curiously essential condensed-milk tins and matches. With the dolly they crushed the samples in the dolly pot. One old milk tin filled with powdered rock should leave a tail of gold in the pan at least the length of a safety match. This would mean about 30 g of gold to a ton of ore.

In this vast jumblebox of mineral treasures the prospectors found chert which contained relics of the earliest known form of life, fossil algae. There were complex chemical elements which only future science will apply to man's technology. But gold was the main thing, and one small alluvial discovery followed the other, all profitable but limited in scope.

French Bob found one such alluvial deposit in a stream which bustled along at the bottom of a deep gorge feeding into the Kaap Valley. There was a tremendous argument when a rival prospector

SILENT SYMPHONY (*Overleaf*) The glistening, silvery morning mist . . . the awakening of the forest . . . the luxuriant green of a forest glade. All these, nature has harmonised to orchestrate a symphony of green and silver in the Kruger National Park.

GOLDEN REEF This is the reef that changed the history of South Africa – Pioneer Reef, where French Bob discovered the gold seam that brought a flurry of fortune seekers from all over the world. Beyond the reef are the slopes of the Kaap Valley.

DAY'S FAREWELL The setting sun dips below the escarpment of the north-eastern Transvaal. A lake mirrors the myriad colours of the evening sky. Soon all will be still, except for the night creatures whose forage for food and drink is about to begin.

claimed exclusive rights to the area as a concession given to him by a Swazi queen.

In disgust, French Bob wandered up to the head of the stream. On Sunday, June 3, 1883, he was prospecting. He climbed the high slope, more to see what lay beyond than for anything else. The slopes are steep and still covered in grass and flowering plants, and the view is sublime.

The luck of French Bob

Here, in this supreme setting, fate rewarded French Bob for all his toil and hope. Near the ridge, right on the surface, he found an outcrop of a white-coloured quartz reef. He chipped off a sample and in his hand it glittered with visible gold. This was the Pioneer Reef, the richest gold discovery found anywhere in the world up to that date. News of its discovery created a sensation and brought to South Africa a mass of fortune seekers.

The Pioneer Reef was to prove archetypal of many later discoveries in the Kaap Valley. It was shallow and narrow, less than 1 m wide, but running straight along the ridge, rising and falling for 2 km. It contained many thousands of grams of gold and although the reef required machinery to crush it, the rock was decomposed and easy to work.

The Kaap Valley has never ceased to produce gold since the days of French Bob. In after years he wrote of his disgruntled feelings as, sitting on his claim, he watched the stream of humanity pouring into the erstwhile solitary valley.

'A carrion crow-like gathering,' he wrote. 'They came to snatch the spoil from the hands of the toil-worn and ragged men who had hunted and brought down the prey.'

It was certainly a momentous change in a landscape as ancient as this. The whole area was ransacked and scarred with innumerable workings. Fortunes were made from many of them; delusive finds from others brought misery. French Bob had his share of fortune, lost most of it, and wandered off to other fields. The site of his discovery is now deserted.

From the heights where French Bob sat and watched the arrival of the fortune seekers, the outlook is still Olympian. Overall there is a tremendous stillness. Even the wind seems to move in silence. There is a sweetness to the air from the aromatic herbs and flowering plants. Complex masses of clouds build up and sweep high over the encircling rim of mountains. When the thunder comes it rolls long and slowly across the full length of the valley and then echoes back, sullen and threatening, from the furthest rim. The valley is darkened in shadows. As the storm breaks, the flashes of lightning illuminate a landscape as wildly beautiful as it was very soon after the time when the earth began.

Where splendour tumbles from the sky

*The thunder, flurry, excitement,
whirls, eddies, backlashes and dangers
of a big waterfall are what provide
a river with its episodes of drama and
romance, of adventure or tragedy.*

BOOMING GORGE Suddenly the bed of the Karkloof River vanishes into space. The river hurtles headlong into a gorge that lies a dizzy 115 m below. The roaring of this mighty waterfall echoes in a hilly, tree-cloaked area near Howick in Natal.

*An inferno of spray, chaotic
water and thunder, as rivers
fall off the high plateau*

A RIVER without at least one waterfall would be like a human being going through life without a love affair. It can be done, but it would be rather dull. The thunder, flurry, excitement, whirls, eddies, back-lashes and dangers of a really big fall are what provide a river with its episodes of drama and romance, of adventure or tragedy.

The lie of the land in Southern Africa – the entire area is like an inverted saucer – makes it difficult for any river to find its way to the sea without a waterfall or stretch of rapids. At some stage there has to be a sharp drop in altitude. Even in reasonably flat areas, nature occasionally trips up some easy-going river by placing across its course an obstruction of rock, which forces the stream into a spasm of activity before it once again reverts to its former languor.

Southern Africa's major rivers, the Zambezi, Orange, Limpopo and Tugela, can muster between them two of the world's greatest waterfalls (Victoria and Augrabies) and a host of lovely cascades and smaller falls.

The Tugela River has a magnificent example of such a 'smaller' fall – small only in the volume of water that plummets over it, not in the dizzy height of its drop. The Tugela, which is the principal river of Natal, has its source on the plateau summit of Mont-aux-Sources, in the Drakensberg. This mountain, 3282 m high, is a notable watershed. A stone's throw away from the source of the Tugela, a second spring acts as the source of the Elands River, one of the principal tributaries of the Vaal, itself the major tributary of the Orange, which flows westwards to the Atlantic. The Tugela flows eastwards to the Indian Ocean. A flake of snow falling on the finely graded summit of the watershed could melt in such a way that its water would be shared by two oceans separated by 1500 km of very rugged country.

Three leaps into space

Both droplets of water, however, would have an immediate adventure in common. They would have to tumble off the summit of the mountain and, by means of a succession of falls and cascades, lose nearly 2000 m in altitude within the first few kilometres of their progress. Both rivers provide a

magnificent spectacle in the course of their drops.

The Tugela falls in three successive leaps into sheer space. The upper fall, 800 m in height, is very often frozen in winter into pinnacles of ice. The centre fall is generally partly vaporised. The lower fall sways in the winds as its water condenses and then, gathering strength from several tributaries, forces a way through a gorge sliced as a narrow gash through sandstone rock.

Flowing on to the sea, the Tugela has worn for itself a vast valley, wild and beautiful, with the river, its winding course full of cascades and rapids, providing some classic examples of incisions and meanders. This stretch of the river traditionally formed the boundary between Natal and Zululand. It presents a scene rugged and primitive, fully justifying its Zulu name – *Thukela* (the startling one).

Eight rivers in all have their sources on the western side of Mont-aux-Sources, a mountain which is really a gigantic sponge, its basalt soaking up rain and melting snow, and feeding crystal-clear water out through innumerable little springs. The rivers of the western side all flow through the highlands of Lesotho, gradually unite and supply the Orange.

All of these tributaries have their rapids and water-falls. But it is another of the tributaries of the upper Orange, the Maletsunyane, which has a particularly enchanting waterfall at a place called *Semonkong* (the place of smoke), from the vapours rising

LAND OF CASCADES Southern Africa is shaped like an inverted saucer. Waterfalls abound as rivers tumble off the high plateau.

ENCHANTED VALLEY Maletsunyane Waterfall at *Semonkong* (the place of smoke) in Lesotho tumbles down a gorge which has an eerie atmosphere. It is a place which has given birth to many legends of ghosts. In winter these falls can be frozen into a twisted ribbon of ice.

through the high, clear air.

This waterfall is 250 m high. Like the Tugela Falls, it freezes in winter into a ribbed sheet of ice. This is a remarkable sight; but it is in summer, when the river has its most powerful flow, that the falls produce an effect that is even more remarkable. The river tumbles into a deep gorge eroded into black basalt rock, and the gorge is full of echoes and weird sounds. Perhaps there are prosaic explanations for these sounds, but the local tribespeople are convinced that they are the calls of sirens, and the despairing wails of victims who have fallen into this flurry of white water.

The Orange: from trickle to flood

The Orange River has its own source in the highlands of Lesotho, on the western side of one of the most handsome of the Drakensberg peaks, known as *Mweni* (the place of fingers), because of the sharp pinnacles of basalt which give it a distinctive shape. From this source to its mouth in the Atlantic Ocean, the Orange finds its way for nearly 2000 km through

FALLS OF TRAGEDY An air of melancholy hangs over towering Howick Falls. The son of the first settler in Howick was carried to his death over the 102 m high falls, and since then there have been several other tragedies at the same spot.

THE CONQUEROR When the irresistible force of the Orange River met a seemingly immovable object of a barrier of granite millions of years ago, it was the river that won. And so the Augrabies Falls, a fury of noise and pounding waters, were created.

country which becomes increasingly drier until, in contrast to the downpour and snowstorms at its source, the river reaches its end in the area of the Namib Desert where rainfall is practically unknown.

Of all the world's great rivers, the Orange is subject to the biggest variations of flow. In a single year it can range from little more than a trickle, half lost in the centre of a sandy bed, to a raging flood, eddying through a course up to 7 km wide.

The Hottentot tribes knew the Orange simply as the *!Garib* (the river). To them, it was the river of all rivers, and nothing else deserved that name. Its muddy waters, surging westwards through an arid wilderness, made life possible in areas which without it would have been completely in the grip of drought. Erratic as was its flow, its pools never dried, and the

islands of rich alluvial soil scattered along its length provided wild fruits and grazing for livestock.

In the very midst of the wilderness, the Orange (so-named by Europeans in honour of the Prince of Orange) thunders down a set of falls so tremendous that it ranks as one of the six greatest waterfalls of the world; and the gorge in which it occurs is considered by geologists as the finest example in the world of weathering by water action on a massive formation of granite.

The Orange encountered this barrier of granite

QUEEN OF WATERFALLS (*Overleaf*) Victoria, boiling, seething, glistening, is the undisputed queen of all waterfalls. Its famous rainbow is present by day and by night, when a full moon creates an eerie-looking lunar rainbow.

MILE-HIGH LEAP From the Mont-aux-Sources plateau, the Thukela River takes a gigantic leap into space – the first stage of a descent that will end more than 2000 m below. At one point the water has an uninterrupted fall of more than 600 m.

GOLDEN CASCADE The Lisbon Falls, overspill of the Eastern Transvaal watershed, near *Graskop* (grassy peak). This is an area of many waterfalls, and most of the rivers carry alluvial gold which can still reward a lucky prospector.

millions of years ago. With ruthless energy the river cut a knife-like wound, on average 260 m deep, through the solid rock. In a series of preliminary falls and cascades, the river loses over 100 m in altitude. Then it forces its way through a narrow gap and falls another 100 m in a sheer drop.

At the bottom of this fall there is a deep pool, supposedly the haunt of a huge serpent and certainly the home of several giant mud barbels, a fish reaching a length of 2 m. Fortune seekers also fancy that this pool contains many diamonds, washed down the Orange, over the fall and then trapped deep in the granite gorge.

An inferno of spray

When the Orange is in spate, there are 19 waterfalls tumbling into this gorge. Each is about 100 m high,

DIAMOND GORGE (*Preceding pages*) The gorge of the Augrabies is rumoured to be rich in diamonds, washed down from the Orange River 100 m above. When the river is in flood, as many as 19 separate falls plunge into the gorge.

and the place is a veritable inferno of spray, chaotic water and thundering sound. It is from this noise that the Hottentots named the fall *!oukurubes* (the noisy place). Europeans, trying to pronounce the name without the click, made it Augrabies.

For 10 km the river rushes through its gorge, losing over 350 m in a series of rapids and minor falls. It is joined by several tributary gorges and presents a scene of savage power in the wilderness. The ceaseless, darting flight of swifts adds to the atmosphere of this primeval place.

Some of the most beautiful falls in Southern Africa are found in the smaller rivers. The Mngeni River in Natal has a very rugged course including, for the latter part of its route, the Valley of a Thousand Hills. Near the town of Howick, the river takes a headlong plunge of 102 m into a gorge.

Back in the days of tribal legend, this waterfall of Howick for some reason acquired a sinister reputation. A path forded the river just above the fall, and many Africans in past years were carried away to their deaths. The coming of Europeans saw the path developed as a road, and the waterfall claimed even more victims.

Close to the Howick Falls there are three other falls, all of which have claimed a quota of human lives. One of these falls, the Karkloof Falls, in a tributary of the Mngeni known as the Karkloof, is 115 m high and, tumbling into a deep, thickly wooded gorge, outstanding in its beauty.

Many of Southern Africa's most spectacular falls are in the Eastern Transvaal. Montrose, near Nelspruit; Berlyn, Lisbon, Debegeni; the gorgeous fall of the Elands River at Waterval Boven; the twin Mac-Mac Falls; all are compellingly beautiful features in a region already rich in excitement with its big game and its stirring memories of gold rushes.

Zimbabwe, too, has a rich collection of waterfalls. In the mountainous eastern districts, along the border with Moçambique, there are five waterfalls in such rivers as the Mutare, Nyangombe and Odzani; and there is the tremendous fall of the Mutarazi into the deep gorge of the Muhonde. The very name echoes the sound made by the water as it crashes down. On the Moçambique side there is a 200 m high fall, Martin's Falls, in the Mubvumodzi River.

If legend is to be believed, this waterfall is the home of so many water spirits of assorted shapes and temperaments that the place must have the social life of a medium-sized town.

Where the Great River flows

It is the Zambezi River, however, which contains the supreme waterfall – one of the great natural wonders of the world – the Victoria Falls. The origin of this waterfall is proof that the creative power of nature can have fun in modelling landscape.

The Zambezi has its source in a lonely grove of trees on the watershed which forms the boundary between Zaire and Zambia. For 1200 km the river, known here by the Aluyi tribespeople as the *Lwambayi* (great river), flows in fairly easy fashion across the sheet of lava which forms the central plateau of Zambia. A few rapids and the minor Gonye Falls alone provide any change to the even current. It is a lazy, sulky sort of river, spreading out each year in vast floods, and then retreating in the dry seasons to its course in a shallow valley for another period of somnambulance.

It is at this stage that nature has played a joke on the river. As the 300 m thick layer of molten lava cooled, long before the Zambezi took its present course, great cracks opened up, as if lying in wait for any unwary river that might come their way. These

Alpine swift (*Apus melba*)

The weather bird

Birds are not commonly associated with waterfalls, so it is all the more surprising that one of the sights at the mighty Augrabies Falls is a flock of swifts cruising endlessly up and down the gorge – sometimes just above the boiling waters, sometimes high over the spray.

They are alpine swifts, among the world's greatest flyers. There are several different races of alpine swifts – in Southern Europe, India and East and South Africa – and there is no evidence of any traffic between them.

One thing they have in common – their almost totally aerial existence. Their legs are so seldom used, and therefore so weak, that swifts are practically helpless on the ground, and it is only with difficulty that they can take off to return to their natural element, the air. When they rest from flying they usually cling to trees or cliffs, from which it is an easy matter to topple back into the air.

Not only do they feed exclusively on insects taken in flight, and drink by scooping water as they fly over it; they also mate in mid-air, and collect the feathers and scraps of vegetation from which they make their nests on the wing.

It has even been suggested that they snatch short periods of sleep on the wing, cat-napping on currents of rising air.

Their nests, which they glue together with their saliva, are usually in crevices and under ledges on cliffs. They can act as interesting weather indicators, for they have a habit of flying high before an approaching depression, screaming loudly . . . often so high that only their cries betray their presence. They do this in pursuit of the hordes of insects that move ahead of a cold front, so whenever such a crowd of swifts is seen or heard, bad weather may safely be forecast.

START OF A LONG JOURNEY The Elands River tumbles off the Mont-aux-Sources plateau at the start of its journey to reach first the Vaal, then the Orange. Via those rivers it eventually flows to the Atlantic Ocean, over 1200 km away.

POOL OF MYSTERY The Berlyn Falls in the Eastern Transvaal, like a silvery-white pillar, plummet 80 m into a deep, dark pool. Bushmen told chilling tales of bizarre creatures supposed to inhabit such pools. Certainly, many contain large fish.

cracks, filled with relatively soft material, run east to west, across the course of the Zambezi.

As it slowly scoured out the bed of its present valley, the Zambezi discovered the first of these cracks and automatically began to wash out the soft material which filled it. The river immediately found itself in a trap of its own making. Into this trench the river tumbled happily enough, but obviously could not be quite so happy about tumbling out again. At this stage, in fact, it must have been thrown into a great agitation, with the full flow of water tumbling into the trench and then climbing over the opposite edge in order to continue its journey.

A laborious process began of searching for a weakness in the lower edge of the trench. The dislodgment of one massive boulder would have provided the first gap in this lower edge. The full weight of the river's flow would immediately have been concentrated at this point. The gap would rapidly have been converted into an escape gorge and, with the river narrowed at this point, scoured deep to take the full force of the flow.

By this time a tremendous spectacle had been created. Across its full width the river tumbled headlong into a deep trench, full of mist and thundering echoes. With the river escaping from this trench through a narrow gap, almost the full length of the down-river edge was left dry as a marvellous observation platform.

The next stage was the destruction of the waterfall when a weak spot was found in the upper edge of the crevice. This would be widened and deepened until the whole flow of the river poured through it, as a mighty cascade or rapid. This flow, however, scoured the bed of the river backwards, and soon uncovered another east-west fault in the lava. Once again, the river washed out the soft filling, and once again found itself caught in a trap.

Why Victoria Falls will vanish

During the last half million years, the Zambezi has scoured out no fewer than eight successive trenches, and had to find an escape route from each of them. Each trench, in its day, must have provided a wonderful spectacle from its down-river edge. The fate of each of these waterfalls was precisely the approaching fate of the Victoria Falls.

The present fall occurs where the river is nearly 2 km wide and 110 m high, with 545 megalitres of water tumbling down each minute at average maximum flow. This mighty flow has already found the weakest spot along the upper lip of the present

trench. This is what is known as the Devil's Cataract. Already some 30 m lower than the rest of the falls, the cataract will be deepened until all the water can shoulder its way through this one gap. The rest of the waterfall will then disappear, and the river will flow through one more leg of an involved series of zigzag gorges.

Nature, however, is far from finished with the Zambezi. At least two more faults are clearly visible across the course of the river and there are likely to be several more, as yet invisible. For another half million years at least, the Zambezi is likely to be busy washing out trenches and creating new waterfalls, each with an ideal observation platform running the full length of the opposite side of the gorge.

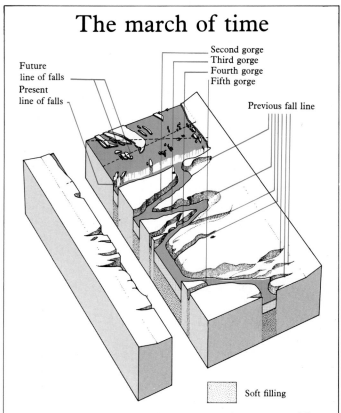

The march of time

The Victoria Falls are for ever on the retreat. The present falls are the eighth to have appeared on a zig-zag path during the past half million years. Each waterfall appears at a fault in the lava bed of the river, which is cracked like crazy paving, with some cracks across its path, and others linking them. The river scours out the soft filling from a fault, and tumbles into the void it has created for itself. Immediately, it begins the task of scouring out one of the 'linking' cracks, cutting back a gorge until it reaches another 'crossways' fault. The Devil's Cataract is such a gorge in the making.

FROM TINY GAP TO GREAT GORGE The queen of waterfalls, the Victoria Falls, tumbling into the great gorge which it has scoured out across its course. At the top is the Devil's Cataract, where the river has found a weak spot in the upper edge of the gorge.

VICTORIA'S MAJESTY In a majestic curtain of spray, the Zambezi thunders over the main falls of Victoria. But mighty as they are, the falls are doomed. The Devil's Cataract is 'stealing' their waters, and in time they will be left high and dry.

LIVINGSTONE'S FIRST VIEW This was the sight that greeted David Livingstone in November 1855 – columns of spray rising high above the falls. He saw them from 8 km away, and later described the falls as 'the most wonderful sight I had witnessed in Africa'.

When all the work is done, the mighty Zambezi will have made for itself a course through so complex a series of gorges that it will have some difficulty in deciding whether it is flowing east, west or even up or down.

Livingstone names the falls

It is below the gorges that the river, flowing through 750 km of some of the wildest country in Africa, receives its name of *Zambezi* (the great river), from the Tonka tribespeople. This name it carries until it reaches the sandy flats of Moçambique, where it becomes the *Kwamo* (river of great floods).

The Victoria Falls also has a variety of names. The now vanished Kololo people, who once lived above the waterfall, named it *Mosi o Thunya* (the smoke that thunders). The Ndebele named it *aManza Thungayo* (the water which rises like smoke). The Kololo regarded the falls with such dread that they never ventured near them. The Tonka chiefs from below the falls offered sacrifices to their ancestors at three tabu places, each within sight of the rainbow, which seemed to them to mark the presence of God.

David Livingstone gave the falls the name of Queen Victoria when he first saw them on November 16, 1855. The missionary-explorer reached the falls by travelling down-river in a canoe from the Kololo country. From 8 km upstream he had first seen the rising plumes of vapour. There were five of them, their white bases standing out distinctly against a dark background of wooded hill, while their summits seemed to mingle with the clouds. The fact that they seemed to become darker as they ascended made the resemblance to smoke remarkably authentic.

Landing on Kazeruka Island, in the middle of the river, Livingstone crept with awe to its extremity and from there, lying face down, received his staggering first view of the falls by peering directly into the prodigious fault which causes the whole spectacle. The next day he returned again to the island and planted some peach and apricot stones, as well as coffee seeds. He also cut his initials and the date 1855 into a tree trunk. This was the only place, as he afterwards confided to the hunter William Baldwin, where, from the west to the east coast of Africa, he had the vanity to leave his initials.

233

Lifting the lid of a treasure chest

Wealth embedded in the rock
is sometimes hidden deep, sometimes
so near the surface
that a mere scratch
reveals the glitter of riches.

A FORTUNE FROM ROCK These gleaming emeralds, seen beside their parent rock, in which some are still embedded, were mined at Sandawana in Zimbabwe. The green lustre of these gemstones comes from the presence of minute traces of chromium.

*The land often reaches beyond
man's wildest dreams . . .
creating bitter heartache*

SOUTHERN AFRICA'S dramatic landscape is the lid of a gigantic treasure chest. To prospectors, geologists and geophysicists who strive to raise the lid, the real wonders of the country are beneath the surface.

Sometimes the treasure is hidden deep; sometimes a mere scratch on the surface reveals a glittering hoard of riches.

Despite its mineral wealth, Africa's most vital underground treasure is water. Rich mineral deposits still lie unworked in many arid areas because of the lack of water to sustain life and industry.

Water which becomes trapped underground first drains through faults, cracks, or porous rocks. Such water, moving about, trying to find its way to lower depths, is known as vadose water. Eventually it reaches what is known as a phreatic zone, beyond which, through lack of porosity of the rocks, it can sink no further. Here the water is contained, saturating rocks and soil, filling faults and crevices, with its upper level forming what is known as the water table.

The water table is not continuous, or even horizontal. It follows the contours of the land surface, at a depth influenced by the amount of phreatic water in a particular area. A heavy rain raises the water table; in a dry season the water table subsides, leaking out faster than it can be replaced.

Heat from the earth's core

The deeper the water, the closer it is to the molten core of the earth. On average, temperatures increase by 1°C for every 50 m of descent into the bowels of the earth. A phreatic deposit of heated water intersected by a valley surfaces as a hot spring.

There are vast numbers of these hot springs in Southern Africa. The hottest is the Zongola geyser, at the confluence of the Gwayi and Zambezi rivers. It emerges with a temperature of 90°C. Most of the others, 73 main ones in South Africa alone, emerge with temperatures of around 50°C. All contain chemicals claimed to have curative properties.

Around some, highly developed spas have grown, notably at Aliwal North in the Cape. Two thermal springs surface there at 34,4°C. They originate at a depth of 1250 m, and artesian pressure forces them to the surface.

The water of these springs is forced upwards because there is a basin structure to the underground rocks. Rainwater flows down the lips, or ridge, of the basin, seeps into the centre under pressure, is heated, then surfaces up some line of weakness. If the lips of the basin were higher, the pressure on the water would force it out of the ground in a jet or geyser, as happens in many parts of the world.

Several hot springs in the Transvaal have been used medicinally since prehistoric times – and not just by man. Bushmen and Bantu hunters believed that elephants wallowed in the mud of hot springs to relieve rheumatism.

When the spring known to the Sotho people as *Bela Bela* (the boiling place) was developed by Europeans at Warmbaths, in the Transvaal, a vast accumulation of skeletons of man and wild animals, but especially of elephants, was found in the mud and soggy vegetation which formed a morass around the spring. This spring, rising at 25 000 litres an hour, reveals the presence of its 49°C water by a column of steam, especially on cold mornings.

The behaviour of some of these underground springs is a puzzle. Near Cradock in the Cape, a group of boreholes contains water which rises and falls in the same rhythm as the sea tides. Yet the spring water is fresh, and the sea is 500 km away.

At Caledon in the Cape, seven springs surface

NATURE'S BOUNTY With two notable omissions – oil and water – nature has been prodigal with her gifts to Southern Africa.

236

close together. Six of them are at a temperature of 50°C; the seventh is cold. All are rich in iron.

More than 450 000 boreholes have been sunk in Southern Africa to tap underground water. Most of them are worked by wind-pumps, and these simple but efficient devices make arid areas of the country habitable to man and his domestic animals.

In the Cape, South West Africa and Botswana, the water is saline but still drinkable – human beings can consume water containing up to 1500 parts of salt per million before it becomes unpalatable. In some arid areas, the inhabitants have never tasted what is known as 'sweet' or pure water. Livestock actually seem to prefer this mineral water, and can absorb about 6000 parts of salt per million.

Some springs, such as that in the salt pan at the western end of the *Soutpansberg* (Salt-Pan Mountains) in the Northern Transvaal, have such a concentration of salt as to be undrinkable. The water is clear green and very cold. It is pumped into evaporation pools where the pure salt it leaves is collected.

Alkali-flavoured water is found in springs in the Northern Transvaal and around Lesotho. Carbonate water comes from the south-western Transvaal and the Northern Cape, while saline-chloride water comes from Natal and the Eastern Cape. The concentration of sulphuretted hydrogen or nitrogen in some of the springs is so strong that it catches alight, and burns at night with an effect like will-o'-the-wisps. At Aliwal North, the gas escape is so considerable that for years it was trapped and led off to be used for heating in the kitchens of the spa's restaurant.

About 1,5 million tons of salt are recovered each year from salt springs and salt pans in Southern Africa. Depressions in low, poorly-drained parts of the central plateau accumulate salt washed down by rainwater. Salt pans occur in areas of high evaporation. During dry weather, salt is swept from the surface, while boreholes feed the water into evaporation pools. The colour of each pool—ranging from blood red to snow white, almost as though ice is forming on the surface in defiance of the hot rays of the sun – depends on the extent of evaporation and the concentration of salts.

A dream sea of gold
Springs and run-off water have been responsible for some extraordinary mineral concentrations. The gold deposit of the Witwatersrand, the greatest subterranean treasure so far found by man, was created by water action, although the details of how this actually happened are complex and controversial.

It seems most likely that there was, about 1000 million years ago, an inland sea or lake on the site of the Witwatersrand. It was to become a strange dream sea of gold. Into this sea, rain washed a rich spoil of erosion. Included in the spoil, apart from pebbles and silt, were carbon, uranium, iron pyrites, chromite, gold and silver, as well as small green diamonds.

This mixture was deposited on the sea floor in layers. Their nature varied because of changes in climate, water currents, and the material available as spoil for the eroding water. The sea level also changed. Eventually, the basin was filled and dried up. The bed solidified. Over the ages it was subjected to immense pressures. It was twisted, tilted, faulted and exposed to extremes of heat and cold. Lava from subterranean deeps intruded into it. Its minerals were partly dissolved and redistributed.

The whole was transformed, to the extent that if there was indeed an ancient sea it has vanished completely, but has left behind a shroud of gold and other precious things – a shroud below which no life ever made a home.

Something like 1000 million years passed, with this strange series of rocks and sediments, like a huge saucer, buried deep beneath a later overburden of volcanic and sedimentary material. The saucer tilted. Its rim reached the surface to form the *Witwatersrand* (ridge of white waters).

This was the lid of a real treasure chest of nature. Prehistoric man lifted it a little and extracted iron. Pioneer Europeans found specks of gold in streams, but their origin was a mystery.

An 1801 map of the South African interior showed the Witwatersrand, and marked it as rich in gold, but prospectors searched without success. The 73 families who farmed along the ridge eked out a living, isolated from markets for their produce, their nondescript homes huddling in hollows for shelter from winter's cold, dry, frosty winds.

Riddle of the Rand
The man who found the answer to the riddle of the specks of gold arrived in December 1885. In that summer month, when the Witwatersrand was green and warm, a shabby-looking man who spoke with an Australian accent, George Harrison, tramped up to the Witwatersrand and secured a job building a house for Johan Oosthuizen, on the farm *Langlaagte* (the long dale). Harrison was on his way to prospect in the Eastern Transvaal but, short of money, he took on this constructional work to help him on his way.

Harrison, taciturn and almost illiterate, fossicked

around during his spare hours. He never said anything then or afterwards about how it happened, but some time in March 1886 he crushed, as others had done before, a sample of the conglomerate. The sample he panned came from the Main Reef, at one of the few places where it was exposed. He panned it in one of the streams and without great hope looked down into the battered black pan and saw the dirt dissolve and swirl away. Suddenly, there was a marvellous glitter. The treasure chest was open.

Harrison made little from his find. He registered it, and received the usual free discoverer's claim but, an alluvial miner at heart, sold it for £10 when the great rush started, and vanished. There is a legend that he passed that way some years afterwards, looked at the boom city of Johannesburg in disgust and opined that he was sorry he had ever done it.

The extent of the Main Reef is still unknown. More than R1000 million worth of gold has so far been extracted from it. The deepest gold mines in the world probe down into it. The E.R.P.M. (East Rand Proprietory Mine) shaft at Boksburg goes down 3240 m, and ore is known to extend deeper than 15 000 m. The limits of recovery are set, not by the extent of the reef, but by technical problems and costs. Every day, 40 000 tons of ice are used in the E.R.P.M. shaft to provide a reasonable temperature.

Apart from gold, the Witwatersrand reefs are prolific producers of silver, to the extent of 1 part silver to every 10 parts of gold; and of iron pyrites, a pale, brass-yellow coloured mineral composed of 53,4 per cent sulphur and 46,6 per cent iron. Once known as fool's gold because it was thought to be valueless, iron pyrites is today used to make sulphuric acid. Uranium oxide (uraninite) is also abundant.

The basin containing the Witwatersrand System is about 300 km by 150 km and is tilted southwards, deep below the Karoo System. Using magnetometers, geophysicists have traced the gold-bearing reefs to the west of the Rand, where they are buried under such thick masses of water-saturated dolomite that to reach them miners have to resort to the most extraordinary feats of applied science. At Blyvooruitzicht, one of the world's richest gold mines, they had to plug an influx of nearly two million litres of water an hour which suddenly burst through a fissure 500 m below the surface as the shaft was being sunk.

In the Orange Free State, the gold-bearing reefs, known there as the Basal Reefs, were traced as a result of the sinking of more than 500 boreholes. More than 100 brought significant quantities of gold to the surface. One, on the farm *Geduld* (Patience),

produced from a depth of 1300 m a sample which contained nearly 20 per cent of pure gold. Its assay of 23 037 inch-dwt staggered the mining world, as it was the richest ever found.

Near the centre of the sea of gold, there is an island of granite. This mass of granite forced its way up through the bed of the sea in the shape of a great dome. The complete succession of Witwatersrand beds, shattered and overturned, is exposed around this Vredefort Dome. Unfortunately, not much gold was deposited here and prospectors are tantalised simply by traces.

The coming of diamonds
Diamonds came to Southern Africa in a totally different manner from the gold of the Witwatersrand, and most of the deposits are far more recent. Towards the end of the Cretaceous Period, about 65 million years ago, there was a spurt of volcanic activity. Groups of volcanic throats, or pipes, were blown up through the earth's crust from very deep levels. These pipes allowed a flow of soft, waxy, blue-coloured volcanic rock, known as kimberlite, to reach the surface. Exposed to the atmosphere, the kimberlite weathered to form what is called yellow ground. The material, being soft, was easily eroded away, and the crater cones disappeared, dispersed over the land surface by the wind and the rain.

From the surface down, however, the pipes were filled with the blue-coloured kimberlite – called blue ground near the surface, and hardebank at depth. In this kimberlite there are often considerable numbers of diamonds. How they get there remains uncertain. Diamonds are made of carbon under tremendous pressure, but kimberlite itself contains no carbon. It simply acts as the host to the diamonds, which must have been formed deep down, where the pressures are immense. Kimberlite is actually a volcanic rock of exceptionally deep origin, deeper even than basalt.

The diamonds are found as well-formed crystals, broken crystals or cleavage fragments. Their colour also varies. There are white stones tinged with yellow – known as 'Capes' and 'Silver Capes' – greens, greys, blacks, browns, rare blue-white and several other shades. Of the 150 pipes so far found in Southern Africa, 30 contain diamonds in commercial quantities, and each produces diamonds with its own identifiable characteristics. Contained in the kimberlite are several other 'passengers'. Coming from the depths, it picked up fragments of the older rock formations penetrated by the pipe, including ancient material not found anywhere on the surface of the

THE TRUE . . . When gold is as easily seen as this in its parent rock, prospectors know that they have discovered an immensely rich deposit. Compare this sample of gold-bearing rock, from Zimbabwe, with the fool's gold illustrated overleaf.

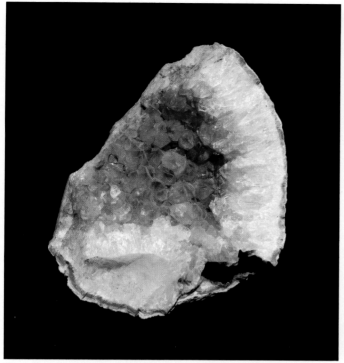

THE EYE OF THE BEHOLDER . . . Amethyst (above) is a form of quartz, one of the most widespread minerals on earth. The difference between a gemstone and any other mineral is a matter of how much it is valued by man for its beauty and rarity.

SPANNING THE CENTURIES Beryl (above) as well as producing emeralds, which have been used in jewellery for thousands of years, is the source of beryllium, a metal that is used in atomic science, and in the production of modern lightweight alloys.

earth. This material ranges in size from pebbles to huge masses weighing millions of tons.

The pipes do not seem to have any particular relation to one another. The diamonds may have been picked up from some deep zone below, or gaseous compounds of carbon may have infiltrated the kimberlite and been formed into diamonds by pressure. They probably had a variety of origins. Each successive upheaval of kimberlite in the pipes contains diamonds slightly different from the others. The kimberlite must have risen up the pipes in a series of convulsive movements.

The message of the leaves

Best known of the volcanic pipes containing diamonds are those at Kimberley, the Premier Mine near Pretoria, the Finsch Mine in the Northern Cape and the Orapa Mine in Botswana. The Williamson Mine in Tanzania is also a diamond-bearing pipe.

Other pipes still await discovery, for many have eroded away and lie hidden. If the kimberlite is near the surface it can affect vegetation, and a prospector

. . . AND THE FALSE Many an old-time prospector has had his hopes dashed because what he thought was gold turned out, on analysis, to be iron pyrites – fool's gold. But today this once worthless mineral is a source of sulphuric acid for industry.

needs to be a botanist as well as a mineralogist, closely observing changes in the colour of the leaves of trees, or in the nature of grass.

In November 1961, Allister Fincham, a miner prospecting for asbestos, observed just such a vegetation change a little to the west of Kimberley. It led to a R4,5 million fortune for Fincham and his partner, a trader named Schwabel who had grubstaked him. What he had discovered was the great diamond mine that was to be named, after both partners, the Finsch.

The exact origin of some diamond deposits remains a mystery. On March 13, 1926, Jacobus Voorendyk, with an African labourer, was digging holes for fence poles on his farm *Elandsputte* (the wells of the eland) in the Western Transvaal. As they dug the last hole, the African suddenly exclaimed 'Here is a diamond'. The two men looked at the small 0,75 carat chip in disbelief. They washed it in a bucket of water, but they knew nothing of diamonds. It could have been glass.

Voorendyk saddled a horse and rode into Lichtenburg, where his father was postmaster. They took the chip to the science master at the local high school. He was sceptical, but he put it in a bottle of acid and left it for the weekend. On Monday morning the men almost tiptoed back to see it. It sparkled cheerily at them.

The rush that followed was one of the most frenzied ever known. Within 12 months there were 108 000 people on the Lichtenburg diamond diggings. More than 30 000 men took part in some of the claim-pegging races organised by the authorities. Some were hired athletes, others scampered to the diggings on crutches. Many magnificent gemstones were found. The rush which started on *Elandsputte* wandered like a tornado over the veld, following what was apparently once a river valley.

The diamonds were found in irregular patches or runs of gravel. They were maddeningly unpredictable. There could be a fortune made on one claim, and prospects of starvation on neighbouring diggings. The gravel, resting on dolomite, filled unexpected depressions, but suddenly thinned out or vanished if

the dolomite approached the surface. Occasionally there were sink holes or pot holes, where the dolomite had collapsed. These pot holes, such as King's pot hole, could exceed 30 m in depth and contain a collection of diamonds, as though a prodigious jewellery box had been tipped into them.

If the Witwatersrand was originally a dream sea of gold, then this was a dream river of diamonds.

Men searched for its beginning, but it seemed to come from nowhere. At the height of the rush there was a cloud of dust over the whole area so thick that motorists had to keep their headlamps burning in daytime as a safeguard against collision.

The great rush to Lichtenburg petered out in 1953, but a few hopefuls still fossick in the area today and sometimes find a few diamonds which the multitude

DESERT ROSE As well as being generously endowed with gemstones, precious metals and minerals of all kinds, Southern Africa is prolific in descriptive names for its underground wealth. Gypsum (above) is aptly named 'the desert rose'.

overlooked. The landscape for kilometres has the appearance of a vast battlefield, scarred and devastated like a no-man's-land.

The classic diamond pipes will always be those at Kimberley. This town has a particular place in the hearts of the women of the world, for from these great pipes have come the gemstones for countless engagement rings and gorgeous pieces of jewellery.

The Big Hole of Kimberley is the deepest open pit ever excavated by man. It has a diameter of 500 m and a circumference of 1,6 km. Three Empire State Buildings, one on top of the other, would comfortably fit into it. The Big Hole was excavated as an open-cast working for 400 m, then continued down for another 900 m, as an underground working. More than 25 million tons of kimberlite were removed and 14 504 566 carats of diamonds recovered before operations ceased in 1914 (1 carat equals 200 mg).

The Big Hole started off as a hillock known as Colesberg Koppie, on which three diamonds were found on July 18, 1871, by a very drunk servant named Damon employed by Fleetwood Rawstone, a digger working a claim near by at Du Toits Pan. Seven hundred claims were pegged on top of the great pipe at Colesberg Koppie. At first each claim was separately worked. Chaos came as the diggers worked deeper into the volcanic throat. Individual workers tried the most ingenious ways of reaching their own claims and hauling away the kimberlite, but this became impossible. Amalgamation into one vast working was the only solution, and so it was that the organising genius of such men as Cecil Rhodes and Barney Barnato brought them to almost unbelievable fortune and control of the diamond industry.

Four diamondiferous pipes are still worked in the vicinity of Kimberley. The output from them is about 19 carats per 70 000 kg of blue ground. The richest pipe worked in Southern Africa is the Premier Mine near Pretoria. Its diamond output is 29 carats per 70 000 kg of blue ground. Discovered in 1902 by Thomas Cullinan, this huge pipe for long produced the bulk of South Africa's gemstones.

The world's finest diamond

It was in this mine, at 5.30 p.m. on January 26, 1905, that a miner called Fred Wells, just before knocking off for the day, found a colossal diamond, 3106 carats in mass – by far the most valuable diamond ever found. It was named the Cullinan Diamond, and General Louis Botha, the Prime Minister of the Transvaal, suggested that the State buy the diamond and present it to the British monarch as an expression of gratitude for the granting of responsible government to the Transvaal.

The State already owned 60 per cent of the diamond through taxation and other rights. The mining company sold its 40 per cent for a nominal sum. The diamond was taken to Amsterdam, where it was cut and polished by a master cutter, Joseph Asscher. It ended as the 530 carat 'Star of South Africa', the smaller Cullinan II, III, IV and several brilliants – all set in the British Crown Jewels.

The bottom has not been reached in any of these diamondiferous pipes. As with the Witwatersrand gold mines, the deeper the mine the greater its working costs. But for at least 50 years to come diamonds will continue to be produced from the Premier Mine, the various Kimberley mines and other pipes such as Jagersfontein and Koffiefontein. New pipes, such as the Finsch Mine, will certainly be found.

Fissures filled with diamond-bearing kimberlite are also mined in the Vaal River area. With other vast deposits in Namaqualand and South West Africa, it is not likely that South Africa will ever be short of diamonds. Since that momentous day in 1866, when a 15-year-old boy, Erasmus Jacobs, found a glittering stone on a farm near Hopetown in the Cape, and the magistrate at Colesberg tentatively identified it as a diamond by scratching the letters 'DP' into the window of his office, an astronomical fortune in diamonds has been found in South Africa with more than 7 million carats, valued at more than R90 million, being the current annual production.

Gold, copper and iron were the earliest minerals mined in Southern Africa. In prehistoric times these three metals were mined extensively, especially in Zimbabwe, and practically every surface outcrop in the country was worked.

On a strange, isolated, flat-topped hill known as *maPhungubwe* (place of jackals), in the Northern Transvaal, a long-vanished tribe known as the Leya had a settlement which has left modern archaeologists with a rich treasure trove in beads, bangles, ornaments and plates, all made of solid gold.

These ancient miners all seem to have been women. The male smelters poured the molten metal, iron as well as copper, into moulds scooped in the ground and, for some reason lost in tradition, shaped like cooking pots with clusters of small legs at the bottom. These were standard trade items, accepted all over Southern Africa.

In the late 1890s a white hermit, called Wild Lotrie, who lived in the wilderness, told a prospector in Rhodesia, John Grenfell, about the primitive mines. Only after the South African War did Grenfell manage to reach the area. He was guided to the numerous workings by a man who was the last-known survivor of the original mining tribes. His people had long abandoned the area, leaving to it the name of Musina, which Europeans corrupted to Messina. Grenfell was staggered at what he saw. The area was a veritable landscape of copper, overgrown with a wild garden of baobab and mopane trees. There were numerous disused shafts and adits, many having been abandoned when they were flooded at the water table. Grenfell pegged the area, and the great modern copper mines of Messina came into being.

The original miners had wandered southwards looking for new copper deposits. Legend has it that chance led them to a vast, savanna-covered plain, rich in wildlife and with a cluster of strangely shaped, isolated hillocks rising up abruptly through the bush. It was an area with an atmosphere of aloofness, unfriendliness and strangeness; and, indeed, there was something very peculiar beneath the surface. The wandering prospectors found signs of considerable mineralisation, but they had not the technical knowledge to understand the clues. The prospectors continued the search further south, but were disappointed. They then returned to the scene of the first discovery and named it *Phalaborwa* (better than the south). They settled, and later mined some of the area's rich deposits of copper and iron.

European prospectors observed the ancient workings

TWO SOURCES OF DIAMONDS Kimberlite (left) is a volcanic rock which is a primary source of diamonds. But the diamonds can be carried far from the site of the original eruption by such forces as floods, and then picked up in alluvial deposits (right).

and the broken-down smelters and forges. They pegged claims and started a number of little mines, working against fever, isolation, heat and a prodigious population of big game. Then, in the early 1930s, a German geologist, Dr Hans Merensky, realised the economic potential of the area.

About 2000 million years ago a gigantic volcanic eruption had taken place. The level area with the fragmented hillocks was the base of a vanished crater. The throat was choked with an assortment of minerals as astonishing as the kimberlite in the diamondiferous pipes. The mouth of the vast pipe occupied 18 square km, and it contained to an unknown depth such minerals and metals as apatite, copper, gold, iron, mica, vermiculite and zirconium.

The deposit of vermiculite is the largest in the world. This is a mineral related to mica and much used for heat and sound insulation in modern industry, and in the hydroponic cultivation of plants. Merensky started mining vermiculite in 1938. Then the apatite deposit was mined. Apatite is a phosphate of lime combined with fluoride or chloride of lime, and is in great demand as a fertilizer. As with the vermiculite, the depth of the deposit is not yet known. Its extent is prodigious – sufficient for all the needs of Southern Africa and much of the world for hundreds of years to come.

Close to the apatite there lies a deposit of copper estimated at 300 million tons. Magnetite (iron ore) is also mined from a huge deposit in the same volcanic throat. Zirconium and uranium oxide, of great value in nuclear reactors, are also mined.

Dr Merensky, the geologist who discovered the potential of the Phalaborwa Igneous Complex, as it is known, was also closely involved with the discovery of platinum in Southern Africa. Platinum, sometimes known as white gold from its appearance – brilliant white ranging to blue-grey – is found in small quantities in the Witwatersrand gold-bearing reefs. It has different groups: palladium, ruthenium and rhodium are lighter than gold; platinum, iridium and osmium are heavier.

Apart from jewellery, platinum has considerable use as a catalyst in refining petrol and in the purification of exhaust fumes. Small quantities were extracted from the Witwatersrand reef and from lodes found elsewhere, but without very profitable results. Then, in May 1924, a prospector named A. F. Lombard panned platinum from a dry watercourse near Lydenburg. The samples were sent to Dr Merensky for analysis and he began substantial prospecting. In 1924 he and his group, including A. F. Lombard,

A DAZZLEMENT OF DIAMONDS This emperor's ransom in cut and uncut diamonds comes from Kimberley. There is a mystery about their origin, for diamonds are a form of carbon, yet the kimberlite itself, in which they are found, contains none of this mineral.

found platinum in what was named the Merensky Reef. The reef was traced to several parts of the Transvaal, especially the Rustenburg district. It is a remarkable reef – really a platinum horizon, or level, contained in a basin-shaped layer of a rock called norite. The platinum in the reef is of low concentration, but distributed so uniformly over so vast an area that the deposit is by far the largest in the world. One of the modern mines working it, the Rustenburg Platinum Mine, is the world's most extensive underground working. Some copper, iron, nickel and gold are recovered from the same reef.

Platinum is a beautiful metal, and an arsenide of platinum, known as sperrylite, found in the Potgietersrus district, occurs in huge and spectacularly lovely crystals.

Another metal which is found in Southern Africa to a greater extent than anywhere else in the world is antimony, a silver-white, brittle metal, used in alloys such as pewter (which also contains tin and lead); in printing metal, batteries, bearings, medicines, shrapnel, matches; as white and red pigments in paints; and in other products of the world's factories.

In 1870, a party of prospectors found gold traces in a

range of mountains in the Eastern Transvaal which they named after Sir Roderick Murchison, the renowned British geologist. Nothing much resulted from this find, but in 1888 there was a new discovery and a rush took place to the area. Gold was what the diggers wanted, but they found it exceedingly hard to extract. No matter what they did, they could not get rid of the antimony. The gold mines closed down and the Murchison Range was for a while an area of ghost mines, haunted by mosquitoes.

The world's deepest base metal mine shaft

Then antimony came into demand as a strategic metal and for industrial use. The mines were reopened, this time to produce antimony, with gold as a by-product. One mine in the area, Consolidated Murchison, is the largest producer in the world, with its Alpha shaft the deepest sunk by man to recover a base metal.

Cinnabar, emeralds, feldspar, mica and silica are also mined in the Murchison Range. Cinnabar is sulphide of mercury, or quicksilver, the only common metal that is liquid at normal room temperatures. It is used in medicines, paints and various chemical processes, some concerned with gold recovery. Cinnabar is a beautiful cochineal-red in colour, and is made up of 86,2 per cent mercury and 13,8 per cent sulphur.

Emeralds are a crystal variety of a mineral called beryl, their lovely green colour coming from the presence of small amounts of chromium. Beryl is the source of the metal beryllium, which is used in atomic science and for the production of very light alloys. It occurs in the Murchison Range and other parts of Southern Africa. The best emeralds come from the Belingwe area of Zimbabwe, where they were discovered in 1956. As in the Murchison Range, they occur in a rock called actinolite schist which has been invaded by a type of granite called pegmatite.

Apart from green emeralds, there are other crystal varieties of beryl. A blue-green variety is known as aquamarine, with good specimens from Urungwe in Zimbabwe, Rössing in South West Africa, and the Murchison Range. A pink variety, called morganite, is rare, but is occasionally found in Namaqualand and the north-east Transvaal; while the handsome yellow variety known as heliodor comes from Rössing in South West Africa.

Feldspar, also mined in the igneous rocks of the Murchison Range, as well as in Namaqualand and Zimbabwe, is used in the manufacture of porcelain and enamelware, glass, soaps and other products. Crystals of it form the colourful semi-precious stones known as amazonite (green), sunstone (golden), moonstone (white) and labradorite (purple).

Mica is another strange mineral mined in the area of the Murchison Range, and also in Zimbabwe near Miami. The name mica actually covers a group of silicate minerals with similar properties. All form the same kind of crystals – layered like a stack of tables; all are transparent; all are poor conductors of heat and electricity; all cleave perfectly; and all occur in thick deposits known as books, with individual sheets easy to separate. Muscovite and phlogopite are the two most important members of the family from a commercial point of view, being used in electrical and electronic devices, heat insulation, lubricants, wallpapers and roofing.

Mica occurs in great dykes and humps, known as lenses, in the old granite of the primitive system. Some of its crystals, especially of muscovite, are several metres across. The railway station named Mica in the Murchison Range area is a great centre for the mineral. Huge books of it are mined in the vicinity and loaded for dispatch, with waste material scattered over the surrounding countryside, glittering and sparkling in the brilliant sunshine of the Eastern Transvaal lowveld.

Mica is an improbable-looking mineral to find in its natural state. It seems rather to be the left-overs from some prehistoric glassworks. Asbestos is another peculiar material that could well be the petrified remnants of vanished vegetation rather than the mineral which it is. Asbestos is actually the commercial term applied to a number of silicate minerals, the most common of which, in Southern Africa, are chrysotile, crocidolite, amosite, tremolite, anthophyllite and actinolite. All of these related minerals are fibrous. Southern Africa is the third-largest producer of asbestos in the world, after Russia and Canada.

Chrysotile, or white asbestos, is most commonly used in industry for asbestos-cement products, brake-linings and insulation products. It occurs in serpentine rocks, and the seams of white fibre make a striking appearance set in the green-coloured serpentine. The big producing mines are Shabani in Zimbabwe, Havelock in Swaziland, and Diepgezet in the Eastern Transvaal.

Crocidolite, or blue asbestos, has properties some-

'GRAPES' FROM THE KAROO Nothing is too strange to come from the weird landscape of the Karoo, with its flat-topped koppies and endless distances – not even this cluster of what looks like petrified grapes. They are, in fact, a mineral called prehnite.

what different from those of chrysotile. It is stronger and more resistant to acid and the corrosion of sea water. It is found in the Transvaal, but principally in the Northern Cape. Southern Africa is the world's largest supplier of this variety of asbestos. A beautiful and unique offspring of crocidolite is the oxidised and silicified semi-precious stone known as tiger's eye when it is golden-coloured; as bull's eye when blue; hawk's eye when grey-green; zebra's eye when yellow and green; cat's eye when bluish to greyish-yellow; and devil's eye when red. These gemstones are amongst the most popular of all semi-precious stones, and are in great demand by jewellers in Germany.

Amosite, another form of asbestos, is produced only in South Africa, mainly in the rugged mountain country of the central Transvaal, at the great Penge Mine and in several isolated workings, some of them precariously situated high on the faces of rocky precipices. Amosite is the largest of the asbestos fibres, up to 150 mm in length and as much as 300 mm thick. It is used in marine and jet engines, in fire-resistant partitions for ships, and in many other places demanding high resistance to corrosion and the ability to withstand great heat.

Tremolite, anthophyllite and actinolite are forms of asbestos found in parts of Natal and the Transvaal and spasmodically mined to supply specialised demands in asbestos pasteboards, cement, tiles, filters and other purposes. The treasure chest of Southern Africa is unique in that it contains vast reserves of six classes of asbestos which are needed by man for various industries.

The best rubies
Another mineral found in several parts of Southern Africa, notably the Northern Transvaal, Zimbabwe and Namaqualand, is corundum, an essential grinding material in industry. It is the second hardest substance after diamond, and is found in a variety of colours – grey, blue, black, brown, red-brown and pink. Precious varieties of it are also found, and these are known as rubies and sapphires. The best rubies and sapphires in Southern Africa are found in the Gwelo area of Zimbabwe.

Southern Africa also has colossal deposits of iron. Near Postmasburg and Sishen, and the ingeniously named *Hotazel* (hot as hell) in the Northern Cape, lie over 1000 million tons of high-grade iron ore, the largest and richest deposit in the whole of Africa. Zimbabwe, the Transvaal and Natal all have vast deposits of such iron-bearing minerals as magnetite, hematite, geothite, limonite, siderite and chamosite.

Associated with these iron ores are immense deposits of chrome and manganese, both essential to the manufacture of steel. The largest deposits of chrome ore in the western world are found in Zimbabwe and South Africa. Most of the stainless steel produced in the western world owes its shine to the ore obtained from these nearly inexhaustible deposits.

Manganese is used in the production of ordinary carbon steel. It was actually the first metal discovered by Europeans in Southern Africa. In the sandstones of the Western Cape it appears very commonly as dark-coloured bands. Fragments are easy to find in the form of heavy black lumps of rock. The first prospectors were deluded that it was silver ore, for its exotic nature and use were quite unknown to them. The name of 'Silver Mine' still lingers rather wistfully over an area in the mountains near Cape Town where in 1687 the first prospecting adit in Southern Africa was sunk by early Dutch miners into a lode of manganese.

Several little mines worked manganese deposits in the Western Cape, but the deposits proved to be irritatingly patchy. The huge deposits of ore lying on the surface in the Northern Cape, and in Botswana, now produce as much as is required, with Southern Africa the world's third-largest producer, after Russia and India.

Vanadium is another constituent of steel, increasing its powers of resistance to shocks, and is also used in the production of anilene dyes and as a photographic developer. It is found in the Cape, Natal and the Transvaal.

Fluorspar and fluorite are also much used in steelmaking and in the production of optical lenses. They occur widely in the Transvaal. Fluorspar is a beautiful and interesting mineral occurring in groups of cubes, coloured purple, yellow, blue, green and pink. Especially notable is the fact that some of its crystals show one colour through transmitted light and another under reflected light. From this property comes the word 'fluorescence'. The mineral is also phosphorescent. Hydrofluoric acid and its derivatives are made from this material and are much used in Japan and America in the manufacture of aluminium, for etching glass, in aerosols and in refrigeration. This acid is very corrosive.

In most countries where tin is found in its ore form, mainly cassiterite, it was mined from very ancient times. The tin mines of Zimbabwe and South Africa are today established on the sites of earlier workings made by people who vanished so many years ago that even legends of them no longer exist.

The silvery-white lustre of tin has always attracted man. It is easy to mine, easy to smelt and to work, and has great flexibility when alloyed with other common metals such as iron or copper. Cassiterite, like so many other minerals and metals, occurs in lodes connected with the intrusion of the old granites of the primitive system and associated volcanic disturbances. Found with it are such metals as wolfram, or tungsten, used in steel and electric-light filaments. Southern Africa has an ample store of these materials for all its own uses, and is a considerable exporter.

A metal for the Space Age

Zincblende, the sulphide of zinc, is found in the Transvaal, Zimbabwe and South West Africa, while galena, the sulphide of lead, is found in the Transvaal and Zimbabwe, although not to the extent of the prodigious Broken Hill deposit at Kabwe in Zambia, where the underground works glitter and shine in the light of the miners' lamps.

Titanium is another silver-white metal. It is lighter than iron, almost as strong as steel, nearly as corrosion-proof as platinum, and resistant to heat up to temperatures of 1500°C. Jet engines, space rockets, sputniks and numerous industries all use titanium. It is actually the ninth most abundant element in the earth's crust but, although present in many areas, is not too often found in deposits sufficiently concentrated as to be workable.

Along the beaches of the eastern and western seaboard of Southern Africa there are huge mounds of reddish-coloured sand which contain concentrations of ilmenite, an oxide of iron-titanium. Some of these mounds cover substantial areas. At Umgababa, on the south coast of Natal, there is a sand mound covering 324 hectares and containing at least 2 million tons of ilmenite. At Richards Bay, and along the lonely coast of Zululand, the sands are so richly coloured with this oxide that the pioneer Portuguese navigators named the area *Medeos dos Oros* (sands of

VEGETABLE OR MINERAL? Southern Africa is one of the world's leading producers of asbestos, a strange looking mineral that could easily be mistaken for petrified wood. The three types here are (*clockwise from top*): Amosite, Crocidolite and Chrysotile.

gold). Turtles bury their eggs in sands which may yield the metal for some spacecraft of the future – blazing a trail to distant planets while the unwieldy old reptiles still seem to be living inoffensively in prehistoric times.

An entire group of minerals of the atomic age are the so-called 'rare earths', of which there are 17. They are divided into three groups: the light or cerium group; the medium or terbium group; and the heavy or yttrium group. Some of these earths, such as thulium, fetch almost preposterous prices of around R150 000 per 500 g. The cerium group are used in carbon-arc lighting, gas mantles, glass making and as neutron absorbers. The yttrium group are used as catalysts in the petroleum industry, in special metal alloys, and as control rods in atomic reactors.

The rare earths have extraordinary properties for atomic science. They are found associated with the old granites. The prospectors who find them have to be knowledgeable in the peculiar demands of atomic science, and recovery is a highly specialised task. Uranium and thorium often occur with the ores of the rare earths and this makes them radio-active and detectable by a Geiger-Mullercounter or a scintillometer.

The Northern Transvaal, Namaqualand and the north-western Cape are the sources of the rare earths. Tantalum, niobium and thorium are closely related to the family of rare earths. Zirconium is another metal of the world of electronics and atoms. It is found in considerable quantities in the sands of the east and west coasts.

The beautifully lustrous metal nickel is found in the Transvaal and Griqualand East. It is used in the minting of coins, in electro-plating and as the catalyst in many chemical reactions.

Many non-metallic minerals are found in Southern Africa too. There is alum, in considerable quantities at Vioolsdrift in Namaqualand. Andalusite, sillimanite and kyanite, all silicates of aluminium, and used as refractories in the making of pottery and glass, are found in the Transvaal. Barytes, used in paints, rubber, linoleum and paper, is found in the Transvaal, the Eastern Cape and Namaqualand. Limestone and its marble variety which can take a polish are found in many places, particularly in the Transvaal at Belfast, Kairo and Marble Hall, and in the Cape at Vanrhynsdorp and Port St Johns.

Many different clays, kaolite, Fuller's earth, magnesites, feldspars and other ingredients of china, porcelain, scouring soaps and powders, are found in Southern Africa. Gypsum, graphite, Iceland spar, Kieselguhr, mineral pigments such as red oxide, umber, and yellow and red ochre, are widespread.

Mineral pigments have been exploited since prehistoric times by the rock artists. Ochre became the national colour of the Xhosa tribe. Every woman dyed her clothing with ochre to achieve the handsome golden colour which custom decreed essential. Ochre mines in such areas as the south-western Cape have richly coloured surface workings, with the surroundings turned golden by wind-blown powder.

Gemstones or semi-precious stones are as lovely and varied in their crystal form and colour as wild flowers. In some of the most arid parts of Southern Africa the absence of plant cover reveals innumerable gemstones on the surface, as though nature had compensated for the lack of vegetation by bestowing a wealth of minerals.

Gemstones in industry

Apart from their ornamental value, gemstones have many practical uses. Tourmaline, for instance, with its multi-coloured crystals ranging from pink to green and blue, is found in South West Africa, the north-western Cape and Zimbabwe. With its strong absorption of light it is used as a polariser, while its capacity to modulate or influence an electrical current has put it to work in microphones, gramophone pickups and sound-measuring devices.

Rubies, sapphires, garnets, chrysoberyls, spinels, zircon, topaz, rock crystals and agates all provide bearings or jewels in watches and scientific instruments. Sapphires, diamonds and rubies are the stylus points in gramophone-record pickups. Garnets, rock crystals, quartz, topaz and powdered corundum, including sapphires and rubies, are used as abrasives.

Amber, found in the Northern Cape, is used to produce resin and other by-products. Jasper and other varieties of quartz are crushed to make insecticides, and have many other industrial applications.

But it is mainly for their beauty that these gemstones are known. Jasper is found in Zimbabwe and the Northern Cape. It is really an opaque, impure variety of quartz. Depending on its impurities, it comes in a wide and beautiful range of colours. Brown, yellow-brown, green and brilliant red are the main colours of jasper. Some specimens are banded or speckled with different colours, and these are carved into ornamental articles such as vases, tabletops and statues.

In the same quartz family as jasper is agate which,

since before the time of Christ, has been used to make mortars and pestles. Agates are found as the banded infilling of cavities in lavas. Vast numbers are found in the Drakensberg basalt and other volcanic remains throughout Southern Africa.

Amethyst, cairngorm, rose quartz and smoky quartz are found in the Transvaal, South West Africa and Namaqualand. Carnelian, brown-red to red, is found in the Northern Cape. Chalcedony is closely related to agate, and a lovely blue variety is found at Mont-aux-Sources in the Drakensberg. Green quartz is found in the Soutpansberg district and in the Murchison Range. Rock crystal, used in the production of electricity, and for making prisms and lenses, is found all over Southern Africa.

Cordierite is a silicate of aluminium and magnesium. Blue is its most attractive variety and it is often mistaken for sapphire. It is found in the Cape granite at Hout Bay, and near Cape Town. There are also yellow, green, brown and colourless varieties.

Epidote or okkolite of mixed colours is found in the Northern Cape near Keimoes. Garnet varieties such as dark red almandite are found in the Soutpansberg district of the Northern Transvaal and in Zimbabwe. South African jade is another variety of garnet. Properly it is grossularite, a lime garnet with an exquisite green colour. Other varieties are pink, pale blue and cream, but these are very rare. It is found in the Rustenburg district and the area of the Bushveld Igneous Complex. True jade or nephrite is found in Mashaba, Zimbabwe.

Pyrope, sometimes called the Cape ruby, is blood-red in colour and found in the gravels of the Vaal and Orange rivers, in Namaqualand and in most of the diamond pipes. It is a variety of garnet, as is uvarovite, an emerald-green, chrome-calcium gemstone. Prehnite, discovered by Colonel Prehn, a Governor of the Cape Colony at the end of the 18th century, is a green stone found in the Karoo districts.

Verdite, a variety of serpentine, is coloured a rich dark green and found in the area of the Kaap Valley. It was used to decorate the interior of the Bank of England and South Africa House in London. Stichtite is a lovely lavender-coloured stone from the same area, as is also a banded green-and-white fine-grained quartzite called buddstone.

Spinel, deep green in colour, is found in the Northern Transvaal, but is very rare in crystals large enough to be used as gems. Lapis lazuli (azure stone), deep blue or blue with white spots, comes from the vicinity of Upington in the Northern Cape, but is rare and expensive. Marble onyx, yellow or banded, is found in Namaqualand. Obsidian, blue and green in colour, comes from the north-eastern Transvaal. Olivine in green shades is found at Barkly West in the Cape.

There are opals in Namaqualand and the Northern Cape in numerous colours. Turquoise, blue in brown rock, comes from Upington in the Cape while hyacinth, a brownish-red variety of zircon, comes from Barkly West. Topaz, pale brownish-yellow or blue, is found in the Miami area of Zimbabwe. Alexandrite, a variety of chrysoberyl, with the peculiarity of being green in sunshine and red in artificial light, is found in Zimbabwe.

1000 million tons of coal

Nothing could be in greater contrast to the beauty of gemstones than coal. But coal is vital to the well-being of any country. Not only is it a fuel, but innumerable industrial processes and chemical derivatives are also based on it. Like subterranean water, it is a treasure that was buried from the surface; for the seams of coal are the graves of the giant forests of antiquity.

South Africa is fortunate in possessing huge deposits of coal of considerable variety, though mainly of low grades. In the Transvaal, Natal and Zimbabwe there are deposits of coal estimated at over 1000 million tons, while lower grades of coal are found in the Cape and elsewhere. Anthracite and torbanite are also found, with torbanite very restricted.

Coal is usually near the surface, and relatively easily found and worked. From prehistoric times, man has mined it in Southern Africa, using it for warmth, cooking and for smelting ore. Europeans observed the African people using it when they first came to Southern Africa, and the outcrops were easily found in northern Natal and the Eastern Transvaal. The development of the mining industry at Kimberley and the Witwatersrand with its demands for power, and the need for bunker coal at the ports, started coal mining. Today it is being developed on a massive scale, is exported to many countries, is used in the thermal generation of electric power, and is converted into numerous industrial chemicals.

South Africa has the world's only oil-from-coal plant, now being duplicated on a vast scale to make the country even more independent of imported fuel.

What other treasures are still to be discovered beneath the sunny landscape of Southern Africa remains a fascinating speculation. Certainly, the lid of the treasure chest has even now not been fully opened.

The majesty and mysteries of the high forest

The monarchs are the giant trees which, in years of battle with their fellows, have shouldered aside all opposition and reached such a size that nothing can threaten them save man or old age.

KING OF THE FOREST A huge yellowwood tree, festooned with creepers, dominates a dense mass of smaller trees in the classic high forest of the Groot River Valley. Yellowwoods can live for a thousand years.

*Forests that still seem
to be haunted by
memories of past battles*

SOUTHERN AFRICA, rich in almost all of nature's gifts but rain, is essentially a savanna, prairie and desert country rather than a land of forests. The moist air coming in from the warm waters of the east coast brings heavy rains only along the coastal terrace, against the edge of the central plateau and against the central basalt island of the Drakensberg and Lesotho, where it is too high and cold for forest trees to flourish.

It is only along the narrow coastal terrace, therefore, that temperate and subtropical forests grow in Southern Africa. They occur as long, narrow belts of trees, or as dense patches of forest crowded into a relatively limited area.

The largest high forest covers an area 150 km by 15 km along the coast between George and the Storms River in the south-eastern Cape. This Southern Cape Forest Region, as it is officially known, has

a spectacular setting. The National Road leading through it is justly known as the Garden Route.

The charm of the area comes from the subtle contrasts of scenery, colour and types of vegetation. To the north it is bounded by a long, high wall of mountains.

To the west stretches the *Langeberg* (long mountains). In the centre is the Outeniqua range. To the east, the mountain wall continues as the *Tsitsikamma* (glittering water), a well-watered world of high rainfall (over 1000 mm), dense high forest (so called because the trees are tall, not because they grow at high altitudes) and particularly handsome peaks. One of these, named *Formosa* (beautiful) by the early Portuguese navigators who admired it from the sea, is a mountain classic in its elegant shape, and the way it dominates the countryside from all sides.

From the shoreline, a series of terraces rises inland until eventually, at an altitude of about 600 m, they reach the foot of the mountain range. Each terrace has its own rainfall, and a diversity of vegetation flourishes in narrow bands along these terraces. As an additional scenic complication, the original shoreline has occasionally veered inland to form shallow bays. These have become converted into lagoons or lakes,

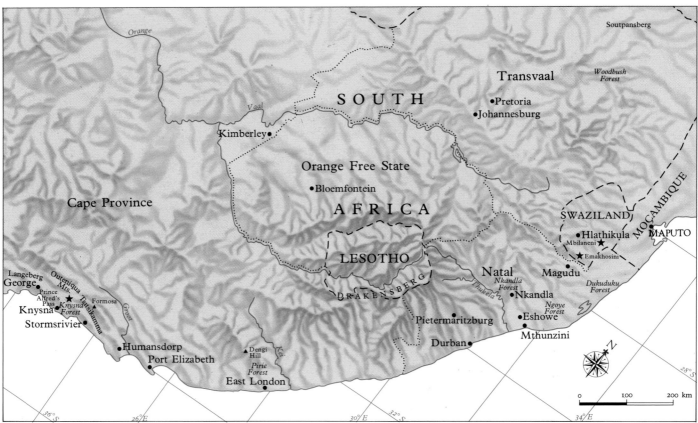

WHERE THE TREES ARE The diversity of vegetation in the high forests (shaded areas) is accounted for entirely by differences in altitude and rainfall, for the soil is consistent throughout. Forests demand at least 750 mm of rain a year.

fed by rivers. In places, huge sand dunes have been built up by the winds, completely separating the freshwater lakes from the sea.

On this varied base, the vegetation ranges from dry scrub and forest, through a temperate and humid succession of terraces to a wet high forest, with a very wet scrub covering the summit of the mountain range. What might be described as the characteristic vegetation of the area is found in the intermediate zone, a medium-moist high forest which occupies 40 per cent of the area. The rainfall averages 900 mm and is reasonably spread throughout the year.

The battle to grow tall

In the dense mass of vegetation it is difficult to single out individual trees from the rest of the forest. The more obvious monarchs are the giants which, in years of battle with their fellows, shouldered aside all opposition, and eventually reached such a size that nothing can threaten them save man or old age. The shade of their canopies is so dark, their root systems so demanding, that little else, including their own progeny, can take root and compete, until death brings some vast tree crashing down, producing a gap in the forest canopy through which the sunlight pours. Then begins a bitter struggle amongst would-be successors, all aspiring to replace the fallen monarch.

One of the most important of the giant trees is the common yellowwood, a tree reaching heights of 50 m and living for about a thousand years. The handsome yellowish colour of its timber and its hardness have made it greatly in demand for furniture. Its wood was widely used as structural timber in the days when even farmhouse cottages could have elegant gables, ceilings and floorboards.

There is a smaller yellowwood, which reaches heights of 30 m. Its wood, straight-grained and pale yellow, is considered superior even to that of the common yellowwood and is often given the name of real yellowwood. Like its taller brother, this tree is usually draped with beard lichen and vines of the wild grape.

The second largest tree species in the forest is the black ironwood, which, with its long, generally smooth-barked trunk, reaches a height of 35 m. The extreme hardness of the dark-coloured wood made it ideal for railway sleepers. Nowadays, with concrete sleepers, fewer trees are felled. The durable wood of the ironwood trees is now used for flooring and veneers. Around March, the ironwood trees produce their cream-coloured blossoms and the forest canopy is a glorious sight.

Smaller than the two giants, but with equally excellent timber, is the stinkwood, which reaches a height of 25 m. The wood, ranging in colour from yellow and gold to dark brown, has a piquant odour when cut, but this fades and the matured timber is odourless. Hard, handsomely coloured and well-grained, stinkwood was an essential constituent of Cape Dutch buildings and furniture.

The strength of stinkwood also made it ideal for wagons. The South African trek or tented wagon had the reputation of being about the toughest transport vehicle ever devised by man. Without it, the wilderness could not have been penetrated. (See box, p. 256.)

Many of the other tall trees of the high forest are invaluable to the carpenter. They include the Terblans, named after the woodcutter who first exploited its hard, dark red wood; the red alder, with its red-coloured, straight-grained timber; and its white alder cousin, whose dark timber is used for prestige furniture, veneers and frames. The freshly cut, pale red timber of the red stinkwood has a strong smell of bitter almonds, but it loses this odour when dry, and yields a very hard, heavy timber suitable for cabinets and face veneers. Carpenters also admire the pale yellowwood of the Cape ash, a member of the mahogany family; the light brown, beautifully patterned timber of the Cape beech, or *boekenhout*, which is used for furniture and was also used in wagonmaking; and the whitish-brown wood of the white pear, used for furniture, carts and rifle butts. The timber of the hard pear has a yellowish hue, and is prized for panelling, flooring and wagons. Many of these tall trees produce wood of great toughness and resilience, able to stand up to hard wear. The grey-green timber of Cape holly is useful for items such as the heels of women's shoes and the handles of tools. The pinkish timber of the wild peach was once the standard material for wheel spokes and the backs of chairs. And the blackwood is so tough and resilient that its timber makes good hammer handles. The wild elder, too, is used for tool handles.

Flowering trees daub the forest with colour

Many smaller trees live in the high forest, and some of these produce the finest shows of flowers. The keurboom is particularly lovely, covered in sweetly perfumed, pink-coloured, pea-like blossoms. The white sugarbush produces huge creamy-white flowers, full of sweet nectar which is the delight of birds, insects and man. The Hottentot's bean has masses of brilliant red blossoms which produce rusty-brown seed pods containing large, roundish beans which are very palatable to man and beast. The bush boerbean also produces showy red blossoms.

The Cape chestnut, a lovely medium-sized forest tree, growing to about 15 m, has leaves which are lemon-perfumed, and lilac-coloured flowers of gentle, delectable perfume, very generous in their display. The stock rose is a spectacular flowering shrub with large white and purple blossoms.

The dewberry has elegant, lilac-pink flowers, and stems which provided early Hottentots with the shafts of their spears. For this reason, Europeans named the tree the *Assegaaibos* from the Arabic word *azzaghayah* (a spear).

Other decorative smaller trees of the high forest include the false olive, the wild sage and *Halleria lucida*, the tree fuchsia with its red, orange or cream-coloured flowers. The wild pomegranate has brilliant orange-red flowers and odd fruit vessels with pointed lobes resembling the horns of miniature buffaloes.

Splashing the high forest with delicate colour are the pale yellow blossoms and large, round, decorative fruit of the wild gardenia. Another two species generous in blossoms are the white water alder and the camphor bush, the latter exuding its characteristic odour from its wood and leaves. This bush has featured in funeral ceremonies in every land in the

WAGON THAT WON THE WILDERNESS

Creaking and groaning, jerking, tilting and crashing its way through bush, incessantly complaining but never giving up the struggle, the tented wagon of a century and more ago went where no other vehicle could possibly have gone. Mountains, bush and deserts were more its normal terrain than roads. For in the age of ivory hunters, wandering traders, missionaries and pioneer settlers, the lumbering wagon, known popularly as the *kakebeen* (jawbone) from its shape, opened up the wilderness. If conditions became impossible the wagon could be taken apart, the separate sections placed on the backs of oxen and conveyed to a more congenial area.

As it was made entirely of wood – mostly stinkwood from the high forests – the only spares a traveller needed were nails, nuts and bolts. Travellers could replace broken parts simply by cutting down a tree and roughly fashioning a replacement. But in the Cape the craftsmen who built them proudly boasted that a charge from a bull elephant could not break their wagons. The kakebeen could be floated across flooded rivers or skidded down mountains. Only fire could totally destroy it.

The wagons varied in size and shape, but there was a ponderous character to them which, like the majesty of the law, had been devised and learnt as a result of long years of bitter experience.

The tented wagon, for all its lack of luxury, made an excellent and comfortable home. Travellers loved it. Its elevation made it very difficult for predatory animals to raid the larder, or to feed on the travellers.

Each wagon was a mobile stronghold. When arranged with other wagons in a circle, with wheels locked together and thorn bushes packed into all gaps, the result was a formidable *laager* or fortified camp.

A wagon was usually drawn by five to eight pairs of oxen, but sometimes 12 pairs might be yoked up, depending on the load. On level, open ground it travelled at a leisurely 5 km an hour. Stages were generally about 9 km at a time, and the oxen were then outspanned and allowed to graze or water.

Most of the oxen were of the Afrikander breed, with a hump betraying their zebu ancestry. These big, stoically patient, powerful beasts left their bones, as landmarks of man's explorations, littered over the interior of Africa, along with the bones of a number of their owners.

VIEW THAT CHARMED 'Nature has made an enchanting abode of this beautiful place', wrote the 18th century French traveller Le Vaillant when he first entered the foothills of the Outeniqua range in the Southern Cape. The area has changed little since then.

world in which it is indigenous.

Some of the plants of the high forest are parasites, depending for support and nourishment on the trees which have leaves that convert sunlight into food. Among these parasites are several species of beautifully flowered tree orchids; beard lichens, which give the forest trees an enchanted, old-world appearance; tree club moss, which flourishes particularly on the stinkwood trees; mistletoe, which can sometimes overwhelm the tree selected as its host; forest pepper, which prefers the rotten bark of old tree trunks; the dodder and the false dodder, both of which thin out the forest by killing off their host trees.

The lichens can also have catastrophic effects on trees. Some of them, such as the strangling twiner, wrap themselves so tightly around saplings that they literally choke them to death. The monkey rope or wild grape is particularly spectacular in the way it drapes itself over the forest.

Lichens may be the delight of monkeys and of boys playing at being Tarzan, but to the forest trees they are a curse. There are many of them: traveller's joy, lemon capers, climbing saffron, milky rope, bush birdweed, David's root and others. They often completely envelop their unfortunate host, leaving little of it to see the light and weighing it down with their tremendous mass. The ultimate collapse is a vast jumble of expiring tree and dismayed parasites.

Sunlight penetrates only fitfully to the floor of the forest, which is the home of ferns, shrubs, some grasses and several herbs. The most spectacular fern is the tree fern, which grows to about 4 m in height, with a large, spreading crown of green compound leaves. There are flowering ferns such as *Todea barbara*, climbing ferns, bracken and its near relative the seven weeks fern. The *Dal van Varings* (dale of ferns) is a particularly beautiful area near the foot of Prince Alfred's Pass in the Knysna main forest.

The elephants of the high forest have adapted successfully to its conditions, their padded feet protecting them from the wet ground. These bush elephants have always been renowned for their size – the evolutionary result, it is said, of living in an area where the tender new shoots are high in the trees.

Bush pigs also roam through the forest, acting as mobile garbage-disposal units, eating everything from

THE SILENT WOOD A feeling of peace and stillness pervades this forest of aromatic eucalyptus trees in the Knysna area. The trees were planted to replace a section of the original high forest that was destroyed by fire long ago.

carrion and rotting vegetation to insects, reptiles, fruits and seeds. These tough, courageous animals have no serious enemies in the forest. The cat family does not like wet ground, and man has great difficulty hunting in such a tangle of plants. The boars weigh about 113 kg and their tusks reach about 180 mm in length. Although plentiful in the forest, they are very seldom seen. They lie up during the day, and roam the dark forest at night.

The leopard is the natural enemy of the bush pig, but not many of these beautiful cats like to hunt the high forest. Their lairs are in the mountains. Occasionally they raid the forest and take a bush pig for a meal, or snatch a monkey from the canopy. But leopards normally prefer a drier hunting area, and the mountain slopes are the home of creatures such as baboons, dassies and numerous antelope, all of which make excellent eating.

Vervet monkeys, which also provide favourite fare for leopards, are particularly happy inhabitants of the high forest. They live in the sunshine on the canopy, feeding on berries, nuts, fruits, eggs, young birds and insects, and seldom descend to the ground. From their perches on the canopy, there is a steady downpour of half-eaten fruit, seeds, and droppings filled with undigested seeds. Such free-and-easy eating and sanitary habits are an asset to the high forest, for they provide a seed-dispersal service.

A fallen tree, blown down in a storm or collapsed through old age, makes an attempt at rejuvenation by lowering a mass of aerial roots and sprouting a vast number of coppice shoots. Bushbuck feed on the succulent shoots. The old stump is provoked to produce still more coppice shoots and the fallen trunk swells to provide even more space for such shoots. For years there can be a battle between bushbuck and stump. Eventually one or more of the coppice shoots will evade the bushbuck by being inconveniently situated, or protected by nibbled-off shoots. And so new trees are born.

The only other antelope species which flourishes in the high forest is that delightful little creature, the blue duiker. This tiny, ineffably dainty animal, about the size of a large hare, lurks in the depths of the forest, feeding on ferns, herbs, leaves and fallen branches. Blue duikers seem to be very conservative animals, and this is often their undoing. They make definite paths for themselves through the thickets, and hunters snare them without difficulty.

The crowned eagle is a great hunter of the high forests. From vantage points in the canopy it watches the floor of the forest for the slightest sign of movement from creatures such as blue duikers, moles, mice or other small animals. Monkeys are also included in its prey and the forest is often disturbed by a sudden, vast clamour when some unfortunate member of a monkey troop is carried away, the rest of its fellows shouting abuse at the departing bird.

Bird life in the high forest is fairly rich, but easier to hear than to see. Most birds remain in the canopy, where food and sunlight are to their liking. Owls of several species hunt in the forest, as do various flycatchers and bulbuls who feed on the insects; but the majority of birds keep to the upper storeys. The same applies to snakes. The boomslang lives in the canopy, feeding on eggs and chicks, and is seldom seen. Further north, the green mamba is also found high in the trees. Both snakes are very poisonous but not aggressive, invariably gliding silently and gracefully away at the approach of any large mammal.

Up the east coast beyond Port Elizabeth, patches of high forest exist. They are confined mostly to rainy mountain slopes, the most notable forest being the Pirie Forest. Tree species are much the same as in the Southern Cape Forest Region, except that stinkwood is rare and its place is taken by excellent timber trees such as the sneezewood.

Last battle of the wars
The forests of the Eastern Cape and the Transkei were the natural retreats of the Xhosa people during the nine Kaffir Wars of the last century. They were ideal hiding places for women, children, cattle and warriors retreating from defeat or planning attacks. Some of the fiercest clashes took place in these forests, and they are full of memories of ambuscades, killings, escapes and wild adventures.

Perhaps it was fitting, if tragic, that the last fight in this long sequence of vicious little wars took place in one of these forests. On May 29, 1878, a patrol of Fhengus, led by two Europeans, surprised a group of Xhosa warriors in the high forest at Dengi Hill. The Xhosas fled, leaving 16 corpses behind them. But hidden beneath the leaves after the fight lay one grievously wounded Xhosa.

When eventually his troubles were over, some forest scavenger ate part of his face and right arm. When the Europeans eventually heard about this occurrence from a prisoner, they went and searched for the body and buried beneath the trees with all honour the great chief Sandile, a man of high courage and resolution. With his death the Ninth Kaffir War ended, and a long peace was established between Europeans and Xhosas in the old Cape Colony.

In Transkei, the high forests consist of patches, mainly close to the coast and often in most dramatic scenic settings. Their composition steadily changes with the warmer climate in the north. The Natal mahogany, the Umzimbeet, and the flat-crown start to dominate the trees, while sundu palms give way to lala vegetable ivory palms, which grow so gracefully all the way north up the coast.

The Natal high forests are small, dense, island-like concentrations of trees in a surrounding sea of grass-covered undulating hills. In the coastal forests the mdoni, or water-myrtle trees, are dominant, with many palm trees, such as the lala and the nkhomba.

Zululand has many of these lovely, self-contained high forests, most with very beautiful Zulu names: *Dlinza* (place of meditation) near Eshowe; *Dukuduku* (place of the beating heart); *Ngoye* (place of seclusion); *Mthunzini* (the shady place), where at the time of the Zulu war the strange white chief John Dunn lived with his 50 wives – all well fed, clothed, housed, tolerably happy and reputedly faithful; and *Nkandla* (the place of exhaustion), so named on account of its rugged topography.

The Nkandla forest is one of the loveliest in Southern Africa. It grows along the precipices overlooking the eastern side of the prodigious valley of the Thukela River. Giant trees, festooned with creepers, reach upwards to the sky. It is a forest of immense antiquity and majesty.

It was in this forest that the Bambatha Rebellion played out its bitter course, and it would be hard to imagine a more difficult terrain for man to select as a battleground. Bambatha was the chief of the small Zondi tribe, a man of violent temper with an intense dislike of paying taxes. In 1906 he became the central figure in a revolt against the Natal Government which had recently imposed a new poll tax.

Where Cetshwayo found rest

The Nkandla forest had a profound mystical attraction for Zulus. In the centre of the forest there is a deep gorge, 3 km long and 700 m deep. Through this gorge flows a stream known as *Mhome* (the drainer). It is a place still remote and secluded from the outside world, with a beautiful waterfall tumbling down into the stream from the heights.

In this gorge there lived a small tribe of Lala origin who were the traditional spear-makers and metal-workers to the Zulu royal house. When Cetshwayo, the Zulu king, died in 1884, he was buried in this gorge, beneath a mound of stones. The site was tabu, a place of prayer to ancestral spirits, and of commun-

Knysna lourie (*Tauraco corythaix*)

Heard, but rarely seen

A forest is usually a dark place, with its canopy filtering out the daylight. This explains why canopy-dwelling birds, such as the louries, are often heard but seldom seen. It also explains why these birds are so brilliantly coloured, for they need to be able to locate others of the same species or they would become extinct. One of the most brilliant of all is the Knysna lourie, resplendent in scarlet-and-green plumage, handsome with its crest of hair-like feathers, and so well adapted for life in indigenous forests, such as Knysna, that it never ventures into any other habitat.

It feeds on fruit, climbing and jumping among the branches almost like a squirrel. A feature which contributes to this agility is the design of its feet. One toe is set at right-angles to the others, and can be turned forward or back, to grip branches.

The bird's colouring comes from a pigment manufactured in its body – a pigment so different from any other in the entire bird world that a special name has been given to it – turacoverdin. The source of the red pigment, too, is unique among birds: it is derived from minute traces of copper in the lourie's diet.

ion with the remote spirit of creation *Nkulunkulu* (greatest of the great).

In this stronghold, fortified by assurances from their witchdoctors that they had a special magic which would make the warriors impervious to European bullets, Bambatha and his followers staged their revolt. They were confident of the support of the ancestral spirits and, although the magic of the witchdoctors proved a dismal failure, they stubbornly resisted every effort to prise them out of their retreat. It was an area made for surprises, traps and ambushes, and Government troops had an exhausting exercise in forest and mountain warfare, with bodies and pack-animals falling 500 m when skirmishes were fought on the precipice edges.

The affair ended on June 10, 1906. A deserter

betrayed the whereabouts of Bambatha to the Government men, and the rebels were surprised and routed.

Bambatha tried to escape by half crawling, half swimming up the stream. Without knowing who he was, two African warriors on the Government side saw him. They attacked with spears. He fought back, and the stream was soon red with their combined blood. Then an African policeman shot Bambatha through the head. There was still some fighting elsewhere in Natal, but in the Nkandla forest the whole backbone of the revolt had collapsed and after a while, and a little more killing, peace came.

The Magudu forest in northern Zululand is renowned. It is reputed to be haunted by malevolent spirits which guard for eternity the graves of the chiefs. Many tales are told of intruders who have sought to hunt, explore or cut down trees in this forest. They have aroused a fury of winds, whispering and shouting around their ears: 'Wah! Wah! . . . Who comes here? Do you defy us?' And then, with a great barking of invisible hounds, and a shower of sticks and stones, the intruders are driven away.

Defeat of the Ndwandwes

The Ndwandwe people were the great rivals of the Zulus early in the 19th century, at the time when Shaka was welding the clans and tribes of Zululand into nationhood. After several clashes, there was a final battle. The Ndwandwes were defeated and their last great chief, Zwide, was driven away, and fled into the Transvaal. On his death he was carried with great stealth all the way back to this forest and buried there. It is said that his descendants also find their way there when they die, although no man sees the funeral cortège, which travels at night and hides during the day.

In the Transvaal, patches of high forest cling to the heavy rainfall belt along the seaward edge of the escarpment right the way up to the Soutpansberg. The largest forest is in the Woodbush mountains and this is a superb area of trees and vast views from sites at the edge of the escarpment.

The composition of the Woodbush Forest is very similar to that of the forests of Natal. Heavy rainfall and rich granitic soil make it ideal for such trees as the red stinkwood, the cabbage or kiepersol tree, yellowwoods, and such special local trees as the lovely *Ochna o'Connorii*, a redwood, which starts its spring leaves in a blood-red colour. Then they change to green while its masses of flowers are brilliant yellow in late spring. Its seeds are crimson.

The ironwood flourishes, growing to a formidable size, the largest specimen in the forest being 42 m high and 5,5 m in circumference.

The Woodbush Forest is well inhabited. Wild pigs, bushbuck, leopards, porcupines, lynxes and monkeys, both vervet and samango, are numerous. The samango monkey is an entirely forest-dwelling creature, and most handsome, with its long, fine fur always in great demand by the warrior tribes of Africa for their dress of skins.

In former years, the Tlou tribe had their home just below the escarpment and used the forest as their stronghold. In 1894 this tribe revolted against Government authority and started to raid farms and mining settlements in the vicinity. A punitive force was sent against the tribe. Led by their chief, Makgoba, they retreated into the forest and for 12 months defied every effort to prise them out.

The Woodbush area is as beautiful and almost as difficult a battleground as the Nkandla in Zululand. Armies could lose themselves in trees, valleys and mountains. Lovely waterfalls, such as the Debegeni, where the tribespeople traditionally left offerings of food and beer to appease the water spirits, tumble down into dark valleys. There are caves and hideaways very difficult to find.

The high forest still seems to be haunted by memories of this little war. Makgoba (called Magoeba by Europeans) had about 500 warriors only, but mist, rain and malarial fever were also his allies. The war became a deadly game of patience. The Government force tried to hem the rebels in with a series of forts. Patrols searched the forest while Makgoba's warriors slipped outside in the night and raided for food. Only in June 1895 did the matter end.

A patrol of Swazi warriors, fighting on the Government side, caught two women in the forest. One they killed and the other they tortured a little until she told them where to find Makgoba.

Deep in the forest, about halfway up the ravine which is known as Magoeba's Kloof, they found him. Gleefully they formed a ring and their leader challenged him to mortal combat. In the shadow of the tall trees, Makgoba and the Swazi champion battered each other with clubs and spears until Makgoba fell to his knees and died. The Swazis cut off his head and carried it away as proof of his death.

The catcalls, shouts and screams died away. The trees were left with their shadows; the birds and monkeys played in the branches; the leopards, the lynxes and crowned eagles hunted their prey, and stillness again wandered hand in hand with solitude, down green and silent aisles.

261

Land of mountains and mysteries

The strangest ruins on earth echo the hopes, triumphs and tragedies of forgotten civilizations.

ROCK OF AGES A granite dome near Mutare in Zimbabwe. The most ancient of datable rocks, these petrified explosions from the bowels of the earth have withstood the ravages of time and the erosive forces of nature for something like 3000 million years.

*The wind whispers the legends
of each mountain and ruin,
each river and waterfall*

FOR ROMANTIC BEAUTY there are few places in Africa that compare with the Eastern Highlands of Zimbabwe. It is a jumble of superb mountains and luxuriant vegetation, with a vast assortment of some of the strangest ruins to be found anywhere on earth, a richness of legend, and a singular atmosphere of vanished primitive civilizations. The hopes, triumphs and tragedies of many forgotten people, who disappeared long before history came to be recorded in Southern Africa, linger in this wilderness that combines the oldest of all geological systems, the ancient granites, with the Iron Age of man.

The northern part of these granite heights is dominated by the highest mountain in Zimbabwe, the 2595 m high Nyangani. This great pile of rock looks out on a vast and staggering view over a surrounding African world of immense, sun-drenched space and rugged beauty. Oddly shaped peaks project upwards, and deep gorges carve a way into the mountains. Immediately to the west there is a high moorland forming the summit of a plateau on the range. To the east, the bush-covered sand plains of Moçambique stretch away to a horizon that always seems to be lost in haze and heat.

This is a peculiarly Zimbabwean landscape. If the flat-topped mountains of the Karoo System are the scenic emblem of South Africa, then the ancient granite domes are typical of Zimbabwe. Integral with this landscape are the puzzling remnants of the total wreck of a former civilization.

Vast though they are on a human scale, the ruins begin to dwindle and recede when they are measured against the scale of the African continent. Lying at the foot of prodigious, petrified explosions of granite, they take on the appearance of propitiatory offerings, laid by man as a penance at the altars of primeval gods of stone.

It is difficult to comprehend the full purpose of these buildings. Around the impressive granite peak known as Ziwa, 1744 m high, there lies the equivalent of a ruined city covering 13 000 square km of country on either side of the Nyangombe River. Ziwa and two smaller granite mountains were the pivots of this forgotten African city. On the southern slopes of

Ziwa stand the ruins of several substantial buildings, approached by a pathway guarded by walls. Here the political head and religious leaders of the tribe probably had their headquarters. At the period these buildings were occupied, the worship of the god Mwari had already evolved, with complex rituals and an elaborate priesthood. Mwari could always be approached through an oracle, and granite mountains such as Ziwa were the usual centres of worship, especially if they possessed a cave with the right acoustics. From such caves would emerge the booming voice of the god,

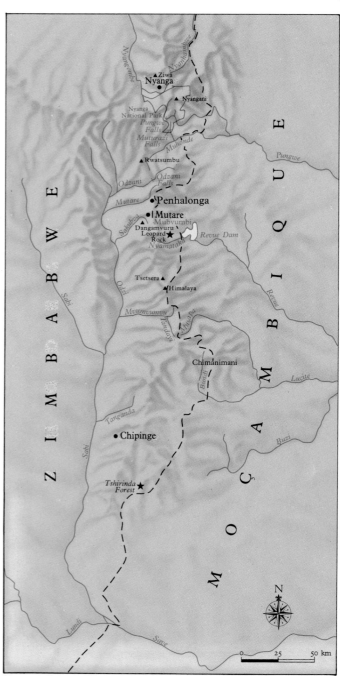

EARTH'S OLDEST ROCKS The great granite domes of Zimbabwe's Eastern Highlands were created some 3000 million years ago.

answering the questions put by supplicants sitting anxiously in the courtyards below.

Around the slopes of Ziwa, the countryside is completely covered with terraces, low parallel walls and circular enclosures, all made of fragments of granite. The purpose of the circular walls at least seems obvious. They protected clusters of huts or sheltered livestock. Many of them are so well preserved, with the grinding stones of the women and the seats of the men scattered around, that it seems as though the occupants have only recently abandoned the place. The foundations of the mud huts in which they lived may still be seen, and fragments have been found of their pottery, utensils and ornaments.

Mystery of the walls

The mystery of this colossal ruin is the almost endless terracing and low, parallel walling covering kilometre after kilometre of country. These walls appear to surround central residential areas in concentric fashion. But they are so low they would be obstacles only to dwarfs. They meander about in seeming foolishness of purpose, poorly made, with no foundations, mortar or design, only a purposeless squandering of heavy material. The builders must have wasted generations in fetching and carrying these heavy blocks of granite for long distances, each just within the carrying capacity of one human being.

The arranging and rearranging of the stones in order to get them near to some inexplicable human desire might indicate a tribe of stone worshippers whose motivation was logical to its members, but is totally puzzling to any uninitiated outsider.

One thing only is certain about these ruins: as with the prehistoric mines of Africa, the drudgery was done by women. That was the rule from the beginning of time in Africa, and it prevailed throughout the continent, no matter how custom or religion differed from tribe to tribe. With these ruins, perhaps an order was given by some lordly ruler to his female subjects, simply to stop talking and build walls. Nobody taught them how, why, when or where, and they never learnt. They simply started, then went on building walls for generations. It became their habit and their custom, and they would admit no other. Whichever ruler ordered the building to begin was long since dead and gone, but still they uncomplainingly persisted until the whole countryside was littered with peculiar constructions. Eventually they stopped, and again nobody knows why. Perhaps they just ran out of stones. Perhaps somebody tripped over one of the walls, hurt himself, boxed their ears and ordered them to stop. Possibly the work was finished.

Near to Ziwa is another massive pile of granite which was for long a centre of human settlement. This height is named Nyahokwe. As with Ziwa, the name comes from later years, when headmen of those names lived in the vicinity. Nyahokwe was the centre of human settlement for many centuries, and the relics different people have left there provide clear evidence of their way of life. There was an early, primitive culture lasting until the 11th century; a transitional period lasting until the 15th century when the first terraces were built; a peak period of stone building between the 16th and the end of the 18th centuries; and then a final period of occupation by the Nyama tribe who had no interest in stone and allowed the place to go to ruin.

These two groups of ruins are in the warm lowland area, on the western side of the highlands. Up on the high moorlands, the climate is completely different – brisk enough to be a tonic for modern visitors to what is known as the Nyanga National park, but very trying to individuals whose dress consists of little more than a loin cloth. Nevertheless, a vast number of ruins remain in this area and indicate that there was once a substantial population there.

The ruins on the highlands, however, are very different from those on the lowlands. They have all the signs of embattlements. People did not live in them out of choice. They were probably built and occupied during times of military pressure and abandoned for the warmer lowlands as soon as times were quieter.

The hill slopes are terraced to an extraordinary extent. The amount of labour invested in the construction of these terraces must have been totally disproportionate to the value of any crops that could have been reaped from them. What crops were produced is conjectural. The modern staple crop of maize was only introduced from America to Africa by the Portuguese in the 16th century – after the terraces were built. Beans, calabashes and millet were the probable crop of the terraces. With their confined space and thin, stony soil they could not have been very productive. A prodigious amount of human energy was simply squandered in a way of life which seems senseless by modern standards.

Ruins in the wilderness

In far more recent times, a renowned healer-diviner named Sanyanga ruled over this area as a vassal of the Nyika chief, Bvumbi. To Europeans the area became known from the name of its ruler as Nyanga. Cecil Rhodes bought the area and bequeathed it to the people of Rhodesia as a National Park. Wandering through the mountains provides visitors with the aesthetic pleasure of superb scenery; a rich botany of everlastings, proteas, ericas and long grass; and the ineffable mystery and sadness lingering on over the wreckage of wasted effort and abandoned human homes.

Some 5000 square km of this wilderness are covered in ruins. The whole wild valley of the Nyanhambwe River is littered with stone cairns, monoliths, clusters of forts, pit ruins, endless terraces, and the signs of ancient mining on hills such as Rwatsumbu, where iron was found. The iron was no doubt traded, as was the gold, or *Ndarama*, found in the mud brought down by rivers. Much of it ended up in the romantic little ports of the east coast, where the Arabs from the days of Sindbad came down on the monsoon winds in their dhows and traded beads, baubles and cloth for gold, ivory and slaves.

There are some superb scenic views in these highlands. The river, known as the Muhonde, from the Karanga name for the *Euphorbia ingens* trees which flourish in its hot valley, has worn for itself one of the most spectacular gorges in Africa. Into this gorge

from the wet upland watershed of Inyanga, there tumble a number of waterfalls of tremendous height – some of them plunging 250 m. On the floor of the valley stands an extraordinary cluster of rocks known as *Masimiki* (the rocks that stand upright). These are natural monoliths that dominate the valley as though they were gigantic idols.

In this valley settled the baRwe tribe. Under chiefs with the hereditary title of Makombe they spent centuries squabbling, raiding and warring with the Nyika people who lived on the highlands, and the Hungwe people further west. Fighting the Hungwe must have had its difficulties, for the chiefs had so strict a tabu against ever seeing the face of neighbouring rulers that at any meeting they had to be separated by an impenetrable fence.

Many rivers have their sources on the moorland summit, which in parts is a boggy sponge. Some of these rivers flow directly east to the Indian Ocean. Others, which fall off the western slopes, have to make long detours in the lowlands before they can find a way around the northern or southern ends of the mountains, and eventually swing eastwards to reach the sea. The Pungwe River cascades down an impressive gorge as it descends from the highlands.

The Odzani and the Nyangombe rivers also have

Riddle of the slave pits

Thousands of what must be among the most peculiar habitations ever devised by man dot the hill slopes of Inyanga, in Zimbabwe. Stone walls have been built out like half moons from the slopes; the area between wall and hill has been filled with rubble; the rubble has been levelled to make a platform; and a pit has been sunk into each platform, then lined with stone.

To Europeans, they are known as slave pits, but to Africans as *Matangi epasi* (cattle enclosures). But what manner of slaves or cattle could have been kept there? The pits average about 6 m in diameter and are from 2 m to 3 m deep. They were entered by a tunnel passage, and a hole in the roof of the passage led to the floor of a hut built on the platform.

It seems that through this hole was passed a post which partially blocked the tunnel, and had its top connected with the wooden headrest of the owner of the livestock. Anybody or anything attempting to enter or escape from the pit at night would have to force a way past the post – and so rouse the owner, who would have slept with spear or club at the ready.

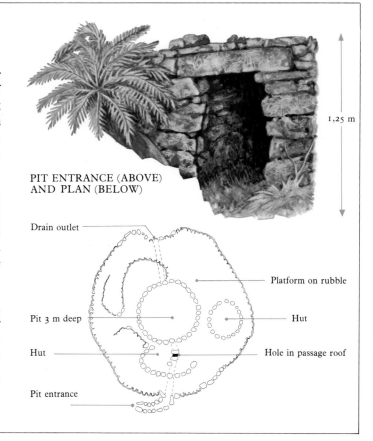

PIT ENTRANCE (ABOVE) AND PLAN (BELOW)

1,25 m

Drain outlet

Platform on rubble

Pit 3 m deep

Hut

Hut

Hole in passage roof

Pit entrance

THE VANISHING MIST The Pungwe River cascades through its gorge in Zimbabwe's Eastern Highlands. The sound of the word *Pungwe* is said to represent the incessant closing in and clearing of the mist that swirls up in the gorge.

fine waterfalls, while the Mutare possesses a superb cascade. The name *Mutare*, or *Umtali* in the Ndebele-Shangane form, means a place of ore. The valley of this river has been mined continuously by generations of workers, and its slopes are littered with adits and trenches. In 1889, J. H. Jeffreys, at the head of a syndicate of Barberton prospectors, pegged two clusters of these ancient workings near the head of the valley and these were developed by Europeans into two of the most profitable gold mines in Zimbabwe – the Penhalonga Mine and the Rezende Mine.

South of the Mutare River lies a tremendous jumble of granite mountains. Each of these great domes

and whalebacks of rock has its name and legend. Vegetation is rich, and especially notable are the musasa trees which turn the countryside so red in September with the colour of their new leaves that it could almost be on fire.

Mutare, one of the most beautifully situated of all towns, lies in the valley of the Sakubva stream. The granite domes crowd all around it. To the south looms *Dangamvuru* (the place where the rain starts), so named because it is said that the seasonal rains first reveal their approach by clouds piling up around this mountain. To the east stands a whole range of granite heights known as the *Mubvumbi* (mountains of drizzle). This enormous ridge of granite, called by

Europeans the Vumba, has a justifiable renown for its sheer splendour of scenery, the vastness of its views and the magnificence of its vegetation.

These heights were occupied about 400 years ago by the Jindwi tribe, who found that the caves and forests there offered sufficient shelter from the high annual rainfall of 1500 mm. The traces of many forgotten villages built by these people may still be found. Nearly each ruin has a tale to it. One such village flourished on the slopes of the height known as *Tshinyakweremba* (the place of tired feet). To the village, one day, there came a stranger, old, weary and decrepit. He requested hospitality. The villagers were drinking beer and inclined to be jocular. Some wag noticed a peculiarity in the old man and the people jeered at him. Angered, he withdrew, muttering vengeance against the villagers.

Only one woman felt sorrow for the stranger. She followed him and offered food. To her he explained himself. In reality he was a spirit from the paradise of ancestors. He had returned to earth to discover how the descendants were keeping the traditions of the past. So far as the villagers were concerned, he had found them sadly wanting. That night he intended to destroy the place. The woman might save herself if she fled before sunset.

In terror, the woman carried the tale to the village elders. In their drunkenness they simply derided her. On her own she abandoned the village. As she fled she looked upwards, and on the mountain top she saw the stranger. With the setting sun he called upon the power of nature to destroy the accursed village. A crash of thunder shook the mountain. A bolt of lightning hurtled down from the cloudless dome of heaven. Where the stranger stood, the mountain collapsed. With a mighty rumble, the rock face engulfed the place, and even nowadays it is said that the cries of the buried villagers can be heard, breaking through the silence of the night.

The scene of this old disaster is buried entirely now by an enchanted forest at the foot of a 200 m high precipice. It is a place filled with the whisper of winds and the sound of louries and rock pigeons, singing drowsily of forgotten days. A family of leopards for long made a home there, sunning themselves by custom on a vantage point known today as Leopard Rock. Above this place, the grey face of the

RAINY HEIGHTS Cool air and heavy rains make the Chimanimani Mountains in Zimbabwe's Eastern Highlands a paradise for flowering plants. *Tshimanimani* means 'squeezed together', and the range is named after the narrow gorge of the Musapa River.

cliffs looks down, stained with the crimson of flowering aloes, like drops of blood left behind on the rocks by the ancient tragedy.

Living in mountains always has its peculiar dangers. Even living in the valleys gave man many problems. African Coast Fever was endemic in these parts, while the rivers were subject to such violent floods that most of them have ominous-sounding names such as *Nyamataka* (the place of mud); *Munyanyazi* (the one that causes things to disappear); *Tshitora* and *Mutora* (both meaning the one that takes away); *Mutoramapudzi* (the pumpkin taker); *Mutorahuku* (the fowl taker); *Mutoragadzi* (the woman taker); and *Mutoradundu* (the bundle taker).

From the heights of the Mubvumbi there is a tremendous view across the Burma Valley to another vast pile of granite mountains, known to Europeans as the Himalaya. This range, 2633 m high, is richly covered in proteas, yellow arum lilies, everlastings, and yellowwood and cedar trees. In its warmer valleys the colourful musasa trees grow thickly.

To the tribespeople, this range is full of evil memories. One of the great trade paths of former years found a tortuous way across the mountains and then down to the lowlands of Moçambique. The skeletons of many travellers caught by the cold winds of the heights have been found along this path, and from this the name of *Tsetsera* (hurry on) was given to both path and mountain.

One of the principal rivers draining the western slopes of the mountains is the *Mvumvumvu* (the river of plenty), and at least its name has a happier sound to it than the coldness of Tsetsera. The valley of the river is warm, with rich alluvial soil, and is densely settled by people of the Mbire tribe. The river itself is a rushing, bustling type of stream with its source in the heights where the descendants of a renowned witchdoctor, named Zvihunzi, have their homes and still practise a peculiar technique of divination using the pods of the mungwato trees. The way the pods fall, and whether they have seeds in them or not, decide the diagnosis. Many illnesses have been treated from these seed pods. The message of the pods is regarded as infallible.

One of the tributaries of the upper Mvumvumvu is the *Tandayi* (the encircled one), so named because its valley is completely surrounded by high mountains. From the heights where the stream has its source there is another view over a vast panorama of mountain and bush-covered lowland. Over the watershed, to the east, there is a plateau which serves as the sponge for a stream flowing eastwards. This stream,

which has its source in a curious sink hole, flows a short way to the edge of the plateau. There, at a point marked by a solitary cedar tree, it takes a glorious leap into space, falling over 1000 m to be caught in the branches of a lovely rain forest which flourishes on the spray and mist into which the winds turn the water of the stream.

Attached to the plateau is a buttress summit projecting onto an outlying peak. The view from this peak is breathtaking. The lowlands of Moçambique make a handsome sight, but the view also embraces in one enormous vista the whole 45 km length of a quite separate range known to the tribespeople as *Mawenje* (the rocky mountains).

Peaks that sparkle

This range presents a glittering contrast to the grey-blue granite of the main massif. The fact that it is of an entirely different geological origin is readily apparent. With its jagged 2600 m high peaks made of sugary-white quartzite, it is the unique remnant in this part of the world of what is known as the Frontier System. Literally sparkling in the brilliant sunlight, this short but magnificent range presents one of the most spectacular scenes in Africa.

The Frontier System consists of water-deposited sediments which have consolidated into sugary-white quartzite, quartz schist, limestone and calc-schist. The system is ancient. It was deposited about, or just before, the time of the creation of the Witwatersrand, 1250 million years ago.

Europeans know the range as the Chimanimani. This name, however, is correctly applied only to the passage of the Musapa River through the range. The name *Tshimanimani* (to be squeezed together) perfectly describes the narrow gorge through which the river finds a way. It has a tortuous and dramatic passage through the mountains. Along its banks an ancient pathway also finds a way from Moçambique into the interior of Zimbabwe.

The trade pathways of Africa have been tramped deep into the ground by countless thousands of pairs of feet. If their story could be told it would be a strange romance of slave raiders, safari traders, ivory hunters, bands of warriors searching for trouble, runaways, explorers and a restless stream of individuals. Each traveller was intent on some special purpose which justified a long walk through all the dangers of predatory man and wild animals.

A few kilometres further south, another pathway finds a route from the coast to the interior by climbing directly over the range. The scenery traversed by this adventurous pathway is superb. From the western side it climbs steadily up the mountain slopes, finding an ingenious way up a beautifully wooded slope, shady nearly all the way, with a cold, clear stream rushing down beside the path.

To the botanist, the journey is particularly eventful. There are so many interesting flowers and plants to see, so many handsome vistas unfolding as the path climbs higher and higher that the walker is diverted from any weariness. The conditions for plants in these mountains resemble those of the Western Cape. The quartzite erodes into sand as white and as fine as salt. In this rather surprising soil there flourish cedar trees which, in ideal conditions, can reach 30 m in height with trunks 2 m in diameter. Their timber is aromatic and their boughs, when used for firewood in camp, perfume the air with a pleasant odour. Another fine tree of these mountains is the yellow-wood, notable for sparkling silver leaves and excellent, yellow-coloured timber.

Four different varieties of protea, *P. gaguedi*, *P. angolensis*, *P. madiensis* and *P. welwitschii*, produce handsome flowers. There are several species of erica, leucospermum, and a golden-coloured everlasting, *Helichrysum nitens*, all of which contribute to the general resemblance to a Western Cape wild-flower garden. Closer inspection soon reveals that, mixed up with these Cape families of flowering plants, there are many lovely plants which are also found in the island of Madagascar, lying on the same degree of latitude. Ferns, orchids and aloes grow in great numbers and variety. One of the prides of these mountains is the orchid *Disa ornithantha*, with its gorgeous red blooms to be seen in the marshlands in January and February.

The pathway approaches the top of its climb and emerges onto a grassy plateau covered with a weirdly shaped collection of gaint rocks. Then it twists and meanders past a regular freak gallery of shapes – dwarfs, giants, monsters and demons, all petrified into stone and seeming to glare balefully at human passers-by.

The path tops a rise and seems to pause a while at the spectacle, now revealed, of the inner heart of the range. The thickly grassed upper valley of the Bundi River, with many a crystal pool to reflect the shapes and colours of the surrounding peaks, finds its source here in a vast natural sponge. Herds of sable and

MAN-MADE LAKE Sunset over the Odzani River, near Mutare in the Eastern Highlands of Zimbabwe. The rivers in this jumble of mountains flow swift and stong, but this stretch of the Odzani is placid, because the river has been dammed.

271

THE SENTINEL The high peak of Gurungurwe Mountain, a solid mass of granite, keeps endless vigil over the well-watered slopes of the Eastern Highlands. Trees have established themselves on its lower slopes, but the mountain's ancient head is bare.

eland graze in this valley, while baboons and leopards wander along the overlooking slopes.

The path descends to the stream and passes a strange pool, known as *Mtseritseri* (the boiling place), where a powerful spring churns up the white sand at its bottom with all the flurried appearance of the inside of a cooking pot well on the boil.

Now the path starts to climb the opposite side of the inner valley. At its peak it reaches a saddle known as Skeleton Pass. From here there is a grand view down and over the lowlands of Moçambique. A cold wind blows over this high saddle. From the warm lowlands to the east a number of paths converge on this pass, and the reason for its name is obvious.

Travellers from the east, thinly clothed for tropical conditions, were, and are, often caught by mists on Skeleton Pass, and the sharp change in temperature has killed many of them.

From Skeleton Pass, one path veers south along the eastern slopes of the mountains. It finds a way below towering cliffs, crossing many streams cascading down from springs in the heights. Clumps of high forest shelter in the hollows, while baboons bark from the heights and bushbuck move silently through the shadows.

Presently, the path climbs to a broad grass-covered ridge. This is a watershed. South of it, the streams unite to form a handsome river, the Mubvumodzi, full of deep pools in a well-grassed, high-lying valley. At the end of this valley, the river suddenly forces its way through a barrier of rock and tumbles in a fine double leap 150 m down what is known as Martin's Falls. Gideon Martin, a pioneer settler of the eastern mountains of Zimbabwe, was the first European to see them. The waterfall named after him is complete with a rainbow and enough legends about mermaids, water sirens and assorted supernatural creatures to fill a book of fairy tales.

Legend of the rainmakers

This whole lovely area of mountains is particularly rich in folklore. Most of its inhabitants are elements of the Rozvi tribe who fled there for sanctuary from sundry fights and disagreements. According to tradition an individual by the name of Nyakuyimba stole the rain charm of the Rozvi king, Murimo. With his two brothers, named Tshikanda and Tshimotwo, he fled to the eastern mountains. A Rozvi army followed in hot pursuit. In the mountains the three brothers and their followers separated and searched for sanctuary. Nyakuyimba fled to the southern end of the mountains, to what is known as the *Dondo* (forest area). With the Rozvi army following him, Nyakuyimba gave the rain charm to his wife. She hid in the forest while he turned at bay. The Rozvi killed him and cut off his head to carry back to their king. On the way the head started to swell. It grew and grew the further the Rozvi carried it. Eventually it burst and from it, says the legend, the Save River had its source.

When the waters of the river flowed past the mountains, Nyakuyimba's wife knew that her husband was dead. She was safe, however, and in the deep forest of mahogany trees known as *Tshirinda* (the refuge), nowadays corrupted to Selinda, she gave birth to a son.

To this young man, in time, his mother gave the Rozvi rainmaking charm. The family entered business in what has always been one of the most profitable branches of black magic in Africa. They became chiefs, and their reigning title was *Musikavanthu* (the creator of men), for it was said that from their rain the food of men arose. Their emblem became the hippopotamus.

The Tshirinda forest is notable for the size of its red mahogany trees. One giant reaches 72 m in height and nearly 20 m in diameter. Ironwoods and wild figs also flourish there.

The mountain country settled by the Rozvi people has always ranked as one of the most beautiful parts of Zimbabwe. Apart from its handsome views it possesses many remarkable natural marvels such as the colossal cleft in the ground, 150 m deep and 3 km long, known as *Mumwoho* (mermaid's grotto). This place, buried in thick vegetation, was the local hiding place in times of war. Its reputation as being the home of a variety of water spirits is one commonly held by many dark pools and waterfalls. The famous Bridal Veil Falls, known to the tribespeople as *Mutsarara*, from the sound of the water falling, is also by repute the home of a *Nzuzu* (water nymph).

Most of Tshikanda's people preferred the warmth of a lower altitude. The area around the buttress known as *Tshipinga* (the impeder), where the administrative post of Chipinga stands today, was a centre for the Rozvi. Their principal home today is the bush-covered valley of the *Tanganda* or *Tandanga* (the flooding river), especially where it flows through the sweltering hot baobab forest to join the Save.

The Save River is one of the great rivers of Africa, flowing into the Indian Ocean. Europeans tend to confuse its name with that of the Sabi in the Eastern Transvaal. Its proper name, however, is *Mutsave* or Save (pronounced Sah-veh), and the role it has played in the story of Southern Africa is both ancient and honoured.

The valley of the Save is noted for its relentless heat and for the magnificence of its baobab trees. They thrive in this area in many thousands, and reach gigantic proportions of bulk and height.

Africa is a continent of abrupt contradictions of climate and weather. The eastern mountains, looking down on the Save River, are well watered, cold and green. The Save Valley is an oven, with its floor baked hard.

River of mercy

The river itself is full of deep pools. Like the people of the mountains, the local residents also have a legend about the origin of this river and its name. They say that when their ancestors settled in this area there was no river and the land was stricken by drought. The sister of their leader was a woman of infinite compassion. Her heart broke at the plight of her people. She died and from her grave there came the *Mutsave* (perpetual dampness), from which sprang the stream which was the beginning of the river. To the Duma tribe, the Save was from that day forward the source of their prosperity in this hot wilderness. They say that the great river comes from the heart of a woman, and the *Moyo* (heart) is the emblem of their tribe.

Enchanted green hills of blood and legend

It has been said that Zululand is green because it has been so generously fertilized with human blood. There are very few parts which have not been the scene of battle.

WHERE SHAKA RAIDED The Mzimvubu River, flowing through a countryside steeped in legend, and over which Shaka led his feared Zulu *impis*, follows a meandering course to the sea, through the jumbled hills of Pondoland.

*A land of weird echoes, where
Zulu spirits roam among a
jumble of hills and rivers*

A SCAR need not always disfigure a face or landscape. It can add distinction, or even a strange kind of beauty. So it is with the scenery of the eastern downlands and seaboard of Southern Africa, which can well be described as a beautiful scar, left behind by the ceaseless chafing and erosion of the elements.

Entire surfaces have been carried away, with only a few fragments remaining. Rivers have washed deep gashes into these eroded surfaces. Their courses, sometimes rushing deep in precipitous valleys, sometimes meandering lazily around the base of countless hills, are the principal feature of this area. Unimaginable quantities of spoil have been carried down these rivers to the sea. They are the fingers of creation, probing and pummelling the inert dough-like mass of land, changing and modelling it.

The sign of this continuing activity is seen each rainy summer, when the annual floods stain the sea dark brown with silt, and the wave action is made sluggish by the loads of flotsam, trees, vegetation, debris, drowned animals, and quite a few live ones, clinging desperately to floating vegetation.

When Dick King made his great 900 km ride in ten days from Durban to Grahamstown, to secure aid for the besieged British garrison, it was estimated that he had to ford 122 rivers. The number reaching the sea north of Durban is also considerable, and the part they have played in history has been almost as important as their role in creating the landscape.

This portion of Southern Africa was settled at the beginning of the 17th century by the tribes who today form the great bloc of Zulu-Xhosa-Pondo-Swazi people, all speaking a related language and sharing a similar culture. From the time of their arrival, the rivers have wielded a major influence on their lives. It is intriguing to visualise this land as they found it at the end of their long migration from the north.

According to tradition, the first migrants were led by a man named Nguni. They were part of a larger group led by another chief named Dlamini, and they were said to have originated from a legendary place known as eMbo, far to the north, in the area of the great lakes of central Africa.

Their migration route was down the coast. Somewhere in Moçambique, the host split up. The van-

guard, led by Nguni, went ahead and found their way into the lovely jumble of hills and rivers which is now called Zululand. There were already some people in this area. In the traditions of the newcomers, these earlier people are little more than phantoms. Their voices are said to make the echoes that can be heard in the hills. Some of them were metal-working offshoots of the Karanga people of Zimbabwe. Others were bushmen hunters, for this area was once one of the finest of all the big-game areas of Africa.

Essentially, it was a land of savanna and grass, with

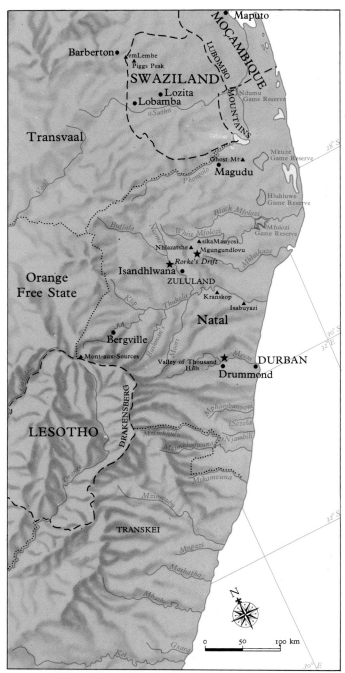

LAND OF RIVERS The rolling eastern downlands are well supplied with rivers, and a natural home for game.

patches of dense bush and high forest. Acacia trees in vast numbers dominated the savanna. The spectral fever trees with their yellow bark grew along the watercourses. Huge wild figs crowded the banks of the rivers so densely that their boughs touched in the middle, and the rivers made their way for many kilometres down long green tunnels of shade. *Erythrina caffra,* one of the most extravagantly beautiful of all trees, made the savanna gorgeous each spring with masses of crimson flowers.

Naming the animals

Altogether, a wonderful wilderness with an extraordinary population of big game. And to each of these wild creatures the newcomers gave a name.

The lion was *iNgonyama* (a wild beast of prey); the elephant was *iNdlovu* (the trampler); the black rhino was *uBejane* (the vicious one); the white rhino was *uMKhombe* (the bulky one); the hippopotamus was *iMvubu* (the fat one); the giraffe was *iNdlulamithi* (taller than the trees); the crocodile was *iNgwenya* (a lawless criminal).

Vast numbers of antelope grazed on the luxuriant grass. Eland, impala, sable, bushbuck, kudu, duiker, zebra, wildebeest, inyala, all were common, along with a multitude of smaller animals, monkeys, baboons, porcupines, warthogs and others. It was altogether a hunter's paradise. Bird life was equally prolific, with the observant newcomers naming them and interpreting their calls. (See box, p. 278.)

With their livestock driven behind them, and their impedimenta packed on the heads of the women, the migrants travelled down close to the eastern slopes of the *Lubombo* (the ridge), a basalt remnant of the geological past when the whole of the area was covered in the same igneous material as that which formed the Drakensberg.

Where the Lubombo petered out into undulating hill country, the migrants found themselves at the gateway to a land close to their hearts' desire. The hill slopes offered grazing and a freedom from the tsetse fly, so lethal to livestock in the bush. The river valleys were alluvial, with excellent soil for agriculture. Rainfall was generous and dependable, and the water in the rivers perennial.

Nguni's following divided into family groups and clans, each searching for the most desirable valley in which to settle. Amongst these people was a man named Malandela who, with a handful of followers, found a home in the valley of the river they named the *Mhlathuze* (the forceful one), from the strength of its current. There they built their beehive-shaped

dwellings and there Malandela eventually died, leaving two sons who divided between them the small inheritance of followers and possessions left by their father.

The younger of these two sons had the pleasant name of *Zulu* (heaven). With his mother and following, he moved away seeking a home of his own. What he found was a basin in the hills drained by a stream known as the *Mkhumbane* (river of the hollow). This is a hallowed place indeed in the lore of the Zulu people, for it was the cradle of their kind.

The basin was covered in savanna forest. Fine canopied acacia trees, like huge sunshades, and several species of decorative euphorbias dominated the area. It was well grassed, and on the heights above there was a spring of fresh water called *Mthonjaneni* (the place of the little fountain). Looming over the basin was a circle of high hills, like a crowd gathered to watch the future events with one great landmark, *Nhlazatshe* (the mountain of green stones), standing as though to direct man to the place.

In this hollow, Zulu settled. All around him other little groups of migrants were making similar homes. Well behind these pioneers, the main bulk of the migrant body, the followers of Dlamini, had also moved south and were busy dispersing into favoured areas.

Thus were laid the foundations of many clans and tribes. Of the man Zulu, little more is remembered. He lived in peace and died in his valley. His people, the *abakwaZulu* (people of the man named Zulu), planted over his grave a euphorbia tree, as was customary, and ever afterwards referred to the site as *kwaNkosinkulu* (the place of the great chief).

The spirit of Shaka

Zulu was succeeded by his son Phunga, and he by his son Mageba, and he by Ndaba, then Jama, then Senzangakhona, who had a son named Shaka. All except Shaka are buried in this valley. He was destined to create the bones of history, to turn the Zulus into a nation, to lead them to great glory, and then to be miserably assassinated, far from the valley of his ancestors.

But his spirit haunts this place, in proud company with his forebears, and in later years, the Zulu army went to this valley before battle to pray at the ancestral graves. When they thundered out, one regiment after the other, chanting the grim salute '*Ngathi, impi!*' ('Because of us, war!'), it was to Shaka that they particularly appealed for the aid of the power of the spirits.

What the birds say

The early Bantu tribes of Natal and Zululand lived very close to nature. Every herb and plant had its name, and many were prized for their medicinal qualities. Every wild creature was observed, its habits remembered and the strange language of its sounds interpreted. The calls of the birds seemed to have a particular fascination for these primitive tribespeople.

The emerald cuckoo was named *uBantwanyana*, for its rather plaintive cry was: '*Bantwanyana ningendi*' ('Children, don't get married').

The quaintly serious hammerhead crane, *uThekwane*, always staring intently into lagoons and rivers, was humorously thought by the tribespeople to be looking not only for food, but also despondently at its own reflection and saying, over and over again: '*Thekwane, Thekwane, nganqimuhle kodwa ngonowa yilokhu nalokhu*' ('Thekwane, Thekwane, I would have been a handsome chap but I am spoilt by this and that, and that').

Insinqizi, the foolish-looking ground hornbill, amused the tribespeople with its apparent pomposity. There seemed no doubt that the female had good reason for her cry: '*Ngiyemuka, ngiyemuka nqiya kwabethu*' ('I am going away, going away to my people'). To this the male replied gruffly: '*Hamba, hamba, kad'usho*' ('Go, go. You have been saying so for a long time').

Juba, the wild pigeon, old enemy of many an African corn-wife, had a merry, bubbling song, constantly repeating: '*Amdokwe avuthiwe*' ('The kaffir corn is ripe').

The strident voice of *iNkankane*, the black ibis or hadadah, echoed down the rivers with: '*Ngahamba, ngahamba, ngahamba*' ('I travel, I travel, I travel').

One of the most striking of the bird cries was the song of *iNkanku*, the red-chested cuckoo or Piet-my-vrou, who announced the approach of spring with: '*Phezukomkhono*' ('On your shoulder'). Thus it told the tribespeople to put their hoes on their shoulders and be off to the fields. With the approach of autumn the same bird changed its cry to: '*Khawulu, khawulu*' ('End the work, end the work').

The most wistful of the calls comes from *isiKhombazane*, the bush dove: '*Ngibe, ngiyazalele lapho, ngithathelwe; ngibe ngiyazalele lapho, ngithathelwe, ngize ngizwe inhliziyo yami ithi to-to-to-to-to*' ('Whenever I lay eggs I get robbed of them, until my heart goes to-to-to-to-to').

Birds of the night had their special songs. The large black owl, *uMandubulu*, sang: '*Vuka, vuka, sekusile*' ('Get up, get up, it has dawned').

It has been said that Zululand is so green because it has been so generously fertilized with human blood. There are very few parts of it which have not been the scene of battle. Like the beds in which Queen Elizabeth slept in Britain, the number of pools and precipices reputedly used by Shaka as places of execution are legion. In fact, if all the claims are true, there would not have been population enough in the whole country to supply victims.

The personality of Shaka was so powerful that, wherever he went, he left his mark upon the landscape. Looking down, for instance, upon the precipitous valley of the Thukela River, there is a flat-topped mountain by the name of *iSabuyazwi*. A typical Shaka legend tells how it received this name.

One day Shaka, with two of his regiments, was travelling past the slopes of this mountain. As they marched the regiments sang war songs, whistled and chanted the praises of their king, while the game animals scurried away and hid in the darkest depths of the forest.

When they arrived at the foot of the mountain, one of Shaka's servants shouted out for the man whose task it was to milk cows for the king. The servant shouted, 'Hey, so-and-so!' and his voice echoed from the mountain.

Shaka heard the echo and laughed, and his laughter also echoed from the listening mountain. Then, to praise their king, the regiments shouted, '*Bayede, Zulu!*' ('Hail, Zulu!'), rattling their shields and whistling, and the sound travelled down the long files of men and was repeated by the echo.

'So,' said Shaka, 'this mountain is *iSabuyazwi*' (the returner of sound). And the regiments thundered out their appreciation of the name and the wisdom of their king in bestowing it.

The valley of the Mhlathuze River was the scene of many battles and hunts, for its dense bush and level floor made it ideal for surprise attacks and secret retreats. In the process of welding together the various clans of Zululand, Shaka fought several battles

BIG-GAME COUNTRY A bull rhinoceros stands against a backdrop of one of the beautifully forested hills of Zululand. In its heyday, Zululand was a paradise for big game, and even today it is still rich in wildlife.

IN THE WILDERNESS A fever tree makes an umbrella that provides shade welcome to man and animal alike on the big-game plain of the Makathini Flats, near the Mkhuze River in Tongaland. Behind the tree looms the Lubombo range.

there, notably against his principal rival Zwide, chief of the Ndwandwe tribe.

The final battle for control of all Zululand was fought in 1819 in the upper reaches of the valley. In the muddy waters of the river the warriors fought it out, while for many kilometres down its course the crocodiles slid gently off their favourite sandbanks and swam up to the ever-increasing stain of blood.

The Ndwandwes were holding their own, stubbornly preventing the Zulus from reaching the north bank of the river. Shaka sent his last reserves secretly up the river. They crossed it and then went down behind the Ndwandwe host. Taking the Ndwandwes in the rear, the Zulus surprised them and started a rout. The Mhlathuze saw a sad slaughter that day.

Zwide fled with the remnants of his army, while the Zulus overran his tribal territory. The Ndwandwes were so scattered that Zwide never saw his homeland again. On his death he had to be carried by stealth to the ancestral burial ground in the tabu

forest of Magudu. His general, Soshangane, fled into the lowlands of Moçambique, and by conquering the local tribes established there the so-called Gasa empire. However, even this proud warrior-chief, when he died, was carried furtively along strange paths to be buried with his ancestors in the heights of Ghost Mountain in the Lubombo range.

Ghost Mountain is a sharp-pointed peak, 528 m in height, and known to the Africans as *eTshaneni* (the place of the small stone). Strange lights and flickering fires are said to be often seen at night around the fissures and crags of the summit. Weird noises and calls are also reported. The mountain is tabu and only the hereditary witchdoctors of the Ndwandwe people know the location of the burial cave and the secrets of its contents.

Shaka, with all Zululand in his power, turned his attention to the area in Natal south of the Thukela River. His shadow fell heavy on that fair land. The resident tribes were systematically attacked, absorbed or driven away. Those that clung to their ancient homes had a precarious time and survived only through the fortunate possession of a natural stronghold.

Mountain of refuge

Where the Mngeni River makes its way through the prodigious spectacle of the Valley of a Thousand Hills there is one such stronghold, an immense pile of sandstone, with a flat-topped summit 957 m high. This is a geological blood brother to Table Mountain, and is known to Europeans as Natal Table Mountain. The Africans call it *emKhambathini* (the place of the giraffe acacia tree). It dominates the whole valley, its steep slopes thickly covered in the various acacia species whose profusion in this valley gives the river its name of *Mngeni* (place of the acacia trees).

The Debe people who lived in the valley used this mountain as a refuge, not only from the Zulus, but also from cannibals who hunted men in the valley with packs of savage dogs. As in Lesotho, cannibalism was the last resort of many people reduced by Zulu raids to a state of utter destitution. The Debe people survived in the sanctuary of the mountain, and devised a technique of hiding in the deep pools of the river, breathing through reeds.

The mountain is a superb scenic spectacle. Its summit is an undulating meadow, richly grassed,

THE KRAAL Cradled by the hills of Natal, these native huts cluster together as if for mutual warmth and comfort. In kraals like this, generations of tribal Africans have passed their lives, herding cattle and growing a few vegetables.

with its own hillocks, valleys and wooded grottoes. The whole atmosphere is that of an island-world of its own, drifting through the ages in a sea made of the thousand hills and twice as many dreams.

From the summit edge of the mountain there is a view almost beyond description. The thousand hills of the Mngeni Valley lie all around in a superb jumble. Eastwards there is a glimpse of the distant ocean. Westwards, on the far horizon, looms the great range of the Drakensberg. In between is the full width of Natal.

On the island summit there are many curious natural marvels. On the right of the main pathway to

Blue crane (*Anthropoides paradisea*)

Dancer of the veld

South Africa's national bird, the blue crane, is, like the springbok, a creature of the open grassland. It may be seen wherever conditions are suitable, often accompanied in late summer by one or two young birds, all of them elegantly stalking across the veld, picking insects and seeds from the grass with their long bills.

The dancing display of the birds in courtship is both heart-warming and slightly absurd, with its sudden leapings in the air and ungainly landings. It is perhaps for this reason that the birds are often kept as pets – despite the injuries they can inflict with their savage beaks.

Southern Africa has two other species of these handsome birds, besides the blue crane. One, the wattled crane, is rare, and therefore a cause for excitement in any bird-watcher who spots one. The other, the crowned crane, is more frequently seen, though only in the eastern regions. The blue crane itself is quite common.

In this, it can count itself fortunate. For two of the world's 15 species of cranes are so reduced in numbers that they are in imminent danger of extinction. It could be that they will survive only in the zoos of the world, often the last refuge for an endangered species.

the summit, at the foot of a grassy knoll, a pleasant little spring bubbles to life, where the coolest of waters may always be found.

Near by stands a small clump of shrubs and tree ferns. This is the secret entrance to a veritable fairy glen. A narrow gorge, almost hidden by overhanging shrubbery and ferns, meanders down through a forest of greenery, mosses, crimson-stemmed begonias, lichens and fungi, then suddenly opens onto a natural terrace, a private veranda for some mountain spirit to regard the view.

The main path around the edge of the summit leads to a grotto from which water springs in a lovely fountain, flows to the edge and then tumbles headlong to the forest 200 m below. Beyond this grotto the pathway winds around a headland, revealing an ever-changing panorama, with kraals scattered over the valley floor far below.

Through beds of watsonias the path continues to a witches' cave lying in a wooded gorge on the eastern side of the mountain. Down this gorge, through a forest of tree ferns, and hidden in a thicket, lies the entrance to a dark cave. Humans are barred from entry by a chasm across the floor but, for the bats and the spirits, the cave burrows on into the bowels of the mountain.

Beyond this cave, the path leads through bracken to a terrace and the so-called Devil's Kloof. Here the mountain has been riven asunder in some past rage of nature, and this enormous fissure – the greatest wonder of the mountain – was formed. The terrace leads to a natural bridge made of mammoth rocks wedged and suspended over the gaping mouth of the chasm.

From the east side a narrow path leads downwards. To the left, halfway down over big boulders, lies a dense thicket falling away to the valley floor. The path finds a tortuous way through the thicket to a ledge of rock, where water drips in silver tears from the overhang. Beyond is a deep, primeval forest of giant yellowwood trees, with tree ferns whose stems reach 10 m high.

Ferns in astonishing profusion – maidenhair, silver ferns, flowering ferns and many more – flourish in this secret paradise. Creepers stretch across the path. The shadows and the stillness seem full of enchantment. The intruder stands spellbound by the silence until suddenly some wild creature, a bushbuck perhaps, which has been watching in breathless suspense, takes fright and goes crashing off through the trees. Behind, the birds twitter, the wind whispers through the leaves, the intruder sighs, and the forest comes alive again.

Where Looks Deceive The waters of the Usuthu River, near Umdumu in Tongaland, look inviting and peaceful. But appearances can be deceptive. As well as having aquatic birds and tiger fish, the Usuthu abounds in hippos and crocodiles.

Basking Killer A crocodile lazes on a tree trunk in the Mkhuze River, Tongaland, dreaming of its last meal . . . or its next. It has been said that crocodiles have been responsible for more deaths of human beings than any other wild animal in the world.

Another immense river valley in Natal is that of the *Mzimkhulu* (the great home of all rivers), and its tributary the *Mzimkhulwane* (little Mzimkhulu River), reaching the sea on the south coast of Natal. Towering sandstone cliffs, red-orange in colour, look down on deep gorges. A luxuriant tangle of shrubbery covers the floor of the gorges of the two rivers. Baboons and leopards wander along the slopes. Duikers, bushbuck, monkeys and a variety of wildcats roam through the forest, while many beautiful birds rest in the branches of the trees.

In Shaka's steps

There are several other notable rivers on the south coast of Natal. In 1828, Shaka led his army on a great raid down this coast and into the Pondo country. As usual, his footsteps remained in the sand, and several of the prominent heights and rivers take their names from events connected with this raid.

Thus it was that when the army reached a certain river, Shaka's personal attendant filled a calabash with water and carried it to his master to drink. Shaka, resting in the shade of an umDoni tree, sipped the water tentatively and was pleased. '*Kanti amanz'a mtoti*' ('So, the water is sweet'), he said. The army, as usual, acclaimed his saying, and the river was thenceforth known as *aManzamtoti* (the sweet

waters).

The *Mphambanyoni* (the deceiver of birds) was so named because its course was so involved as to make even the birds lose their way. The river called *iSezela* (the one who smells out) was so named from a notorious man-eating crocodile which frequented its waters. Shaka heard about this reptile and decided he wanted its skin. His army had great sport. In long lines they waded and dived into the waters, probing with their spears until they flushed the crocodile from its lair, caught it by hand, carried it to their king, and killed it in front of him.

Another river, *uMakhosi* (the river of the chief), pleased Shaka so much with its beautiful scenery that he decreed it to be his own. On pain of death, no man dared to swim or fish in it, and in the course of years the protective tabu made the fish so bold that they played upon the surface of the waters, leaping and lazing and basking, for all men to see.

On another occasion, Shaka gave the same name to two streams – one big, the other small, flowing swiftly parallel towards the sea. He thought of them as two dogs coursing after an antelope, which they caught where the rivers meet. The sea is the antelope. So came the name *iNjambili* (the two dogs).

The greatest of all the rivers of Natal and Zululand is the Thukela, whose vast valley forms the historic frontier between the two countries. It lies in a valley of immense majesty and size, awe-inspiring in its rugged strength and solitude and fully deserving of its name of *Thukela* (startling). A line of high peaks looks down into this valley. One of them is *iTshe lika Ntunjambili* (the rock with two openings), known to Europeans as Kranskop.

The almost inaccessible summit of this 1232 m high mass of sandstone is capped with a crown of trees and linked to the precipice edge of Natal only by a natural bridge, 90 m long and 4 m wide. A giant tunnel pierces the rock beneath the bridge, and legend tells of a second cavern, now closed, which gave the mountain its name of the rock with two openings.

Within this sentinel mountain, the Zulus say, there dwells a spirit whose siren song can be heard coming from the caverns. It is fatal for any traveller to pause and listen to the song, or to watch the entrance of the caves. The song of the siren draws a traveller into the mountain, where he will for ever be lost. Many stories are told of people lured into the mountain. Girls, weary of carrying water up to the heights from the river, were frequent victims. 'Oh rock with two openings,' they would say, 'let me come into your

house.' The great cavern would open up to receive them like the cave of Aladdin. Once in, they were never released and their sighs for freedom and love linger around the precipice face.

The Thukela River (known as the Tugela to Europeans) has a particularly dramatic journey from its source to the sea. In the process of this journey it has cut so deep a gash across the face of Natal that the whole rock skeleton of the country is clearly revealed, as if the river were an autopsy knife in the hands of a surgeon.

From its beginnings on the basalt summit of Mont-aux-Sources in the Drakensberg, the Thukela tumbles down its high waterfall, passing, as it does so, the cave-sandstone level of the Stormberg Series, and then reaching the surface of the Beaufort Series of the Karoo System. The river then flows off eastwards, steadily losing altitude until, approaching the town of Bergville, the Beaufort Series gives way to the lowest series of rocks of the Karoo System, the Ecca Series, which contains the rich coal deposits of northern Natal.

The surface of the Ecca Series in this part of the country is splendidly grassed, making it first-class

THE LOST SILVER MINE

The spectacular valley of the Thukela River is the home of many intriguing legends. One of them concerns a group of early miners of the Lala tribe who lived in the area long before the coming of the Zulu people. They were skilled miners and workers of metal. When the Zulu-speaking people entered the country, these Lala metalworkers were left unmolested, for their skills were valuable.

They manufactured iron hoes, spears and battle-axes for the Zulu army and, from a secret lode of silver, made armbands of particularly striking designs. When Shaka became ruler of all Zululand, these Lala metalworkers paid him tribute of ironwork and the rare and beautiful silver armbands. The armbands became the sign of his special favour and a mark of great honour, awarded only to select dignitaries and nobles of the Zulu nation. Unfortunately for the miners, an obscure skin complaint affected some of the individuals honoured by the armbands. The diviners called in to discover the cause of the affliction accused the miners of treachery. They pointed out to Shaka that the miners were descendants of the earliest people to live in the country.

These people were said to be fragments of the Karanga tribe of Zimbabwe, the same people who mined metals there and built the stone walls of Zimbabwe. The Karangas hated and feared the Zulus for having conquered them, and had conceived a diabolical plan to bewitch and destroy all the leading men of the Zulu nation by infecting them with poison from the armbands.

Shaka was not a man normally gullible in matters of black magic. Nevertheless, he believed these allegations. He gathered in as many of the armbands as he could recover. These were given to a regiment to carry back into the valley of the Thukela. There, in the very pits from which the silver had been mined, the armbands were buried. Then the unfortunate miners and metalworkers were gathered with all their dependants. They were slaughtered to the last child, and their bodies thrown on top of the ill-fated armbands so that their spirits might act as guardians of the tabu hoard. And there they lie today. Many modern treasure seekers have searched for the lost mines, but the spirits guard them well. Only a few surviving armbands and the legend linger on.

'PIED PIPER' MOUNTAIN The great mountain of Kranskop dominates the valley of the Thukela River. A Zulu legend says that a spirit living in the mountain caves can lure travellers inside with its siren song – and they will never emerge.

cattle country; and the river meanders down a course with banks lined with willow trees. This is the easiest part of the river's journey, but it soon flows into serious difficulties. It starts to lose altitude more rapidly, descends through the Dwyka Tillite below the Karoo System, slices easily through the sandstone of the Table Mountain Series, leaves this surface of the midlands of Natal nearly 1000 m above it, and presents its own majestic scenery to man in the form of a valley of enormous proportions.

Journey's end

On the floor of this valley, the Thukela reaches the old granites. It meanders across this hard rock bed,

ceaselessly searching for weaknesses and the easiest route, and being lured into extraordinary 'U' bends and 'S' shapes. There are numerous islands, deep pot-holes scoured out by loose rocks swirled around by eddies in the current, and several hot springs. It is intensely hot and wild country, and an ideal place for witchdoctors, herbalists, diviners and mystics to study the secrets of their calling in complete seclusion.

VALLEY OF A THOUSAND HILLS (*Overleaf*) Even in a language as full of poetry as Zulu there are few names more hauntingly poetic than that given to the Valley of Mngeni. Sunlight dapples some of its thousand hills in this view from Drummond, in Natal.

THE REFUGE Difficult to scale, easy to defend, the flat-topped mountain known as *emKhambathini*, dominating the Valley of a Thousand Hills, provided a place of refuge in the terrible, far-off days of Zulu raids and cannibalism.

Shouldering aside a final barricade of Table Mountain sandstone and Dwyka Tillite boulders, the river emerges at the coast, meanders across the sands of the Cretaceous System, and then pours a heavy load of silt and flotsam into the blue waters of the Indian Ocean. It is not a long river. Its course is about 400 km and its drainage area 30 000 square km, but it has many excellent tributaries, notably the Buffalo, Mooi, Klip and the Bushman's. And the heavy rainfall in its main catchment area in the Drakensberg keeps it well supplied with water.

The Thukela and its tributaries have been involved in many of the great events of history in this part of Africa. To the Zulus it always marked the southern boundary of their country. Beyond it lay only raiding grounds and subject territories. Any foreigner crossing the Thukela or its principal tributary, the Buffalo, was expected to have the permission of the Zulu king, or face the penalty of death.

When the voortrekkers set out in search of vengeance for the murder of Piet Retief and his men, the Zulu general, Ndlela, was ordered to stop them as they crossed the Buffalo. The Zulu army found the trekkers encamped on the high banks of a tributary of the Buffalo, known from its plentiful water and verdant banks as the *Ncome* (praiseworthy one). With no experience in attacking a defensive laager of wagons the Zulus were caught in a death trap, on

288

December 16, 1838. The Ncome River was from that day known as Blood River, for the Zulus paid dearly for their courage. They lost not only the battle, but also the traditional home of their fathers, the basin of the Mkhumbane River. Their capital, *Mgungundlovu* (the secret plot of the elephant), was captured and destroyed, and their king, Dingane, driven away to an ignominious death.

The Zulus long remembered this bitter lesson in tactics. They were to wait 40 years for vengeance against the white man, but revenge when it came was bloody and complete, beneath the brooding shadow of iSandhlwana. (See box, pp. 290–91.)

One of the most romantic and legendary of all the rivers of central Zululand is the *Mfolozi*, so named from its zigzag course. This river, in its middle reaches, divides into two, known to the Zulus as the *Mfolozi eMnyama* (Black Mfolozi) and the *Mfolozi eMhlope* (White Mfolozi) on account of some difference in the colour of the mud. They are rivers of notably violent floods. The Zulus have a proverb about this river: 'The Black Mfolozi chooses its ferrymen for victims.' This is their version of 'a man dies at his trade'.

Another proverb is connected with the stool-shaped mountain overlooking the higher reaches of the White Mfolozi. It is called *isiHlalo sikaManyosi* (the seat of Manyosi). Manyosi Mbatha was a renowned fat man, a toady and court entertainer to Dingane, who showed him off to visitors as the greatest of all gluttons, bloated by colossal meals and drinking. One day he said something out of place and Dingane ordered him to be starved to death. The Zulus still look at the stool-shaped mountain, shrug and say: 'Even Manyosi died.'

Where the Black and White branches of the Mfolozi converge, there is a narrowing peninsula that forms one of the most atmospheric wildernesses in Africa. It is an undulating savanna, with countless beautiful trees and a dense grass covering. It was a perfect home for big game, and a substantial population lived there. Especially notable was the square-lipped, or white, rhinoceros. This massive animal was originally common throughout Southern Africa, but incessant hunting had so reduced its numbers that this secluded area between the two Mfolozi rivers became its last stronghold.

It was fortunate for the game animals that the Mfolozi bush was infested with tsetse fly. European hunters were effectively kept out by these winged 'gamekeepers', whose sting brought sure death to all livestock from the sleeping sickness known to the Zulus as *Nakane*. In such areas, the game animals found a sanctuary. Without the tsetse fly, the white rhino would almost certainly have been extinct. Instead, about 1000 of them survive in the Mfolozi bush, and in the nearby reserve on the banks of the Hluhluwe River where another infestation of tsetse fly kept human hunters out. From Mfolozi, white rhinos have been sent to restock many other game reserves, and to zoological gardens all over the world. The superb expanse of unspoilt Zululand wilderness between the two Mfolozi rivers, however, will always be regarded as their special home and the saviour of their kind. It is now a national park, the Mfolozi Game Reserve.

The traditional northern frontier of Zululand has always been the Phongolo River, one of the tributaries of the uSuthu, the principal river of Swaziland. The country of the Swazi tribe is only 180 km long by 130 km wide, but it is a serenely beautiful little African kingdom, with surprising scenic variety.

The rivers of Swaziland
From the rounded summit of its highest mountain, the 2039 m high *emLembe* (the place of the spider), almost the whole of Swaziland can be seen in one majestic panorama. EmLembe lies on the western border. It is one of the peaks of the granite range known as the *uKhahlamba* (the barrier). West of this range is a prodigious jumble of granite mountains, the basement of the South African central plateau, revealed by the erosive appetite of the shining ribbons of rivers threading their way to the distant sea.

These bustling rivers make Swaziland one of the best watered areas in Africa. They have their headwaters on the South African highveld, and draw for much of their water on the 1500 mm of rain which fall each year on the misty, always green, edge of the central plateau. After they enter Swaziland, they lose altitude rapidly in the fertile middle veld of the country. They then cascade and eddy down to the hot savanna flats, the *eHlanzeni* (place which bears trees), which stretch off in a tangle of vegetation to the long range of the Lubombo, separating Swaziland from the lowlands of Moçambique like a garden wall.

The Swazi people were part of the following of the great chief Dlamini, who led them down on the same migration from the north as the ancestors of the Zulus. While the bulk of the migration pressed southwards, the ancestors of the Swazis, then only a handful of people led by a chief named Ngwane, wandered up the banks of the Phongolo and eventually settled in the hills to the north.

SQUARE THAT BROKE Under the shadow of Isandhlwana, British troops try gallantly but vainly to stem the tide of 20 000 Zulus.

MASSACRE ON THE VELD

Near the mouth of the Thukela River,
in Zululand, there grows a wild fig tree known as
the Ultimatum Tree. The events that began
beneath it stained the veld with blood.

In the shade of the Ultimatum Tree, in December 1878, British representatives presented the Zulus with a series of demands directed against their independence. The Zulus chose to fight, and their general, Ntshingwayo KaMahole Khoza, was ordered by his king, Cetshwayo, to halt the invaders. Unhappily for the British, the Zulu commander remembered the lesson learned at Blood River – that speed, stealth and surprise were necessary to defeat the white man and his guns.

The British Commander, Lord Chelmsford, led his men

across the Buffalo and moved on to a peculiarly shaped sandstone hill known as iSandhlwana, which glowers over a deceptively open-looking expanse of country. Beneath this hill of ill-omen the British made their camp. The hill has its name from the second stomach of a cow, which it resembles in shape. It is a singular landmark in this part of Africa, and has an unmistakable atmosphere of brooding violence.

Unknown to the British, the Zulu general had man-oeuvred his army close to their camp and concealed his

HEROES ALL The morning after a night of carnage at Rorkes Drift.

ZULU GENERAL Ntshingwayo led the Zulu impis at Isandhlwana.

men in a long narrow valley which approached the hill. He had also skilfully used a will-o'-the-wisp diversionary force to lure Lord Chelmsford and a good part of his army out of camp on a wild-goose chase.

So far, so good for the Zulus. But then his diviners warned their commander that the next day was unpropitious for attack. With a curse he ordered his men to lie low. Then fate took a hand in this grim game. A British patrol stumbled on a Zulu advance post. They opened fire and the die was cast. Ntshingwayo brushed aside the diviners. He expertly marshalled his army into battle formation, a chest and two horns, and sent them to envelop the disordered British camp.

Like the shadow of a dark thundercloud, the full Zulu army swept over the veld. The struggle was primeval and savage, but it was also brave and honourable, and if one has to die it is better to die at the hands of men than of cowards. It was over very soon. Fifty-eight British officers, 806 other ranks and 470 native allies were killed. About 1000 Zulus were also killed or wounded – only 55 white soldiers managed to escape.

Towards the end of the battle the Zulu commander detached one of his subordinate officers, Dabulamanzi, to take two regiments and pursue any survivors retreating to the river. At the crossing place over the Buffalo, known as Rorkes Drift, the few survivors had found sanctuary in the buildings of a mission station on the Natal side of the river. Garrison and runaways together numbered only 139. Dabulamanzi thought that under cover of night his men could take the place by storm, and his warriors eagerly swam the river. It was a bad night at Rorkes Drift. But at 4 a.m. Dabulamanzi and his men retreated. Every man left alive in the British force was wounded, but the Zulus had themselves lost 400 men, and this was not what Dabulamanzi had been ordered to do. With the remnants of his two regiments, he recrossed the river into Zululand. As the false dawn came they headed back to rejoin the main army, which was already marching home laden with booty, with many a man helping along some wounded comrade. After the crushing defeat of iSandhlwana, the defence of Rorkes Drift restored British pride. Eleven Victoria Crosses were awarded after the action.

This was a pleasant and fertile area in which to settle. The river gave them water; from the alluvial soil came their food. The hills were free of tsetse fly and had rich grazing for livestock, while the lowlands teemed with game. The settlers flourished. One chief succeeded the other until, at the beginning of the 19th century, they were ruled by Sobhuza. He was the ambitious one who set out to create a nation.

It was an age of great leaders in Southern Africa. Shaka was active in Zululand; Moshesh in Lesotho; and Sobhuza in Swaziland. Sobhuza prudently shied away from the Zulus. He sent his own little army to the north, and they found the great river they called, from the colour of its muddy waters, *Usuthu* (dark brown). From its headwaters on the central plateau, this powerful river flowed eastwards through the centre of the country. Its valley was broad, its alluvial soil deep, the water perennial. The landscape was pleasing, and the granite mountains on either side were full of excellent retreats, caves and hidden gorges where women, cattle and warriors could be securely hidden when the Zulus launched raids.

Sobhuza conquered the Tswana people already living in the valley. By the time of his death there were about 75 different clans subject to his rule, and to them as a nation his son, Mswazi, was destined to give his name. At this time, the early 1840s, Europeans entered Swaziland as traders and prospectors. The landscape of the old granites gave the prospectors hopes for mineral discoveries similar to those in the Barberton area just west of the Khahlamba mountains. They were not disappointed.

An ancient trade path leading from Lourenço Marques to the interior of South Africa had managed to find a way through the mountains on the Swazi border. Along this path one of the most renowned of the Transvaal prospectors, Tom McLachlan, made his way in 1875. Swaziland must have then been quite exquisite in the wildness and freedom of its scenery. The pathway seemed to lead into an earthly paradise. It climbed to the clouds, twisting, turning, rising and falling around the high slopes of the mountains. At the summit of its climb, it appeared to be defeated by a vast ravine high up near the top of emLembe Mountain. Then, in a fine sweep of scenic drama, it made an escape by means of the spectacular *isiKhaleni sebuLembu* (pass of the spider's web), a

natural bridge formed of rock choking up the narrow neck of the ravine.

Beside the path, deep in the mountains, McLachlan and his partners built a shack, and from this base they prospected. In January 1884, one of them, William Pigg, found the so-called Devil's Reef of payable gold near the summit of a height since known as Piggs Peak. This was the first mine in Swaziland, and all of its materials, machines, tools, and its gold output had to be carried on the backs of pack animals.

Other discoveries followed: gold, tin, iron and copper. Much later, in 1923, some Swazi prospectors, working for the caretaker of the Piggs Peak Mine, found chrysotile asbestos in a valley near the mine. In 1928, further finds were made in this area and eventually the great Havelock Asbestos Mine came into production – an extraordinary achievement, with the inaccessible area connected to the outside world by means of an aerial ropeway 20 km long. This ropeway – with 224 carriers moving along it, each loaded with 170 kg of asbestos fibre – has carried out the entire product of the mine, and brought in all the supplies required by one of the world's major chrysotile mines.

The festival of Ncwala

The Swazi people are amongst the handsomest and most colourfully dressed of all African people, and intensely proud of their country. They have always lived intimately with the natural features of the land and, in recognition of this close relationship, the Swazis each year stage one of the world's great mystic festivals, the *Ncwala* (ceremonial dance). The ceremony is held at the time of the first new moon in January, and is staged in the huge corral at the home of the Queen Mother, in the valley of the Usuthu. It is a complex ritual of kingship, a reinforcement of the national spirit, a celebration of the harvesting of the first fruits, a reunion with the forces of nature, and a guarantee of rain for the next season.

At the preceding new moon, officials known as Bemanti fetch samples of water from all major rivers of Swaziland, and also from the sea. When they return to Lobamba, what is known as the Little Ncwala commences, with ceremonies and songs continuing until the moon is full. Then the next phase begins.

On the first day, youths and warriors from Lobamba march to join the men of the king's residence at Lozita. The combined force sing ritual songs and, towards evening, the king sends the youths off

HILL OF DEATH On January 22, 1879, under the grim shadow of a hill called *iSandhlwana*, Cetshwayo's Zulus surprised and wiped out a British army more than 1000 strong. The hill still seems to glower forbiddingly over the landscape.

THE HUNTER An egret searches for prey in a cool, green world of its own on the banks of the Mkhuze River in Tongaland. It will stand motionless until a tempting frog or insect comes along, then make the kill with its dagger-like bill.

to gather branches of the *lusekwane* trees growing at Gunundwini. This is a test of endurance. The youths have to march 40 km to reach the trees before midnight. As the full moon appears over the horizon each boy cuts the largest branch he thinks he can carry. Then they march, singing through the night, all the way back to Lobamba. There, in the morning, they deposit their branches in the cattle corral. Only then do they really rest. This ends the second day.

At dawn on the third day, boys who were too young to do the 80 km return walk to fetch the lusekwane boughs go off and collect branches of the *mbondvo* shrub. These branches are also deposited in the cattle corral. At the western end of this great enclosure, elders then build a *Nhlambelo* (bower) for the king, using the lusekwane and mbondvo branches.

At about 3 p.m. the Bemanti and the various officials of the ceremony arrive and are joined by the king. The warriors muster, dressed in their special Ncwala costumes of skins. Ritual songs are sung – songs which are tabu for the rest of the year. A black ox is then driven into the Nhlambelo and doctored. Outside, the youths have gathered and excitement mounts. The black ox is suddenly driven out and in a surging body they overpower it, pummel it to death

with their bare hands, and carry the carcass back into the bower where parts of it are used in the ritual. Outside, the warriors, drawn up into a great crescent, dance backwards and forwards, like the surging sea, singing the strange-sounding ritual songs, which also imitate the sea. Another black ox is then caught by the youths and taken alive into the bower. This animal is later released, after being used in the ceremonies.

The next day, the fourth in the ceremony, sees the Ncwala reach its climax in the afternoon dancing. The Swazi army, in full costume, is mustered in the enclosure. Official guests arrive and take their seats in a grandstand. If there is a guest of honour, he is escorted by the king to inspect the warriors. The king then joins his warriors and a great dance begins, with the Queen Mother, her ladies and many Swazis participating. Traditional beer is drunk by the guests and then they depart, saying farewell to the king who, escorted by members of his royal clan, now enters his bower.

MOONLIGHT ON THE KEI Night on the Kei River . . . and everything is hushed, save for the call of a bird or the cry of a jackal. But this river, which today marks the boundary between the Cape and Transkei, once echoed to the noise of tribal raids.

DESTROYER THAT BRINGS NEW LIFE Fire rages across the veld of the coastal downlands, destroying everything in its path. But, paradoxically, its ash will fertilize the soil. Soon the black scar will heal, to be replaced by a fresh mantle of green.

The warriors dance backwards and forwards, singing their ritual songs and pleading with the king to return to them for another year of reinforced rule. The king, with some show of reluctance, then leaves his bower. He symbolically tastes the first fruits of the harvests, and from then on crops may be reaped and eaten.

The next day is a sacred day of seclusion and tabu. No work is done.

The sixth and last day sees the warriors march into the hills behind Lobamba. They collect firewood for a huge bonfire in the centre of the cattle corral. In the afternoon this pyre is set alight. On it, the warriors deposit items of their costume worn the previous year. They dance and sing around the fire, begging the ancestral spirits to send rain to put it out as a sign of their favour for the coming year. On nearly every occasion rain does fall, and the ceremony ends with a general celebration of feasting, dancing and singing. If rain does not fall, then certain ceremonies must be repeated until ancestral approval is revealed by means of rain.

The angry waters

South of Natal, the Mthamvuna River marks the border with Transkei, *Mthamvuna* means the reaper of mouthfuls, and the river has this name because of its tendency in flood to erode away portions of the fields of corn and other crops planted along its alluvial banks. It is a river famous for water spirits, and its waters, like the waters of the sea, are said to hate an unclean person. Any traveller attempting to ford such a river has to confess his sins, otherwise the angry waters are liable to sweep him away.

For 250 km south of the Mthamvuna the landscape consists of the beautifully rolling, grass-covered downlands of Transkei. Principal landmarks are still the rivers: the *Mzimvubu* (the home of hippos), which reaches the sea by forcing a final passage between two huge cliffs, densely covered in bush and forest; the *Mngazi* (place of blood); the *Mthatha* (the taker); and many others wind through these hills, past the farmlands and dwellings of such tribes as the Pondo, Bomvana and the Xhosa.

Many of the rivers have waterfalls and rapids, deep gorges, alluvial valleys, and involved meanders – especially the Mbashe River which has a middle course so involved that part of it has the European name of the 'Collywobbles'.

The *Kei* (great) River marks the southern border of Transkei. Close to it flows a river which is linked with one of the most poignant stories in history, the *Gxara* (the river of the precipice). In the river there is a pool in a setting of trees and flowering plants. Here a young medium, Nonqawuse, used to bathe. While sitting looking into its waters she saw faces of the ancestral spirits. Their voices came to her, promising that they would help the Xhosas drive the Europeans away, provided that, as a sign of faith, the tribespeople would destroy all the cattle and crops that they owned.

A great commotion spread amongst the Xhosas at news of this revelation. Men travelled from far to speak with the medium and her witchdoctor uncle, Mhlakaza. Crowds gathered to gaze into the pool, and many claimed to have seen there the faces of their own ancestors, and heard them demanding total faith as the price for support from the supernatural world. Some watchers told with bated breath how they had seen whole armies of ghost warriors waiting to emerge, eager for war and jeering at the timidity of the Xhosas.

Then began a dreadful fever of cattle killing and crop destruction, with the great majority of the Gcaleka section of the Xhosas implicitly obeying the dream voices heard by Nonqawuse. The Ngqika section of the tribe fortunately kept their reason and remained aloof.

For believers the climax was to be on February 18, 1857. Then the sun would rise blood-red, and the land would be filled with fat cattle, new crops and vast armies of reincarnated spirits ready to restore the Xhosa tribe to its past glory and greatness.

It was truly a terrible dawn for many thousands of deluded people when the sun climbed out of the Indian Ocean the same as ever before. The Gcalekas saw before them ruination and starvation. They had nothing. It is estimated that 25 000 people died of hunger, and the remainder survived only through the compassion of neighbouring tribes and the very people they had wanted to destroy – the Europeans, who reached out a hand of friendship and fed them. The discredited medium fled for safety.

She was arrested by European police and ended her days in obscurity on a farm near King William's Town. The pool of the spirits in the Gxara, with its troubled surface and wild surroundings, remains as a memorial to folly. Flowering aloes in winter provide it with a particularly handsome setting, but the area is always beautiful, and the river meanders through the hills until it reaches the lagoon at its mouth. There it rests awhile before its final rush through the barrier of sand to the waiting sea.

A landscape that
burst out of the sea

*Cataclysmic subterranean forces
lifted the continent . . . the angry oceans
lashed the shores . . . and so was
sculpted the coastline of Africa.*

JOURNEY'S END Passing the high cliffs known as the Gates of St. John, the Mzimvubu River reaches the Indian Ocean. Its name means 'home of the hippopotamus', and it is a true river of Africa – brooding, languid, yet capable of great violence.

299

*The sea fought a battle
with the land . . . and
man was the winner*

SINCE TIME BEGAN, there has been a ceaseless battle between the sea and the land. In this struggle, islands and entire coastlines can be submerged and then rise above the surface, perhaps only to be lost again beneath the returning waters or by the subsidence of the land mass itself.

The continent of Africa attained basically its present shape about 150 million years ago, when a central land mass, called Gondwanaland by geologists, and centred roughly over the present-day South Pole, began to split up. Carried on a sea of molten rock, the fragments drifted apart like runaway islands.

Since that time, changes to the face of Africa have been brought about by erosion and variations in level, caused by cataclysmic subterranean forces. The whole continent was elevated by about 1000 m. Then, about 100 million years ago, the southern part of the continent subsided slightly and the sea flowed over the present coastline. It covered most of Moçambique, lapped against the Lubombo Mountains and extended inland at many places, such as the Sundays River Valley in the Eastern Cape.

In the South, the sea swept in over the Cape Flats as far as the slopes of the mountains. Table Mountain and the other heights of the Cape Peninsula, together with isolated heights such as Van Riebeeks Kasteel, were left as islands.

There seems to have been several successive variations in sea level. Some of the variations were the result of the warping, tilting and writhing of the land. Some of these paroxysms had serious consequences. Faults, crevices, cracks and lines of weakness were left, creating areas of instability. One of these is the Worcester fault in the Cape. Nearly 500 km in length, this fault is occasionally the cause of tremors and minor earthquakes.

Along the coast, the effect of these successive changes was to cover considerable areas with shells, thick sand and other detritus washed off the land mass and deposited beneath the shallow sea as a level bed. This material, left behind when the sea retreated once again, forms today the richly fossilised coastal Cretaceous System.

The lagoon that was drowned

Many changes were imposed on the coastal areas by the comings and goings of the sea, and some of them have proved of enormous value to man. Durban harbour is an example of such a valuable change. Originally it was a large lagoon, fed by the waters of several rivers and streams. The rising of the sea drowned this lagoon and turned it into a sheltered bay which became almost entirely enclosed by two sandspits.

Sandspits are features of the Natal coast. Silt

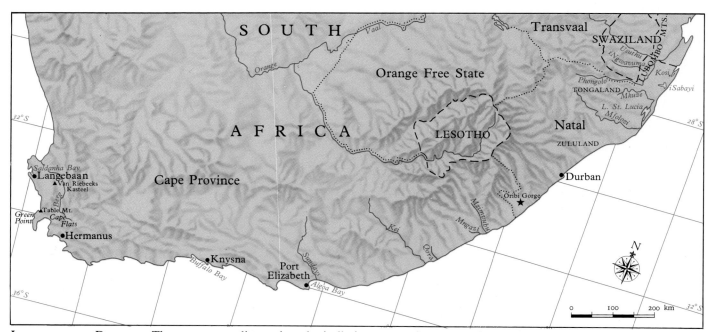

LAND THAT WAS DROWNED The eastern coastline took on basically its present shape more than 70 million years ago, when the sea level fell, exposing vast areas of once-drowned land. Magnificent harbours were created during this period.

brought down by the rivers is carried northwards by the prevailing inshore current, which runs counter to the powerful Moçambique Current flowing southwards several kilometres out from the shore. The silt tends to be deposited immediately north of the mouth of the river, forcing it to deflect southwards to avoid the barrier of its own contrivance.

The two sandspits containing Durban Bay were formed in this manner. On the south side is a high, bush-covered ridge of sand known to Europeans as The Bluff, and to Africans as *isiBubulungu* (the long, bulky thing). This ridge is composed of sand apparently brought down to the sea by the iSipingo River. The bush on this ridge was always particularly thick and provided a hiding place for the small Luthuli tribe, whose survival during the period of Zulu raids was made possible by this convenient retreat in their homeland.

The spit on the north side of the bay is composed of sand brought down by several streams which feed what the Africans know as *eThekwini* (the lagoon), or Durban Bay. It was the discovery of this perfectly protected harbour which attracted pioneer European settlement in Natal. The Portuguese navigators found it, and marked the entrance on their maps as the *Rio de Natal* (River of the Nativity). Passing ships stopped occasionally, and sent small boats into the bay to secure fresh drinking water or to trade with the tribespeople.

Then, in December 1823, a party of British ivory traders in two small ships, the brig *Mary* and the sloop *Jane*, anchored at the entrance. A sudden squall blew up and proved so threatening that they risked sailing directly into the bay, bumping across the sandbar at the entrance. These were the first ships ever to find safe anchorage in the calm waters of that magnificent natural harbour.

At that time the bay must have been a wild and lonely sight in its dense, primeval forest setting. In the centre there was an island covered with mangroves. The waters teemed with fish. There were countless waterfowl and hippos, and the trees were full of monkeys and birds. Big game, including many elephants, wandered around the shores and lurked in the shadows of the trees. To the ivory traders this was paradise. The next year they returned and established a settlement, which was the beginning of the port and city of Durban.

Saldanha Bay, another magnificent natural harbour, also came to be during the Cretaceous Period. Originally, it seems to have been the mouth of the Berg River, which flowed into a lagoon at Geelbek.

The tilting of the southern end of Africa redirected the river to its present mouth. The sea flooded into the former lagoon, creating the harbour, while the southern reaches, known as *Langebaan* (Long Channel), originally the delta of the river, were buried beneath about 6 m of water.

Langebaan is 15 km long and 4 km wide. It is notable for an extraordinary deposit of oyster shells, in such enormous quantity as to be rivalled in all the world only by Chesapeake Bay in North America. The origin of this deposit is conjectural. The oysters were probably casualties of the periodic rising and falling of the sea level. They may have been completely elevated above the sea at some stage and killed by exposure. Alternatively, temperature variations in the water, or silt from the river, could have proved lethal. The shells lie in vast, flat beds 3 m to 7 m thick and intersected by channels caused by tidal flow. Although the cold Benguela Current feeds into Saldanha Bay, Langebaan, the southern cul-de-sac, exposes its water to a hot sun, and the temperature increases progressively until, at the far end, it is at least 10°C warmer than the surrounding sea. This temperature variation creates acute problems for marine life. Seabirds and flamingos are indifferent to it, but fish tend to inhabit clearly defined belts of water where the temperature is suited to their species.

Where sabre-toothed tigers roamed

Close to Langebaan, in the sand-dune area of *Elandsfontein*, there is a fossil site of considerable importance to prehistorians. Originally a small lake in arid surroundings, its fresh water attracted a variety of prehistoric creatures, including extinct species of giraffes, buffalos, lions, baboons, sabre-toothed tigers, zebrine horses, wild pigs, giant boars, elephants, cave hyenas, and early man in several of his evolutionary forms.

There are six islands in and at the approaches to Saldanha Bay. Seabirds and seals have long used these islands as breeding places, situated as they are close to the rich pelagic fishing grounds of the Benguela Current. The first European navigators to explore the area noted the plumpness and vast numbers of these birds and seals, and realised that they must have been feeding on immense supplies of fish.

Such natural riches, and the spacious harbour, would have automatically attracted human settlement. The only disadvantage of the area was a shortage of fresh water. On the southern horizon, the bulk of Table Mountain loomed like the sign of a rival inn, attracting customers to its far more generously provided water and food. Even the name of Saldanha was originally applied to Table Bay when the Portuguese explorer Antonio de Saldanha visited it in 1503. Nearly 100 years later, Dutch sailors arbitrarily changed this name, and the harbour was thenceforth called Table Bay.

The seals of Saldanha attracted the first commercial interest, with a long rivalry between Dutch and French fur hunters. Enormous quantities of seal pelts were obtained, and nowadays from 60 000 to 90 000 seals are killed each year on the various rookeries. Even their carcasses are of value: they are exported frozen to Greenland, for sale to Eskimoes.

At the time of the guano rush to Ichaboe Island (see p. 26), the Saldanha Bay islands attracted attention. In August 1844 there were reported to be over 300 ships loading guano, and several islands, notably Malgas, were found to be covered with it to a depth of about 10 m. Sailors' towns sprang up on the islands, with fanciful names such as 'London Docks' and 'Wapping'. Several thousands shiploads of guano were taken away, and the islands today still yield an annual supply of this rich fertiliser. Phosphatic rock is also found near Saldanha, and this is mined to supply fertiliser.

The most extensive coastal areas, which once lay beneath the sea, are the sand-covered flats of Moçambique, Tongaland and northern Zululand. When the sea finally retreated from these areas about 60 million years ago, it left the rivers with a singularly awkward problem. After making their way from the interior and reaching the original coastline, they found themselves confronted by the unwanted and embarrassing obstacle of an extent of thick sand. This was a hindrance to break the strength of the largest river. They were slowed in their courses and forced to meander in search of a way through the sand, tending to form shallow lakes and pans. Unless their flows were particularly resolute, they were in danger of encountering a final impassable blockade – a wind-erected line of coastal dunes which denied them direct access to the sea. Their courses then terminated in freshwater lakes, linked to the sea only by slow percolation through the sand.

Moçambique has many such coastal lakes. Near the administrative centre of Quissico there is a cluster of

AS EVENING FALLS The glory of an evening sky, and the stillness of the Outeniqua mountains, are mirrored in the barely-ruffled surface of a lake near the Wilderness area of the Southern Cape. This is Africa at its most tranquil.

lakes with fresh water of superb clarity filling sub-stantial depressions just behind the beach dunes. Sparkling white beaches and clean beds are characteristic of these lakes.

The lakes of Tongaland

Tongaland, lying between Zululand and Moçam-bique, has perhaps the classic examples of terminal lakes, and rivers forced to improvise awkward exten-sions to their courses. Tongaland is entirely Cretace-ous in its origin. The high *Lubombo* (ridge) which

runs south to north once marked the line of the coast, with the sea breaking along its eastern slopes. With the elevation of the shell-covered sea bed, the ridge at first looked down on a 70 km wide expanse of almost level sand.

Heavy rainfall soon stimulated the growth of a covering of vegetation on this sand. In a long belt, 40 km wide, a handsome forest grew, with over 200 different species of trees flourishing in a hot, humid atmosphere. Acacias in considerable variety grow in this area, and the white acacia, or fever tree, is

VALLEY OF DARK MEMORIES The Mngazi River, which reaches the sea near Port St. Johns, flows through its peaceful valley. The scene was not always so calm: the river's name means 'place of bloodshed', for the valley was once the scene of savage tribal warfare.

SCULPTED BY NATURE Wind and sea have both taken a hand in creating these sandstone formations overlooking the beach at Buffalo Bay, near Knysna. This coastline arose from the sea millions of years ago. Now the sea is claiming back its own.

particularly handsome. Along the river banks, the forests are dominated by fig trees so huge that for many kilometres the rivers find their way through tunnels formed by their interlocking branches. The Tonga tribespeople have a saying about one of the rivers, the Phongolo: 'The Phongolo will never be found without a fig tree' – meaning that a man will never lack a crony; and certainly this river and its fig trees are inseparable.

On its eastern side, the belt of forest peters out with strange abruptness on a thin line of bog called the *Musi* swamp, because of the musi reeds which grow there. Beyond this long swamp lies a belt of lala palms, then a belt of undulating, open land covered with lush, green, sour grass and scattered clumps of palm trees, wild bananas and assorted shrubbery. Then there is a thin line of coastal forest, a final wall of high sand dunes, a beach of such rich colour that the Portuguese named it the *Medaos do Ouro* (downs of gold), and at last, the pounding surf of the Indian Ocean.

A number of rivers penetrate this 8500 square km

ON THE WILD COAST Undisturbed for thousands of years, the banks of the Qora River, on the Wild Coast, ring to the cries of birds and monkeys. The river itself teems with fish and was once a great place for hippos and crocodiles.

IN THE FOREST Wild banana palms and other sub-tropical plants flourish in the warm, moisture-laden air of the Natal coast south of Durban. The very abundance of plant life brings a problem: it can shut out the sun on which the plants depend for life.

expanse of pure wilderness. In the south, the river known as the *Mkhuze*, from the aromatic trees of that name growing on its banks, forces a passage through a gorge in the Lubombo below the heights of Ghost Mountain. It is a spectacular gorge, noted for its flowering aloes and, until recently, for containing a vast number of human skeletons. They were left there as the result of a vicious fight in 1884 between the Mandlakazi and the Suthu sections of the Zulu people.

Reaching the sandflats of Tongaland, the Mkhuze wilts. It tries to take evasive action and swings southwards, but enters a cul-de-sac where the coastal dunes block its flow. It spreads out over the sand as a large swamp, densely populated by crocodiles and hippos. The waters of the Mkhuze permeate the swamp, finding a way into what the Zulus call *aCwe-beni* (the lagoon), which the Portuguese named Lake St Lucia.

This lake forms a complex estuary system, roughly in the shape of the letter H. The west limb of the H, known as False Bay, is 25 km long, 3 km wide and about 2 m deep. The cross-bar of the H is known as Hell's Gates and is notorious for winds. The east limb of the H is Lake St Lucia proper, 35 km long, 10 km wide and about 2 m deep. Reed-covered islands are scattered over the surface. From the southern end, a shallow channel flows through the sand and joins the Mfolozi River near its mouth, relying on its powerful floodwaters to periodically force a passage through the final barrier of sand, and so reach the sea.

The St Lucia estuary is on the same level as the sea. When its mouth is open to the sea, salt water floods into the estuary, flows north into the upper

WHERE THE ANTELOPE ROAM The Mzimkulwana River in Natal, a tributary of the Mzimkulu (the great home of all rivers), flows through the Oribi Gorge. The gorge is named after the oribi antelope, which find food and security in its dense bush.

FINAL BARRIER Before reaching the sea, the Sundays River has to find its way around one final obstacle: a wind-built barrier of sand dunes. Many rivers along this coast are unable to breach the barrier, and end in freshwater lakes near the sea.

BAY OF BEAUTY The Wild Coast is a place of unspoiled beauty, full of isolated bays like Sinangwana Beach, where the surf of the Indian Ocean hurls itself perpetually against a shoreline framed by the bush-covered, aloe-dotted hills of Pondoland.

recesses and there evaporates in the intense heat. Salt is left behind and, in consequence, False Bay has a salinity of 52,6 parts per 1000, compared to the 35 parts per 1000 of the sea.

The whole estuary teems with life. Salmon, grunter, mullet, mud bream, barbel and tiger fish are to be found in its waters. Preying on them are masses of crocodiles, and over 25 species of aquatic birds, including pelicans, flamingos, fish eagles, ducks, geese, Goliath herons, kingfishers and cormorants. Big-game fish and sharks haunt the entrance, feeding on the fish entering and leaving the estuary. Hippos feed on the reeds, and antelope come down to thickets lining the shore. The area is today a national park.

North of St Lucia lie two smaller lakes, both of fresh water and both quite isolated from the sea by the dunes. The largest of these lakes is *iSabayi*, a name which means an enclosure with no visible outlet. This lake is 30 m deep, with drinkable water so limpid that fish, hippos and crocodiles are clearly visible moving about beneath the surface. The beach is a dazzling white, while the bed of the lake is clear sand. No streams flow into this lake, and there is no apparent drainage to the sea. Underground streams must, therefore, maintain the level against evaporation and seepage.

Still further north, close to the border with Moçambique, there is a chain of deep lakes known to

Europeans as Kosi. The name arises from an old muddle. Naval surveyors in 1822 were looking for the mouth of the Mkhuze, and failed to appreciate that this river had turned sharply south in an effort to avoid the sand. The estuary of the chain of lakes was considered to be the mouth of this river and the name, badly misspelt, was thenceforth marked on the maps.

Actually, there are four main lakes all linked together, with a connection to the sea. The largest is *Hlangwe* (place of reeds), which reaches a depth of over 50 m. It is a superb natural harbour, 8 km long and 5 km wide, lying in a wilderness which man, perhaps fortunately, has not so far managed to tame. The lake, therefore, lies pure and clean in a setting of beautiful trees and shrubs. Fish eagles send their eerie cry over its waters, and fish teem in its depths.

Linked to Hlangwe is a smaller lake, *oKhunwini* (the place of firewood). Beyond it is the third in the chain, *uKhalwe* (the distant one); and then there is an estuary lake known as *eNkhovukeni* (up and down), from the tidal action of its waters. This estuary is connected to the sea, and through it the chain of lakes receives a flow of fish which come to feed and spawn in its warm and protected waters. Sea-pike, grunter, bream and many others make their way up the chain, finding zones of salinity suited to their needs, from the 35 per cent of the sea to the 3,31 per cent of Hlangwe.

Two major rivers find a way through the northern part of Tongaland, and their courses are marked by numerous pans and lakelets where the water spills out into adjacent hollows. The water is rich in foodstuffs, and these lakelets support a dense population of fish, mainly barbel and tiger fish. Crocodiles in considerable quantity prey on the fish. For hippos this water world, in its setting of rich vegetation, is a perfect home. The water is warm, of convenient depth, and has innumerable sandbanks on which to laze.

Fish galore . . . and free liquor

The local tribespeople stage large-scale communal fish hunts in the lakelets. Forming into long lines, and beating the water with sticks, they walk through the lakelets, driving the fish into funnel-shaped traps. Crocodiles and hippos are driven away by the general noise and excitement and, usually, many hundreds of fat barbel are trapped, caught and dried for later consumption.

In addition to this generous supply of free fish, nature has provided what is certainly the world's largest store of free alcohol. The lala palms yield a sap which is tapped by the tribespeople, who cut grooves into the stems and draw the sap into a gourd, where it ferments and is then collected and drunk. The consequence of this free supply of alcohol is that it is possible for people of the Tembe-Tonga tribe to be permanently drunk. Some are even born drunk from the alcohol in their mothers' blood, and die drunk without ever knowing what it is to be sober. It is even said that the mosquitoes, which in these parts are large and aggressive, are also under the influence of the alcohol in their victims' blood. Elephants are partial to robbing the gourds of their contents, and are said to be a particularly jolly crowd of inebriated pachyderms.

The principal river flowing through Tongaland is the *Usuthu* (dark brown), fed by tributaries such as the *Phongolo* (the trough) and the *Ngwavuma*, which takes its name from a species of tree common along its banks. These rivers are classically African in their nature – muddy, hot, feverous, and sullenly sluggish in their flow, but periodically given to violent floods, when huge trees are carried away and hippos and crocodiles are forced to flee onto dry land or face destruction from the force of the current or the weight of flotsam.

Raised beaches, at places such as Green Point on the shores of Table Bay, Hermanus and Algoa Bay, are another legacy of the Cretaceous Period. But the vast, flat areas of Moçambique and Tongaland are its principal product and contribution to the land mass of Southern Africa. Since these areas were last left above the level of the sea, about 60 million years ago, Southern Africa has been quiet from a geological point of view.

Volcanic throats and diamond pipes were blown up from the depths towards the end of the Cretaceous Period, but this was a completely separate spasm of eruptive activity. For the rest of the time, through what is known as the Tertiary, and then the Quaternary Period of today, nature has been altering the surface through the erosive work of rain, rivers and winds. River valleys have been deepened; the area of the wind-blown sands of the Kgalagadi has been expanded; mountains have been reshaped; and odd rocks have been left precariously and temporarily balanced, as though to show that the power of creation is always present. This is the power that has wandered over the land, making subtle changes here and there; never still, never tiring; with only man thinking in terms of time because of his own limited span of life, in a setting which knows of no beginning or end . . . only incessant transformation.

Index

Major entries on a subject are indicated by the use of **bold type**.
Figures in *italic type* refer to pages on which there is an illustration or map.
Other references to a subject are indicated by Roman type.

BIRDS

Stinkwood trees 255
Stonefish 17, *18*
Stormberg Series 111
Strelitzia parvifolia 59
Stromatolites 184
Sudwala Caves **184–91**
  Arctic Chamber 189
  Cathedral Avenue 191
  Corkscrew Passage 188
  Crystal Chamber 191
  Fairyland Chamber 188
  Joint Passage 188
  Penguin Chamber 189, 191
  P. R. Owen Hall 187
  Red Devil 187
  Screaming Monster *180–1*, 187
  Smoking Chamber 189
  Weeping Madonna 188
Sundays River *116–8*, 309
Suricate **115**
Swakop River 102
Swartberg (Black Mountain) range **61–7**
Swartberg Pass 67
Swaziland 289, 293

T

Table Bay 39, 302
Table Mountain *33*, **39–43**, *41*
Table Mountain Series 40, 48
Tablecloth *41*, **42–3**
Tandayi tributary 270
Tented wagon **256**
Terblans trees 255
Termites 168
Tertiary Period 311
Thaba Bosiho 129, 130, 132
Thamalakane River 174
Thorium 250
Thornveld *165*
Three Sisters 112
Thukela River *141*, 216, 226, **283–8**
Tin 248, 249
Titanium 249
Tlou tribe 261
Tongaland 304
Toorkop 64
Toorwaterpoort 64
Tooverberg *114*, 114
Topaz 251
Topnaar Hottentots 93
Tourmaline 107
Transkei High Forest 260
Tree ferns 257
Tremolite 248
Truffles 95
Tsamma melons 95, *169*, 177
Tsetse fly 289
Tshinyakweremba 268
Tshiremba *196*
Tshirinda forest 273
Tshirorodziva 191

Tsitsikamma 254
Tsumeb **106**, 107
Tugela River *141*, 216, 226, **283–8**
Tugela Waterfall 147, 216
Turquoise 251
Turtles 20

U

uKhalwe 311
Ultimatum Tree **290–1**
uluNdi 151
uMakhosi 283
umLambonja River 147, 148
Uranium 280
Ursinia 56
  cakilefolia 59
Usuthu River 154, *283*, 293, 311

V

Vadose Water 236
Valley of a Thousand Hills 281, 282, *286–7*
Valley of Death **207–13**
Valley of Desolation *116–8*
Vanadium 248
Van Hunks, Legend of **42–3**
Veldkos 95
Verdite 251
Vermiculite 244
Verneuk Pan 154
Vervet monkeys 259
Victoria Falls *220–2*, 230, *231*, 232, 233
Volcanics, Drakensberg 136
Voorendyk, Jacobus 241
Vumba 267, 268

W

Wankie National Park 156
Warmbaths 236
Warm-water oyster 75
Water lily *174*
Water table 236
Waterfalls **215–33**

Welwitschia mirabilis 82, *82–3*
Western Cape **45–67**
Whêtse 127
White Mfolozi 289
White rhino 289
White thorn trees 94
White water alder 255
Widdringtonia cedarbergensis 56
Wild banana palms *307*
Wild Coast 21–3, *310*
Wild date palm 95
Witsand, Singing sands of **170**
Witte (White) River 60–1, *61*
Witteberg Series 40, 49
Witwatersrand 237
  reefs 237, 238
Wolvenkloof 61
Woodbush Forest 261
Worcester Fault 300

X

Xalanga 151
Xhosa tribe 297

Y

Yellowwood tree *252–3*, 255

Z

Zambezi River **227–33**
Zastron 108–9
Zincblende 249
Zirconium 250
Ziwa Peak 264
Zongola Geyser 236
Zulu, Chief 277
Zululand **276–89**
Zululand high forests 260, 277
Zulus 288, 289
Zwide, Chief 280

Photographers

The picture credits for each page are arranged from left to right.

Illustrations

Drawings of birds by Michael Woods, except for the Namaqua Sandgrouse on page 168 which is by Norman Lighton, reproduced from Roberts' *Birds of South Africa* (with the permission of the Trustees of the John Voelcker Bird Book Fund)

The type used for the body text, captions and chapter headings in this book is Plantin 110. The text is set in 11 point, leaded to 13½ points, and the captions in 9 point, on a 9½ point base. Chapter headings are in 30 point Roman and 14 point italics.

Typesetting by Cape and Transvaal Printers (Pty) Ltd., Cape Town.

Colour separations by Hirt and Carter (Pty) Ltd., Cape Town.

Printed by Everbest Printing Co., Ltd. Hong Kong.

® 'Reader's Digest' is a registered trademark of The Reader's Digest Association, Inc. of Pleasantville, New York, USA.